Library of Congress Cataloging-in-Publication Data

The Concept of Beauty in Patristic and Byzantine Theology.
Edited by John Anthony McGuckin (1952 -):
I. (Beauty & the Transcendent; Early Christian Aesthetics).
II. Sophia Studies in Orthodox Theology. vol. 5.

These paper were originally delivered at the Academic Conference 'Beauty and the Beautiful in Eastern Orthodox Thought and Culture' held at Union Theological Seminary on Dec 7th 2011 under the *aegis* of the Sophia Institute. The views expressed in this volume of *Sophia Studies in Orthodox Theology* are those of the authors and do not necessarily reflect those held by the Editorial Board or Officers of the Sophia Institute or its Academic or Ecclesial sponsors.

ISBN: (paperback) 978-0-9853596-0-7

Cover Design :
Cover Art: Iconography by Eileen McGuckin.
The Icon Studio. New York. www.sgtt.org.

Sophia Studies in Orthodox Theology vol. 5.

THE CONCEPT OF BEAUTY
IN PATRISTIC
AND BYZANTINE THEOLOGY

Papers delivered at the Sophia Institute

Academic Conference

New York. December. 2011.

Edited by

John Anthony McGuckin

Theotokos Press

New York, 2012

The Sophia Institute, 3041 Broadway, New York, NY. 10027

CONTENTS

Editor's Preface

The Notion of The Beautiful in Greek Thought
and its Early Christian Transfiguration.

J.A. McGuckin.

In a richly suggestive essay on Platonic philosophy, R. J. O'Connell highlights one of the most interesting and problematic aspects of the identification of the good and the beautiful in the Greek philosophical tradition:

> It is a truism to say that, for the Greek mind, the good and the beautiful (*Kalokagathon*) are at one , just as the evil and the ugly are. Use these terms in their moral sense, however, and the gigantic act of 'belief' implied in that equivalence becomes more evident. [1]

The widespread and distinctive Greek idea that moral utility (what was good by virtue of being beneficial) would coincide with socially accepted senses of rightness of action, in more or less the same way as it could be commonly agreed that a 'good' vase or a 'good' horse meant simply one of these things that was at one and the same time an elegant as well as an efficient specimen, was an idea that sounded well, and sometimes worked, but was frequently doomed to failure as a standard of ethics in so far as it did not have the workaday capacity to make sense for the Greeks of those many situations of moral conflict that called for a good action that brought no benefit to its agent. Many can be the occasions when one is called upon to do the 'right thing', to do one's duty, when the result is far from beneficial or advantageous. To the simple idea of utilitarian 'goodness' in early Greek thought Socrates brought a more refined and transcendent notion of aesthetics. To this Plato remained faithful.

---

[1] R.J. O'Connell. 'Eros & Philia in Plato's Moral Cosmos.' in: H. Blumenthal & R.A. Markus. (edd). *Neo-Platonism in Early Christian Thought*. London. 1981. 3-19.

7

Plato's sense of the moral beauty of an act which had to take precedence over any questions of its advantageousness advanced Greek thought into a new realm of moral awareness - one that had begun to take seriously the issue of moral beauty as such. Plato advances this thought (a major development in the history of ideas, not simply in aesthetic theory) in an important section of his *Symposium* and in other dialogues such as the *Phaedrus*.

For Plato the act of belief that the beautiful and the good would coincide, still remained an act of faith, but a faith that was now grounded on a more robust realism. When the two forces of utility and virtue did not apparently or immediately coincide, then the precedence was unquestioningly given to the moral beauty of an act. Knowing that this preference could only be sustained on the ground of an enduring fundamental trust that however difficult the resolution might be, nevertheless the good and the true must ultimately be one, Plato held that the perception of this ultimate unity was a call to an ascending purification of perception (*aesthesis*), one that was religiously inspired and indeed no less than the transcendental imperative.

Such an idea was one of the great forward leaps in the history of human thought and, even for this insight alone, justified the sense entertained by several of the Church Fathers (and certainly some of the church's iconographers who delighted in iconically depicting Plato on the church walls as a precursor of the Gospel) that here was a tradition of thought and belief that, like the Jewish lawyer in the Gospels, was 'not far from the Kingdom of God'.[2]

Plato added more, he understood that such a purified perception, frequently running against the current of human needs and self-referent desires, needed a dynamic motivating force to realize it, and, accordingly, posited love as the supreme virtue, or force [3], that gave the moral aesthetic sense its transcendent dynamic. In his *Symposium* he attributes the key role of teacher of these

---

[2] Mk. 12.34.

[3] The Latin term *virtus* (virtue) and the Greek synonym *arete* denote an energetic movement, a grasping of something not merely an abstract state.

8

mysteries to the 'stranger of Mantinea', the priestess Diotima. In and through her initiations Plato intimates the profoundly religious character of his insight that the person who habitually prefers beauty is thereby increasingly led to an ascent to the Supremely Beautiful. the text is worth quoting in its fullness as it can clearly seen to be a sub-text behind the minds of most of the Christian Fathers who comment upon this theme:

> He who has been instructed thus far in the things of love, and who has learned to see the beautiful in due order and succession, when he comes to the end will suddenly perceive a nature of wondrous beauty ...... beauty absolute, separate, simple, and everlasting, which is imparted to the ever-growing and perishing beauties of all other beautiful things, without itself suffering diminution, or increase, or any change. He who, ascending from these earthly things under the influence of true love, begins to perceive *that* beauty, is not far from the end. And the true order of going, or being led by another, to the things of love, is to begin from the beauties of earth and mount upwards for the sake of that other beauty, using these as steps only, and from one going on to two, and from two to all fair bodily forms, and from fair bodily forms to fair practices, and from fair practices to fair sciences, until from fair sciences he arrives at the science of which I have spoken, the science which has no other object than absolute beauty, and at last knows that which is beautiful by itself alone. This, my dear Socrates,' said the stranger of Mantinea, 'Is that life above all others which man should live, in the contemplation of beauty absolute..... But what if a man had eyes to see the true beauty, the divine beauty I mean, pure and clear and all unalloyed, not infected with the pollutions of the flesh and all the colours and vanities of mortal life, thither looking, and holding converse with the true beauty simple and divine? Remember how in that communion only, beholding beauty with that by which it can be beheld[4], he will be enabled to bring forth not images of beauty, but realities (for he has hold not of an image but of a reality) and

---

[4] That is, by noetic intuition , beyond aesthetic or sensory experience. For a comment on this passage cf. J . Adam . *The Religious Teachers of Greece*. Edinburgh 1908. 390-397. [Gifford Lectures 1904-1906].

bringing forth and nourishing true virtue will properly become the friend of God and be immortal, if mortal man may.' [5]

This extraordinarily lovely and profound passage was to have an immense effect on the Christian consciousness and formed a strong link between the philosophical and Christian patristic traditions in later centuries. In this justly famous speech of the 'Stranger of Mantinea' Plato's theory of the Ideal Forms takes on a status that is more than the merely ideational, and gives him the basis for a moral teleology. His progress towards this insight can be traced in the course of his writings.

In his *Meno* Plato begins his theory of Ideal Forms from the basis of a theory of knowledge: thus we do not approach truth by deductive processes based on sensory reality (*aisthetos*) rather we intuitively recollect the truth in so far as we have already experienced it before birth in a purely Noetic form (*noetikos, anaisthetos*). This starting point of the theory of knowledge is important to keep in mind, but the Theory of Ideas extends its significance in other works of Plato into the metaphysical or cosmological domain. The theory of knowledge, if kept in tandem with the theory of Forms, preserves the character of the Platonic Cosmos as a moral teleology. In the *Symposium* where the Ideal Form of Beauty is most clearly argued, this teleology attains the character of an aesthetic which transfigures into ethic, and ultimately into mysticism. This triadic process, from its roots in Plato's religious sense of the Beautiful, bears the character of an ascent; an ascent which is articulated most fully in religious terms, as we have seen, in the speech of Diotima in the *Symposium*.

The significance of this dynamic of ascent, and its relationship with Christianity, has long been categorized as one of the results of the impact of Neo-Platonic ideas on the church, especially in the period after Plotinus and Augustine. But, more accurately, the tendency to centralize the philosophical *Telos* as the ascent of the soul to the Transcendent Absolute is already the major concern of

---

[5] *The Symposium.* (tr). B Jowett. (edd). RM. Hare & DA. Russell. London. 1970. 224-5.

the Middle Platonists. As such it is a dominant concern of one of the more famous of that school, Origen of Alexandria.

Through him the Platonic notion of ascent is fundamentally moderated in its shape by the twin stimuli of Christian Logos-theology and biblical exegesis, and through him it comes into the Christian mystical tradition. This Origenian strand continues to emphasize the Platonic insight that the ecstatic perception of Beauty is the highest perception of truth afforded to creatures. His *Commentary on the Song of Songs* demonstrates the notion most clearly, and had a marked impact on Christian spirituality in both East and West thereafter.

Origen's legacy was most notably developed in the East by St. Gregory Nazianzen [6], St. Gregory Nyssa, Evagrios Pontike, St. Dionysios the Pseudo-Areopagite, and St. Maximus the Confessor. All of them, in their own way, diffract and mediate the great Alexandrian's own style of theorizing, in the process of artic-ulating a fully-fledged and particularly Christian approach to the problem. After this it is no longer accurate to speak of Platonized Christianity, or Christianized Platonism, for neither reduction does justice to the unique synthesis which the patristic paradigm represents: something which Florovsky wished to designate (in antithesis to Harnack) as the 'Christianization of Hellenism'. It remains true, however, that the Origenian tradition, even when subjected to such a masterly synthesis as that offered by the Cappadocians, remains far stronger in articulating the ascent from base materiality to spiritual perception than it is in describing the transfiguration of materiality which lay outside the ken of Plato, and was reserved as a mystery of the Incarnation.

The ascetical tradition of such monastic theorists as Makarios, and the typical praxis of asceticism of the other monastic teachers such as Pachomios, Shenoude, Euthymios, Saba, and John Klimakos,

---

[6] Further see JA. McGuckin. 'The Beauty of the World and its Significance in St. Gregory the Theologian.' in: J Chryssavgis. (ed). *Eastern Christian Ecology*. Fordham Univ. Press. 2012 (2013).

played an important synthetic role in this regard, because all represented a strongly moderating influence on (even in fact a current against) such a theology of transcendentalist aesthetics in the Origenian aftermath.

The Church's major Christological conflicts from the Fourth to the Fifth centuries also produced a significant body of thought, from the likes of such greats as Athanasios and Cyril, which added to the simpler monastic and moral tradition, and which also grounded its mystical endeavor in an Incarnational theology of Revelation and Theosis. This eventually issued in a high conciliar approach that is partly indebted to Origen but in significant aspects wholly independent of him and more affirmative of the body and sacramental materiality than ever he would choose to be[7]. From Cyril of Alexandria onwards we can decidedly recognize an authentic Christology of 'transfigured materiality': a major divergence from Plato's theology of the transcendence of materiality. Cyril's Christological images of the lily and its perfume to represent the union of divine and human in Christ; or the bond of soul and body to represent the manner of the incarnation of the divine in history, perfectly sum up this newly sharpened sense of 'transfiguration theology'. [8]

This double aspect and character of the genuinely Christian theological concern: namely, the apprehension of God as the Absolute Beauty drawing the soul onward in ecstasy, and the approach to the divine encounter in Christ as the transfiguration of matter, ultimately finds both its polarities reconciled in the late Byzantine synthesis. Maximus already demonstrates this, as does Dionysius the Pseudo-Areopagite. Their co-dependent treatment of theological aesthetics[9] marks them out as dependent on Plato's insight, while simultaneously developing it in a thoroughly Christianized form into new dimensions: a 'sea-change' into

---

[7] The body for him was a temporary corrective measure, a term-limited *paideusis* for pre-existent *Noes* fallen into materiality.

[8] cf. JA. McGuckin. *St. Cyril of Alexandria: The Christological Controversy.* Brill. Leiden. 1994.

[9] Maximus was a very careful reader, and explicit commentator on Plato, Origen, Gregory Nazianzen, and Dionysios the Areopagite.

something rich and strange. Maximus, in his *First Century on Theology* cc. 85-6 (a cardinal passage on Christian aesthetics which will be more closely commented on in my own essay later in this book) demonstrates a masterly synthesis of Plato and the biblical tradition of the image and its relation to the divine archetype. Maximus speaks of entering the Archetypal Beauty in terms of Noetic initiation, and approaches it from the viewpoint of the Theophany of Sinai. Moses pitches his tent apart from the camp of Israel, Maximus notes, and takes this as the soul's transcendence of material limitations as it ascends, darkly, to the immaterial. It is enabled, as a paradox, to ascend to the immaterial as a material creature, because of the divine image of the archetype that has mystically been placed within its own nature. He makes out of his exegesis of this passage a masterly synthesis of biblical typology, moral teleology and transcendental theology.

One of his chief points in this exegesis of Sinai is that Moses comes down once more from the mountain. So too the initiate, for Maximus, ends like a 'Second Moses.' For him then, following Origen and the Cappadocians in this, the highest mystical union does not abandon materiality, but descends, just as Moses does from Sinai, and (though unstated the parallel is implied) like the Divine Logos from heaven[10]. This is a descent which no longer in any sense can be understood as a decline. It is a *Katabasis* of mercy, a stooping down in the biblical sense, like the mother in tenderness to her child. It is a descent of the economy, a coming to save which is the *economia* of salvific revelation and which also prefigures the *Parousia* and which, in the interval, is given as a duty to the Church whose own *katabasis* (con-descension) to the world, after it has encountered the mystery of its Lord, is the economy of its mission in the world, its fundamental and inalienable duty to witness the truth, to proclaim the Gospel.

For Maximus, the descent does not dissipate the power of the vision rather it manifests it in love and mercy in an economy of the transfigured life. This is a recurring dynamic of *katabasis* and

---

10 All patristic exegesis understood the divine theophany on Sinai to be a manifestation of God the Word, second person of the Trinity.

anabasis based on the pattern of the Logos' own ascent and descent as described by the Evangelist John[11].

He returns to the theme in his *Fifth Century of Various Texts*. cc. 83-86, which is one of the most striking departures of all Christian theologians from the Platonic tradition, and which (because of careless readings in the main) has often brought down on his head (and on that of Dionysios before him) the bizarre charge of 'excessive Platonizing'. This too will be the subject of closer scrutiny later in the book. Suffice it so say for now that while Maximus and Dionysios are, perhaps, the two Christian theorists who apply reflection on the *Kalokagathon* most explicitly, and show evidence of the most careful reading of Plato on Beauty, they both write in the ecstasy of mystical fervor in ways that Plato could never have comprehended.

Even the most diffident comparison of Maximus' teachings on the Eros of Divine Beauty, with Diotima's speech, should reveal to anyone 'who has the eyes to see or the ears to hear', the profoundly different emphases that Maximus' apprehension of Gospel imperatives has brought to the fore. Here is Plato's insight, certainly, but subordinated in a powerful Christian confession to the overriding providence of a personal power of Love that seeks to redeem its creatures even to the point of divine *Kenosis*. The God of Maximus who: 'Moves others and itself moves, since it thirsts to be thirsted for, longs to be longed-for, and loves to be loved,' is hardly the God of the Platonists. When Maximus describes the deity radically anew, using the theology of beauty to approach his inner life as an 'erotic force', and speaking of his immanence in this way: 'spell-bound as it were by goodness, love, and longing, he relinquishes his utter transcendence in order to dwell in all things while yet remaining within himself,' we have a major and absolute departure from the *theologia* of the ancient world.

---

[11] The twin themes of *anabasis* and *katabasis* are major literary and theological structures in the 4th Gospel.

Maximus has not only baptized Plato in this Byzantine synthesis, he has also brought home the wild genius of his teacher Origen, and harmonized the latter's visions of the truth and his clear-sighted glimpse of the transcendent divine beauty, with the Church's more developed theology of the sacramental nature of the divine incarnation. This, of course, was Maximus' double intent from the outset.

These notes have simply intended to sketch out the main lines of one of the most important theological and philosophical developments in the life of the Early and Byzantine church. The essays that follow and comprise this book, will take the matter further, and will, I hope, provide a rich resource for future discussions on what is a major but still undeveloped area of theology.

The theology of the Beautiful (so badly misrepresented as a theory of aesthetics) is a topic of perennial importance, but today, perhaps more than ever, the Church needs to look afresh at its mystical and philosophical tradition in a world and an era where the two notions have suffered a fatal divorce in a so-called 'post Christian' context. Let me explain briefly why I believe this theological aesthetics to be one of the most important areas of contemporary theology, calling out for attention and development, even though it is largely relegated to the sidelines [12] and often misunderstood as an exercise in 'cosmetics' [13].

It is my belief that here, in the theology of Beauty, is an agenda for twentieth century theology which will rescue the discipline from its tendency to concentrate increasingly on the peripheral and ephemeral in its growing anxiety that its voice is becoming less and less relevant to contemporary society. Patristic theology, which once dealt so well with the same problems of comm-unicating a vision of truth that was somehow at once familiar and

---

[12] Even despite Von Balthasar's extensive work on the subject: E.T. *The Glory of the Lord. A Theological Aesthetics.* T&T Clark. Edinburgh. 1982.
[13] The Greek term *kosmetika* (cosmetics) means 'beautiful things' but today semantically it has a surface implication (like lipstick!).

yet new to its contemporary world, has an important role to play in this process of intellectual brokering and hermeneutics. To play its rightful part, however, it must first cast off the shackles imposed upon it in so many limited conceptions of academic theology that try to keep patristics relegated to the domain of the merely historical or archival.

The Early Greek Church's deep-rooted tradition of a mystical and sacramental understanding of God that is at one and the same time securely founded on a moral apprehension of self-sacrificing virtue as the Supremely Beautiful (the religion of the Incarnate Lord), is a powerful remedy, or *Pharmakeia*, for western society which, where it has retained any religious sense, is becoming increasingly pietistic and ineffectual in its spiritual dynamic.

Such a trend can be discerned even in some of the churches, but above all in the non-Christian phenomena so often attendant on New Age Religion - soft on rationality, soft on ethics, soft on justice, and soft on truth. And in those many places where society has not retained any vestige of its religious instinct, the entire social fabric is increasingly, and more and more obviously, distorted by the wholesale collapse of the sense of community, idealism, and charity - all the factors, in short, which would be able to work for a new transcendental which alone can raise up a human society beyond the mire of nationalisms, narcissistic greed, and concomitant societal and cultural decay.

The main road of reconciliation possible for a society that is in danger of losing even the distant memories of its religious civilisation, at a time when its preferred religions have turned solipsistic, and its schools of political, philosophical, and artistic thought have elevated short-term self interest to new heights, is no less than the return to a renewed sense of the Beautiful (*to Kalon*). It is, in the Christian reinterpretation of the Greek notion of *kalokagathon*[14], the ideal synthesis of a religious, mystical, and

---

[14] The word, a synthesis of the 'beautiful' and the 'good' was taken up by St. Gregory Nazianzen from Hellenistic general use (as meaning 'A Gentleman'), to signify the state of the cultured Christian, consciously living the virtuous life.

moral transcendental, that new life might be offered to reinvigorate metaphysical foundations that necessarily underpin a society's moral attitudes.

Beauty is, if the Church can still act decisively enough to be the intellectual midwife and interpreter, the one concept and experience that can still be remembered well enough by a generally 'paganized' society to serve as the basis for a new *pro-paideusis* of what civilisation and human aspirations to ascent are all about. If the Church can find the wit, and the voices in the present generation who will be up to the task as were the farseeing saints, founders and teachers, of the past, (who dealt with an equally ambiguous and diffident post-imperial society), then this *pro-paideusis* will be no less than a clarion call to European society which has already declined far from its once high standards of Christian civilisation, and now urgently needs catechizing about the very nature of the simplest truths - what constitutes Beauty; and where lies the reconciliation of Aesthetics and Justice - central ideas constitutive to a civilisation that even a few decades ago might have been thought to be hardly capable of being forgotten in so short a time and so widespread a fashion.

In brief, the theology of Beauty, one of the great jewels in the patristic and mystical tradition of Orthodox Christianity, is far from being played out. It remains to have perhaps its greatest role ever in the history of the church - the reform of civilized standards in the attempt to return to the West its forgotten transcendental instincts. Perhaps the role of the early Christian Fathers in this *kerygmatic* process, is one of the sacraments reserved for the latter age: to witness vividly to Beauty, and by so doing demonstrate the self-evident authenticity and integrity of the Gospel they were called to proclaim in a darkening world. Their patristic wisdom, dressed in the plain garments befitting hierophants, set out to fulfill a great evangelical task of old: to lead the confused and wandering from the obscurities to the illumined places where the mysteries are celebrated 'with unveiled faces'. Their teachings retain this mystical capacity even today.

17

The stranger of Mantinea was perfectly right, such a journey to the Beautiful can only be made if one who has seen leads by the hand, with care and love, the one who desires to see. For such a great and pressing destiny, those who do see and care must be ready, and must be engaged in all levels of the church's interface with society, essentially with inspired strategies of *paideia* and dedicated perseverance in the ways the Spirit refashions self interest into the recognizable pattern of the Christ-life. May this little book, created out of the great energies, lights, and charity of so many young scholars, of such vital promise, bring that patristic light out like a lantern for our times.

John Anthony McGuckin.

President of the Sophia Institute.
New York. December 2012.

PART I. PATRISTIC

Preludium i

How natural a thing it is to look for beauty, and to love it, even if the idea of what it is that is beautiful should differ from one person to the next. But what is more wondrous that the beauty of God? What can you possibly imagine that is more likely to give pleasure than the splendor of God? What desire could be more intense, or more irresistible than that thirst which God himself has inspired in the soul, once it has been purified from all vice, and when it cries out: 'I am sick with love.' (Song of Songs 2.5).

The beauty of God is beyond the power of words to describe. We might compare its radiance to the light of the morning star, or to the moon, or the sun. But we would be as far from an accurate depiction as midday is from midnight.

This beauty is not visible to bodily eyes. Only the Soul and the Nous can perceive it. Each time it illumines the saints it leaves in them a sting, a sense of longing so strong as to make them cry out: 'Alas that I remain an exile still.' (Ps.120.5).

By the terms of our very nature we humans aspire to what is beautiful and love it. But what is beautiful is also good. God is good. Just as everyone looks for the good; so do all look for God.

St. Basil the Great.

The Greater Rules. c. 2. (PG. 31. 909).   (Tr.) T. Spidlik.

Preludium ii

On the Divine Beauty.

Grant, Immortal Monarch,
that we may hymn you;
grant that we may sing of you
our ruler and lord;
through whom is the hymn,
through whom the praise,
through whom the angelic chorus,
through whom the endless ages,
through whom the light of the sun,
through whom the course of the moon,
through whom the great beauty of the stars,
through whom noble Man was made
that as a rational creature we could perceive the deity.

For you have created all things
and given order to each,
governing all things in your providence.
You spoke a Word and so it came to pass.
You Word is God the Son;
of the same being as yourself,
of the same rank as his parent.
he has 'kept all things together' (Eph. 1.10)
that he might rule over all.
And the Holy Spirit, who is God,
embraces all things around
and guards all in his providence.

O living Trinity, I name you
One and Only Monarch,
unchangeable nature without beginning
nature of ineffable being,
impenetrably wise intelligence,
unshakeable strength of the heavens,
devoid of all beginning and boundless;
radiant glory that can never be seen,

yet which looks upon all that is.
No depth lies beyond your gaze
from the earth even to the abyss.

Father, give me your mercy
and grant that I may worship
this awesome mystery through the ages.
So cast away my sins
and cleanse my heart from evil thoughts
that I may glorify the Godhead,
lifting up hands that are pure;
that I may bless the Christ
and bend a supplicant's knee,
that he may receive me as a servant
on the day he comes in his kingly power (Lk. 23.42).

Father, give me your mercy.
And thus I find mercy and peace,
for glory and thanks are yours
to the ever unending ages.

St. Gregory the Theologian.

Carmina 1.1.30 (PG. 37. 508-510)

(Tr.) J A McGuckin.

The Notion of Beauty in Plato

Sergey Trostyanskiy

The notion of beauty was central for Plato's philosophy. Plato left a very subtle and in a sense puzzling account of beauty which is not an easy one to grasp. It is thus a subject of diverging interpretations. Plato's account of beauty can be found in quite a number of Platonic dialogues. There is one dialogue attributed to the early period and two – to the middle period which immediate subject is beauty. Moreover, the notion of beauty can be found in many other dialogues where beauty is given a certain consideration.

The notion of beauty in Plato has various dimensions, so to say, and generally understood as pertaining to the issues of metaphysics and epistemology. Within Plato's metaphysics the question of beauty touches upon four different issues, namely: 1. the nature of beauty itself by itself (*auto kath' auto*); 2. the nature of the particulars (*ta polla*) that participate (*metexein*) in the virtue of beauty and are named after it; 3. the nature of the arts (in particular, that of imitative arts). Thus, the first issue is associated with an attempt to place beauty within the range of beings (*ta onta*). The second issue deals with the question of how and why many beautiful things are beautiful. Finally, the last issue concerns the nature of representational arts (this is the subject of aesthetics proper as conceived by contemporary philosophy).

The epistemological dimension of the subject of beauty, in turn, is meant to elucidate the question of how we know 'beauty' and how we make an epistemic ascent from various manifestations of beauty (beautiful particulars) to beauty itself by itself (which is the final *telos* of the ascent). The possibility of defining beauty (definition being a distinctive mark of the early period dialogues) represents one of the primary epistemological concerns associated with the question of how the *eidos*[15] (or form, here sometimes

---

[15] The noun *eidos* (*eide* in plural) is derived from the verb *eido*, meaning 'I see'. Another noun, *idea*, used by Plato simultaneously with *eidos*, is derived from the same verb *eido* through its infinitive form (*idein*). Therefore, *eide* mean things to

designated as *F*) of beauty can be absorbed into *logos* (discursive reasoning). In the middle period dialogues the primary epistemological concern is the relationship between discursive and non-discursive reasoning and the role of dialectics in 'giving an account'. Thus, in the middle period dialogues the possibility of knowing beauty itself depends on fulfilling two proposed conditions of knowledge (*episteme*), namely, an immediate grasp of primary realities (*eide*) through seeing (*thea, theoria*) and the ability to give an account (*logos*). The epistemic ascent to the *eidos* of beauty through 'vision' and the incorporation of the content of such 'vision' into discursive reasoning are on agenda at the time.

It is evident from the above considerations that the subject of beauty in Plato necessarily presents certain difficulties to the researches as the Platonic corpus is not monolithic and represents a gradual development of Plato's metaphysics and epistemology. Thus, the conception of beauty in the early dialogues differs from that of the middle period due to the development of Plato's metaphysics and epistemology. Therefore, here I will be necessary to provide a brief survey of Plato's early and middle period metaphysics and epistemology and to trace the philosophical development that lead Plato from the *Greater Hippius* to the *Symposium* and the *Phaedrus*. I will give primary attention in the scope of this chapter to Plato's metaphysics and its key issue of the nature of beauty itself by itself as well as to the epistemological issues associated with the epistemic ascent to beauty itself.

The *Greater Hippias* is the only early period dialogue that takes beauty as its subject. This early period dialogue is one of the traditional 'Socratic' dialogues positing the '*What F*' questions (*ti esti arête*). The subjects of philosophical investigation here are virtues in general and the virtue of beauty (*kalon*) in particular. The epistemological concern of Socrates over knowing and defining is focal in this context.

---

be seeing by the eye of the soul, things that show themselves to the intelligible sight.

The notion of virtue within the framework of contemporary intellectual horizon normally refers to ethical issues and the moral excellence. This is the way it is defined in the dictionaries. However, within the mindset of the ancient Greeks the notion of virtue (arête) was not limited within the boundaries of ethics, but extended its domain much further. It is, thus, no surprise to the student of antiquity that Greek philosophers will speak of the virtues of, say, *nous* (intellect), *sophia* (wisdom), *phronesis* (practical wisdom), and beauty.[16] The notion of virtue, thus embraces the spheres of aesthetics and rational discourse along the line with ethics. In other words, here both practical and speculative reasons, so to say, go hand in hand. Thus, the virtue of beauty signifies a certain, not necessarily moral, excellence of human beings who historically manifest beauty. Here, again, the notion of beauty has a greater extension that we might think of and includes physical, moral, and spiritual beauties. This is one of the reasons why the contemporary scholars of Plato translate *kalon* as 'fine' rather than 'beautiful'. This translation apparently attempts to redirect the reader from the narrow conception of beauty associated with sense perception (*aesthesis*) and imagination and connotes the *arête* aspect of beauty.

Another peculiar feature of the intellection horizon of antiquity (that was about to give birth to Platonism) is associated with the perception of virtues as self-subsisting (not mind-dependent) entities. Thus, it is not particular behavioral patterns or a type of knowing and acting that constitute, say, the virtues of justice and beauty, but the pure self-subsisting entities which originate various historical manifestations of the properties of justice and beauty that the particulars possess. Thus pure beauty is the cause of many beautiful things. This metaphysical realism is a distinctive mark of Platonism which posits real self-subsisting entities as referents of properties that 'the many' possess.

The question of what arête is constitutes the focal point of the Socratic dialogues. Here the historical Socrates to a greater or lesser

---

[16] For an excellent discussion on the understanding of virtues in Plato see S. Menn's: *Plato on God as Nous*. Southern Illinois University Press. 1995.

extent is on the stage. It will be useful in this context to look at Aristotle's description of Socrates and his philosophical significance. In the *Metaphysics* 13.4 we can find the following text:

> But when Socrates was occupying himself with the excellences of character, and in connection with them became the first to raise the problem of universal definition …it was natural that Socrates should be seeking the essence, for he was seeking to syllogize, and 'what a thing is' is the starting-point of syllogisms…two things may be fairly ascribed to Socrates—inductive arguments and universal definition, both of which are concerned with the starting-point of science):—but Socrates did not make the universals or the definitions exist apart: they [Platonists], however, gave them separate existence, and this was the kind of thing they called Ideas.

Thus in the early dialogues the question of 'what it is' (*ti esti*) is crucial as a starting point of philosophical investigations. In this context the suggestion of Aristotle that the historical Socrates and his approach to metaphysics in the early Platonic dialogues are different from that which the middle period dialogues will present to the reader (which Aristotle attributed to the 'Platonists') should be taken into account. The issue of what beauty is might not, as a matter of fact, suggest that the virtue of beauty itself in the early dialogues is separated from the particular manifestations of beauty (and can thus exist un-instantiated). Here the most foundational issue of 'one over the many' is at work and signifies the dividing line between the Socratic-Aristotelian solution of the problem through the concept of immanent universals and Plato's approach (distinctive for the middle period dialogues) that posits pure and uniform paradigms, virtues themselves by themselves, and thus, in a sense, separates them from the particulars.[17] However, it should be noted in this context that the ontological grounding of Socratic *eide* (in the early dialogues) is quite uncertain. This uncertainty creates many problems and posits

---

[17] It is still the subject of scholarly debate whether Plato's *eide* are universals of particulars. As of today there is no agreement on how to approach *eide* in the way that might be satisfactory to everyone, including Plato himself.

many questions. In the *Greater Hippias* the dominating theme is beauty itself. Here Socrates asks his interlocutor the following question:

> I asked for the absolute beautiful, by which everything to which it is added has the property of being beautiful, both stone and stick and man and god and every act and every acquisition of knowledge ? For what I am asking is this, man: what is absolute beauty? [292d]

It appears that to answer the so called '*What F*' question (what is form or *eidos* or *idea*) is to give a definition of essence (*horos*). Thus the subject of inquiry is the definition of essential beauty. Here it is worthwhile noting that Socrates is not looking for 'what is beautiful, but what the beautiful is' [287e]. Thus, any particular historical manifestations of beauty are juxtaposed to beauty itself. The subject of definition (*definiendum*) therefore is not a particular beautiful thing (or a set of things), or an aspect of a thing, or an action, but beauty itself, the essential beauty. It is thus evident that Socrates asks for a real definition. As Gail Fine rightly pointed out, 'the ontological correlates of real definitions are real essences, non-linguistic universals that explain why things are as they are'.[18] Thus, the proposed definition is of the *eidos* of beauty, of that which 'imparts' the property of being beautiful into the particulars. The possibility of defining is intrinsically connected with the possibility of knowing as only that which is defined is known. The key assumption in this context is that only forms or *eide*, i.e. intellectual entities, can be defined (definition answering the *ti esti* question). Thus, in order to know an *eidos* one should be able to define it.

It is important to note that the philosophical underpinning of the '*What F question*' is associated with the most foundational issue of the time, namely, the issue of, so called, 'one over the many'. How is it that many things share the same property (say, the property of being beautiful) after which they are all named (as beautiful things)? What is the nature of the property and how can it be

[18] G.Fine. *On Ideas; Aristotle's Criticism of Plato's Theory of Forms*. Clarendon Press. Oxford. 1995. 49.

shared by the many? How can one know F (*eidos*) and know whether a particular thing has the property of F (*eidos* instantiated in the particulars)? These questions were of a crucial significance for antique philosophy. Socrates approached the subject mainly from the epistemological perspective. Thus, 'the possibility of knowledge requires explanation, and this, in turn, requires the existence of forms – real properties and kinds.'[19] However, the metaphysical argument is also offered: 'the existence of many Fs requires the existence of some one thing, the form [*eidos*] of F, in virtue of which they are F'.[20] Thus, the absolute beauty in the *Greater Hippias* is required to explain the being of the beautiful particulars.

In the *Greater Hippias* the interlocutor of the dialogue (Hippias, a famous Athenian sophist and rhetorician in this case) is asked to define beauty. The process of defining runs by positing an F-condition (or a set of F-conditions) and testing the proposed definition on the subject of consistency with F-conditions. These conditions represent Socrates' criteria for the truth of definition of arête. As David Wolfsdorf noted, in the dialogue 'Socrates tests proposed definitions against F-conditions to which he is committed.'[21] Among the F-conditions in the *Greater Hippias* Wolfsdorf listed the following: fineness/beauty (*to kalon*) is not in any way not-fine (or, it is purely fine); fineness makes entities fine; fineness is good. The proposed F-conditions, as one can note, are not supported by overarching metaphysical and epistemological structures. Thus, at the end of the day it is unclear why Socrates chooses and is thus committed to these particular conditions and not others.

The multiple attempts of Hippias and Socrates to define beauty fail and are rejected as inappropriate. Thus, a stick, gold, appropriateness, beautiful public speech, etc. are incapable of defining beauty as being inconsistent with F-conditions. The conclusion of the dialogue seems to indicate that the discourse has ended up in an *aporia*. Both Socrates and Hippias failed to define

---

[19] Fine. 1995. 50.
[20] Fine. 1995. 50.
[21] D.Wolfsdorf. 'Socrates' Pursuit of Definitions.' *Phronesis*, 48. 4. 2003. 280.

beauty. Socrates concludes his speech by quoting the proverb which says that 'beautiful things are difficult' [304e]. However, if one cannot define beauty, it is unknown (knowledge here being juxtaposed to ignorance). But if the beauty itself (the *eidos* of beauty), that which makes many things beautiful, is not defined and thus is not known, how can one judge the particulars as beautiful or ugly? How then will one know 'what sort of things are beautiful and ugly?' [286d][22]

In other words, if the criterion for judging things as beautiful is not established, the beautiful things cannot be known or said to be beautiful or ugly, and thus cannot be named beautiful, cannot share the name with beauty. Here the *eidos* of beauty functions as a paradigm which, being compared to the particular instantiations of beauty, gives one the criterion for judging things as beautiful of ugly. Moreover, the reason why beautiful things are beautiful [288a], in the light of the failure to define beauty, could not be given either. Here the explanatory role of *eidos* is well articulated by Socrates.

This *aporia* will be intensified further on in the *Meno* [71a-b] which will pose the question of how virtue can be taught. Thus, in order to teach what virtue is one should know it and thus be able to define it. If, on the contrary, the definition is not provided, one cannot ascend to knowledge but is destined to stay content with ignorance and opine rather than know. Opinion, on the other hand, is insufficient for the purposes of giving the statement of essence. One of the ways out of this *aporia* is through positing justified belief as a criterion. However, in the *Greater Hippias*, the notion of justified belief is not yet introduced and Socrates has to confess ignorance about what beauty is.

It seems that Socrates and Hippias approach the subject from the different sets of assumptions. Having being questioned about what beauty is, Hippias gives a number of examples that he thinks

---

[22] Similar in the Euthyphro [6e]: 'Well then, show me what, precisely, this ideal is, so that, with my eye on it, and using it as a standard, I can say that any action done by you or anybody else is holy if it resembles this ideal or, if it does not, can deny that it is holy.'

of as sufficient conditions for the ascent to the meaning of beauty. The examples of beauty are meant to fully unfold the subject matter. Thus, to say that 'a beautiful maiden is beautiful' seems to be enough in Hippias opinion for one to make an ascent to the meaning if beauty and to gain knowledge (or, a right opinion) of it. It might be suggested that beauty here is approached from the semantic perspective. It seems that a given example is just right enough for the hearer to grasp the meaning of the subject matter. Here an appeal to the common sense as a starting point of the ascent to knowledge is important.

Socrates, however, has a different set of assumptions: knowable is definable; 'the one' which stands over 'the many' should be defined and used as an explanatory tool for 'the many' and as a criterion of judgment of the extent to which 'the many' possess a certain property. Thus, to answer the *'What F'* question for Hippias is to point to an example which will allow one to ascend to the meaning of the notion (of beauty in this case). For Socrates it is rather to give a statement of essence of the real referent of the notion. Thus, from the perspective of Socrates, 'one cannot achieve definitional knowledge of *F* through the use of instances of *F*.'[23]

Hippias does not seem to share the same set of premises about beauty and tend to take the common opinion of what beauty is as a definition of beauty, thus assuming that a particular manifestation of beauty perfectly exemplifies what beauty means and is thus fully representative of the common notion that many people share. He does not seem to understand Socrates' question of beauty itself as a real referent of the notion.

Socrates objects to Hippias's approach by pointing out that a particular example, a beautiful thing or action cannot be used for the purposes of defining virtue. There seem to be a few reasons behind this deficiency/incapacity on the side of examples to define the *eidos* of beauty. Firstly, from the metaphysical perspective, a particular instantiation of beauty, a beautiful thing

[23] D. Wolfsdorf. 'The Socratic Fallacy and the Epistemological Priority of Definitional Knowledge.' *Journal for Ancient Philosophy and Science.* 37. 1. March. 2004. 36.

or action, is a subject to time, place, origin, and context, and can be viewed as both beautiful (from a particular standpoint of, say, humans) and ugly (from a different standpoint of, say, gods). Thus, the fact that the particulars are signified by the compresence of opposites (are both beautiful and ugly, or beautiful and non-beautiful) [289a-b] precludes them from being capable of defining beauty itself (the notion that will be fully developed in the middle period dialogues). In other words, their being is inferior to beauty itself due to impurity signified by the compresence of opposites.[24] Thus, the proposed definition by the way of examples is inconsistent with one of the F-conditions (that beauty is not in any way not-beautiful; since a particular manifestation of beauty is characterized by being both beautiful and ugly/non-beautiful, it is not consistent with the proposed F-condition). It is thus rejected.

Moreover, as some authors have pointed out, Socrates seems to suggest that a definition that uses a particular instantiation of beauty (the *definiens* of the definition) is not (or, at least, in most of the cases is not) extensionally identical with beauty itself (the *definiendum* of the definition); different sets of objects fall under *definiendum* and *definiens*; thus, the coextension between *definiendum* and *definiens* of the proposed definition is not secured; therefore this type of definition should be rejected as being too narrow, or too broad.[25]

In addition, 'a definition that simply listed the many Fs would be at best a nominal definition'[26] which informs us that some particulars possess the property of F without giving the reason why these particulars are Fs. Thus, the explanatory role of *eidos* is not taken into account. As we already know, the *eidos* of beauty is that on account of which all particulars are beautiful. 'If a beautiful maiden is beautiful, there is something by reason of

---

[24] A very illuminating discussion of the compresence can be found in Fine. 1995, where she distinguishes narrow and wide compresence.
[25] See G. Fine (ed). *Plato 1. Metaphysics and Epistemology*. OUP. Oxford. 1999. 5; and eadem. 1995. 51.
[26] Fine. 1995. 48.

which these things would be beautiful' [288a].[27] As Fine noted, in the *Euthyphro* 'although 'piety' and 'being loved by all the gods' are coextensive, the latter is none the less an inadequate answer to the question 'What is piety?' For being loved by all the gods is an accidental property...of piety, whereas Socrates wants to know its nature or essence...'[28] Thus, she continues, 'being loved by all the gods isn't that by which all pious things are pious; on the contrary, the fact that a thing is pious explains why the gods love it'[29] (pp.5-6). The conclusion is that even if the coextension is secured in this type of definition the *definiens* does not explain why all pious things are pious. Consequently, the proposed definition of beauty by the way of examples is inconsistent with one of the *F*-conditions (that beauty makes entities beautiful and is thus their explanatory principle) and is thus rejected.

It is also interesting to note that the 'many', the particulars under this scenario cannot be known and defined. The proper subject of definition is *eidos*. 'Definitional knowledge is epistemologically prior to knowledge of instances of *F*'.[30] Thus, any references to the particulars in defining *eidos* are futile. The procedure (of defining *eidos*) cannot be accomplished by making references to the 'many' particulars, be it a beautiful maiden, or a sculpture, or an act. This 'contempt' of Socrates for the particular manifestations of beauty is quite remarkable. Some scholars pointed out that this procedure necessarily leads one to paradoxes.[31]

---

[27] 'In addition to preserving coextension, a correct answer must explain the nature of the virtue in question.' Fine. 1995. 5.

[28] Fine. 1995. 5.

[29] Fine 1995. 6.

[30] D.Wolfsdorf. 'The Socratic Fallacy and the Epistemological Priority of Definitional Knowledge.' *Journal for Ancient Philosophy and Science*, 37. 1. March. 2004. 36.

[31] As John Beversluis noted: 'One cannot simultaneously affirm (a) that known instances of X are to be scrutinized for the purpose of discovering the *eidos* common to them, and (b) that one cannot recognize something as an instance of X unless one already knows that *eidos*. Indeed, these contradictory claims exhibit in strikingly limpid form the incoherence of the traditional interpretation. According to (a), the *eidos* common to a number of instances is, in principle, discoverable inductively. Such a view presupposes, of course, that we are capable of gathering known instances of X while lacking a knowledge of their *eidos*.

It should be noted that no account on the relationship between *eidos* and *ta polla* ('the many') is given in the earlier dialogues. Thus, their mode of relation is unclear. For example, the notion of 'addition' of *eidos* to the many in the *Greater Hippias* is not clarified. In other words, the reader is not given an account of how *eidos* is present in the particulars. The middle period dialogues will provide an account of participation in a sketchy way and the *Parmenides* (a late middle-period dialogue) will attempt to resolve the puzzles of participation.

Gregory Vlastos has noted some of the difficulties in understanding the principle of investigation of approach that Socrates used. He called it 'the paradox of Socrates' *elenchus*'. Though Vlastos excluded the *Greater Hippias* from the set of dialogues that uses elenchus, the focal point of the procedure can still be applied to it. Thus, he pointed out that the pattern of philosophical inquiry perused by Socrates it not itself a subject of investigation. 'He never troubles to say why his way of searching is the way to discover truth'.[32] There is no method here and the criteria for the truth of ethical judgments are not established. Therefore, Socrates ends up with the denial of the possibility of knowledge of virtues. The implication of such denial is that *eide* of virtues cannot be defined. For example, all attempts to answer the question of what beauty is fail. We do not really know what beauty is. How do we know then that beautiful things are beautiful? Socrates' disavowal of knowledge of virtues is thus a necessary result of the general lack of metaphysical and epistemological grounding.

David Wolfsdorf developed the same theme by pointing out that in the early dialogues the reason for Socrates' disavowal of knowledge of virtues is not offered. 'I suggest the reason for his

To grant this, however, is to deny the relation of epistemological priority affirmed by (b).' The conclusion is that 'Socrates cannot, therefore, consistently hold that a knowledge of the *eidos* is epistemologically prior to a recognitional ability of its instance.' J.Beversluis. 'Socratic Definition.' *American Philosophical Quarterly*. 2.4. October 1974 (VIII). 334-335. A way out of the paradoxes is by justified or true belief. But as Beversluis noted, this is not an option in the pre-*Meno* dialogues.

[32] G.Vlastos. 'The Socratic Elenchus.' in: G. Fine. (ed). *Plato 1. Metaphysics and Epistemology*. Oxford University Press. Oxford. 1999. 37.

silence on this matter reflects the very reason why he so frequently disavows ethical knowledge: he does not understand how ethical reasoning operates, and, specifically, he does not understand what makes ethical propositions true'.[33]

I addition, Wolfsdorf rightly noted that the general lack of understanding of the proper form of real definitions marks the Socratic dialogues. Thus, 'the early definitional dialogues do not offer a great deal with which to answer this question. Socrates specifies F-conditions that the *definiens* must satisfy, but these conditions pertain to the specific excellences under investigation. They are not general conditions for defining entities. What Socrates lacks is a theoretical ontology to provide a general framework for real definitions'[34]. Thus the ascent to definition takes Socrates and his interlocutors through various steps of positing a definition and testing it as consistent or inconsistent with the proposed F-conditions. F-conditions, however, vary from dialogue to dialogue and do not provide a consistent set of formal requirement for definition. Moreover, it is unclear why Socrates is committed to some particular F-conditions offered in the early period dialogues. The lack of metaphysical and epistemological grounding explains this apparently random choice.

The *Greater Hippias* leaves us with a number of *aporiai*. The possibility of defining the virtue of beauty is questioned either due to the incapacity to fulfill F-conditions and thus to define the *eidos* of beauty, beauty itself. The conclusion, associated with Socrates' disavowal of knowledge and the insistence on ignorance about virtues, follows. Thus, in early dialogues the possibility of defining *eide* is affirmed, but the rules of definition (and of the use of *logoi* in general) are not clarified. Finally, all we know about beauty is associated with F-conditions posited to test the proposed definitions. No other qualifications of the *eidos* of beauty are given.

As we move to the middle period dialogues, the new difficulties emerge. Now *eidos* is proposed to be simple, isolated, and uniform (*monoeides*) paradigm. It cannot participate in other *eide* but can be

[33] D. Wolfsdorf. 'Socrates' Pursuit of Definitions.' *Phronesis*, 48. 4. 2003. 295.
[34] Wolfsdorf. 2003. 305.

participated in by the particulars. These metaphysical assumptions are linked with the new epistemological notions where non-discursive reasoning is emphasized and the nature of the relation between discursive and non-discursive reasoning is posited as a subject of philosophical investigations.

It should be noted in this context that definition implies logical complexity. The new epistemology with the emphasis on non-discursive reasoning associated with 'seeing' (*blepein, theorein*) or 'touching (*ephaptein*) affirms the possibility of giving an account (*logos*) of *eidos*; however, the metaphysical assumption of simplicity, uniformity, and isolation of *eidos* does not really allow *eidos* to be incorporated into the complex structure of definition. This possibility will become more visible during the late middle period dialogues, in particular, in the *Parmenides*, which will allow *eidos* to have a certain extensional identity with other *eide*. Thus, in the middle period dialogues the question of what beauty is could not be answered via definition.

Now the questions to be answered are the following: How can *eidos* be incorporated into *logos*? How can a simple and uniform entity be absorbed into a complex structure of discourse in general and of definition in particular? How is it possible to define essence and thus to answer the question *ti esti to kalon*? At this time the problem seems to be that we know (or can know under certain conditions) *eidos* intuitively, non-discursively, but cannot translate this non-discursive knowledge into *logos*. It is thus understandable that in the middle period dialogues the 'What *F*' question has necessarily faded from the scenery and the proposed answer to the statement of essence is replaced by the self-predication of *eide*. The only thing that now can be said about an isolated and uniform entity is that it is what it is. Thus, beauty is beauty; or beauty is beautiful. Though one might see the distinction between the different meanings of the copula in these sentences (one, indicating an identity statement, and the other one – predication), it is quite clear that now the *eidos* of beauty is classified by beauty. Thus the famous issue of self-predication/self-participation arises. Therefore, it is obvious that the middle period metaphysics and epistemology posit the possibility of giving an account of *eide*

34

(thus, to know is to have vision and to be able to give an account[35]), but do not find a way around the issue of incorporating pure, simple, and uniform *eidos* into the complex structure of *logos* and answering the 'What *F*' question (thus defining or giving an account of what virtue is). As Teloch pointed out, two independent models of knowledge (propositional and non-propositional) are in conflict here.

One way out of this difficulty is to reformulate the notion of *logos/logoi* in the middle period dialogues. Thus now the definitional understanding of logos here seems to be replaced by dialectic which incorporates *eide* into discourse (*logos*) but allows them to stay undefined due to their simplicity. Thus *eide* here are used as the first principles of knowledge that do not themselves require to be defined.

The *Symposium* well illustrates the situation. Here the account of what beauty is, of the nature of beauty as beauty, is not supplied. The nature of forms that all forms share is quite well spelled out (immutable, eternal, etc.). However, the nature of beauty as beauty, not just as one of the members of the intellectual realm remains concealed.

This situation can be partially explained by the separation of *eide* from the particulars. It is obvious that *eidos* does not impart its nature to the particulars. Thus, the particulars do not become immutable and eternal by participating in the form of, say, largeness. Thus the *eidos* of largeness does not impart its eternity and immutability to the large particulars. Moreover, the *eidos* of largeness is not itself large (being beyond spatial conditions and the possibility of being compared in size with other *eide*). The property of largeness that the particulars possess is not the same as pure largeness, the *eidos* of largeness itself by itself. Thus, the *eidos* of largeness does not participate in itself, does not become a large entity. In other words, the *eidos* of largeness does not share the property of being large with the particulars. Though the *eidos* of beauty can be said to be self-participating and beautiful, pure

---

[35] 'And do you not also give the name of dialectician to the man who is able to exact an account of the essence of each thing.' [*Republic*. 534b].

beauty once again cannot be identified with the property of being beautiful which the particulars (whose beauty is impure) possess. This metaphysical gap between *eide* and particulars makes the ascent to knowledge and the epistemic correlation between the levels of reality quite problematic. Though the possibility of knowing *eide* through 'vision' (*thea*) is affirmed, the ascent to the knowledge of the *eidos* of beauty in the *Symposium* is accomplished suddenly, through the leap. The particulars here represent certain reminders that trigger the vision. However, there is no continuity between the most subtle manifestations of beauty in the world of things and beauty itself by itself. Finally, even though the immediate knowledge (or grasp) of beauty is possible, its translation to *logos* (*dianoia* or *logismos*) is problematic.

As a consequence, the nature of the synonymy between *eidos* and the particulars is questioned as the particulars now cannot possess the name (*onoma*) but only an *eponym*[36] Thus a particular can only derivatively said to be large or beautiful. One of the reasons why the particulars are not said to be beautiful or large without qualification is impurity (due to the compresence of opposites). Thus, the separation of *eide* from the particulars reaches its highest point in this context.

This consideration among the others gave some scholars the reason to distinguish between *eidos* and its *ousia* as well as between two type of relation, the ones of being and partaking. Allan Silverman characterized this 'two worlds metaphysics' in Plato as attributing being (*ousia*) to *eide* and classifying the particulars as lacking *ousia*. Thus *eide* are classified by their relation to being; the particulars are characterized by the relation of participation. The epistemological implication of this 'two world metaphysics' is that 'what is defined is essence [*ousia*, the feminine participle of *eine* – being] and since Forms along possess essences [*ousiai*], i.e., of what is definable, it follows that that only Forms can be known.'[37] However, it turns that partaking of being is a non-characterizing relation. Thus, definition here, once again, is

[36] A. Silverman. *The Dialectic of Essence: A Study of Plato's Metaphysics*, Princeton University Press. Princeton. 2002. 87.
[37] Silverman. 2002. 16.

equated with self-predication. It is still unclear on this account how *eidos* can be defined. Thus, the non-characterizing relation of the *eidos* of beauty to its being does not give any definable content to the *eidos* of beauty (in a traditional sense of definition in terms of commonalities and differences).

In the *Symposium* Plato gives us an account of what *eide* are. Here the nature of pure beauty, of the *eidos* of beauty as *eidos* is described in the following way:

> A nature which in the first place is everlasting, not growing and decaying, or waxing and waning; secondly, not fair in one point of view and foul in another, or at one time or in one relation or at one place fair, at another time or in another relation or at another place foul, as if fair to some and foul to others... but beauty absolute, separate, simple, and everlasting, which without diminution and without increase, or any change, is imparted to the ever-growing and perishing beauties of all other things. [211a-b]

Thus, the nature of the *eidos* of beauty (that which it shares with other *eide*) is simple, immutable, eternal, not a subject of time, place, origin, or context. We also learn from this passage that the true, simple, and divine beauty is 'pure and clear and unalloyed, not clogged with the pollutions of mortality and all the colors and vanities of human life.' However, the nature of beauty as beauty, of the self-subsisting virtue itself by itself is not explained. At the end we do not know what beauty is and cannot define it. Thus it is unclear what constitutes beauty itself as beauty.

This pure beauty is accessible only to 'the eye of the soul'. Here 'vision' (*thea*) is not associated with the perception of shape, color, motion, and any products of the faculties of sense perception or imagination. This imageless 'vision' or contemplation (*theoria*) is also unmediated by the discursive faculties (*dianoia* or *logismos*); it is characterized by the immediate grasps of the primary realities (immutable, simple, and divine *eide*) of the universe. Only 'vision' can lay hold on or grasp *eide* themselves by themselves; the faculties of sense perception, imagination, and discursive reasoning approach *eide* as they appear 'in communion with bodies, motions, and other *eide*, thus in the impure form. Therefore, 'vision' here refers to the noetic phase of the soul and the objects of 'vision' are the *archai*, the first principles constituting primary realities of the universe.

We also learn from the Symposium that the soul that beholds pure beauty with 'the eye of the mind brings' forth and nourishes 'true virtue' and become 'the friend of God' and thus becomes immortal. Goodness and immortality here are intrinsically connected. The virtuous person attains virtues by contemplating *eide*. The noetic phase of the soul is primary responsible for the creation of a virtuous character. Virtuous (or good) character is by implication always beautiful. The intellectualism of Plato in the *Symposium*, as one can notice, is quite remarkable.

It is also important to note that the conjuncture between beauty and goodness (also proposed in other dialogues, for example in the *Greater Hippias*) is intensified in the *Symposium*. Here the erotic lust for beauty goes in conjunction with the desire to possess the Good. Therefore, beauty and goodness are identified as spoken of interchangeably.

> When a man loves the beautiful, what does he desire? I answered her 'That the beautiful may be his.'…'the answer suggests a further question: What is given by the possession of beauty?'… 'let me put the word 'good' in the place of the beautiful, and repeat the question once more: If he who loves, loves the good, what is it then that he loves?' 'The possession of the good,'…'And what does he gain who possesses the good?' 'Happiness'…'the happy are made happy by the acquisition of good things. For there is nothing which men love but the good…'…'the simple truth is, that men love the good.'… 'To which must be added that they love the possession of the good?'…'And not only the possession, but the everlasting possession of the good?'…'Then love'…'may be described generally as the love of the everlasting possession of the good?' [204d-e]

Moreover, the notion of immortality is presented here in conjuncture with beauty and goodness. Thus, all mortal creatures strive for immortality which can be partially attained by 'giving birth in beauty'.

For love, Socrates, is not, as you imagine, the love of the beautiful only.' 'What then?' 'The love of generation and of birth in beauty. But why of generation?' 'Because to the mortal creature, generation is a sort of eternity and immortality,' she replied; 'and if, as has been already admitted, love is of the everlasting possession of the good, all men will necessarily desire immortality together with good: Wherefore love is of immortality.' [206e]

Thus, goodness, beauty, and immortality seem to be intrinsically connected and presented as the final ends, as teleological principles of life that grant happiness.

The epistemic ascent to beauty represents the climax of the dialogue. The possibility of an ascent from the particulars to *eidos* is affirmed. Though the gap between the imperfect particulars and perfect *eide* can only be epistemologically bridged through the leap. Thus, behind the seeming continuity there is a cognitive gap. The preparation for the ascent to beauty in the Symposium is depicted in the following way:

He who would proceed aright in this matter should begin in youth to seek the company of corporeal beauty; and first, if he be guided by his instructor aright, to love one beautiful body only - out of that he should create fair thoughts; and soon he will of himself perceive that the beauty of one body is akin to the beauty of another; and then if beauty of form in general is his pursuit, how foolish would he be not to recognize that the beauty in every form is and the same! And when he perceives this he will abate his violent love of the one, which he will despise and deem a small thing, and will become a lover of all beautiful bodies. In the next stage he will consider that the beauty of the soul is more honorable than the beauty of the outward form...until he is compelled to contemplate and see the beauty of institutions and laws, and to understand that the beauty of them all is of one family, and that personal beauty is a trifle; and after laws and institutions he will go on to the sciences, in order that, beholding the wide region already occupied by beauty, he may cease to be like a servant in love with one beauty only, that of a particular youth or man or institution, himself a slave mean and narrow-minded, but drawing towards and contemplating the vast sea of beauty, he will create many fair and noble thoughts and notions in boundless love of wisdom; until on that shore he grows and waxes strong...[210a-d]

This horizontal expansion from immediate instances of beauty to its more subtle manifestations does not yet grant an immediate knowledge of beauty but signifies a preparatory step in the ascent to beauty itself by itself. Then the ascent proper follows:

And at last the vision is revealed to him of a single science, which is the science of beauty everywhere. He who has been instructed thus far in the things of love, and who has learned to see the beautiful in due order and succession, when he comes toward the end will suddenly perceive a nature of wondrous beauty. [210e]

Ludwig Chen pointed out that here the horizontal expansion associated with the instances of beauty, with the beautiful particulars, described metaphorically as 'the vast sea of the beautiful' is followed by the pause for intellectual strengthening and sudden vision. Thus, 'having reached the group of beautiful sciences, the *philosophos* has to wait before proceeding further. This indicates that the transition from the knowledge which has reached this point to the beholding of the Idea is different in nature from the previous successive expansions from knowledge of one group to knowledge of another group. This transition, not foregoing process of expansion, is the ascent proper.'[38] This indicates the cognitive gap between the beautiful particulars and the *eidos* of beauty which the horizontal expansion is unable to bridge. Thus, the philosopher takes a pause to straighten his capacities. 'The interval lasts until the mind has grown strong enough to take

[38] L.Chen. *Acquiring Knowledge of the Ideas.* Steiner. Stuttgart. 1992. 42.

suddenly the upward leap and to cross the gap. The leap is the ascent, the ascent to the vision of the Idea of beauty.'[39]

However, the final result of the ascent satisfies only one of the two conditions of knowledge proper (*episteme*) in the middle period dialogues, namely, to have 'vision' of *eidos* and an ability to give an account [*Rep.* 534b-c]. Now the question is how this immediate knowledge constituted by 'vision' (*thea*) can be used in discourse and thus incorporated into *logos/oi* to grant us the knowledge proper. Though the possibility of defining *eide* is affirmed as in a number of the middle period dialogues, it is not giving a priority (which is quite clear from the fact that the definitions of virtues are not given there). Rather, the other notion is developed associated with the use of dialectic where *eide* are taken as simple entities which for the reason of their simplicity are not subject of definitions.

It is important in this context to look at the *Republic* [511b-c] and the role of dialectic in translating the non-discursive *thea* (vision) into *logos*. It seems that the ambitious task of giving an account of *eide* is understood here as accomplishable. As Michael Mayer noted, in Plato's middle period dialogues 'dialectic is the method of transition from the hypothetical to the anhypothetical.'[40] The anhypothetical in this context is associated with the highest *eide* (as one might suggest) as the first principles of explanation that themselves cannot be explained (reduced to another principle as their cause) and defined (due to their simplicity). In the *Republic* the idea of the Good is the primary manifestation of the notion of the *arche anhypothetos*. It is a teleological principle of all which is not known as such but through its 'offspring'. It is not clear how dialectic (and the method of hypothesis) precisely works. Multiple interpretations are offered in this regard. What seems to be important in this context is that the *arche anhypothetos* cannot be reached discursively (through the stretches of reasoning, *dianoia*) but is supplied by *thea* and absorbed into discourse in the process of dialectical intertwining of *logoi*.

---

[39] Chen. 1992. 43.
[40] M. Meyer. 'Dialectic and Questioning: Socrates and Plato.' *American Philosophical Quarterly*. 17. 4. October. 1980. 286.

The *Symposium* adds beauty to the list anhypothetical principles. Thus, beauty along the line with goodness is presented as one of the highest *eide* that is, in a sense, beyond explanation and definition. In the *Symposium* both the Good and beauty are presented as the first anhypothetical principles; both are classified as the primary teleological and explanatory principles that themselves cannot be explained. As R.E. Allen noted, both are divine, simple, and thus un-definable.[41] Thus, the *eide* of goodness and beauty are proposed to be teleological principles towards which the soul strives and whose being is beyond the grasp for discursive capacities of human beings. However, these *eide* can be successfully incorporated into discourse (*logos*) as anhypothetical principles upon which the discourse is established.

A legitimate question in this context is what can be said about a simple entity? A lot of things! But nothing that pertains to its essence! Rather its causal activity is something that can be spoken of (here associated with the final cause, *telos*). This gives a way for *eide* to be incorporated into discursive reasoning. Dialectic in this case provides all necessary means for the incorporation.

The *Phaedrus* adds some more details on the notion of beauty. Beauty is described in the dialogue as 'the colorless, formless, intangible essence, visible only to mind, the pilot of the soul' [247c]. Here the soul is presented in the figure of a pair of winged horses and a charioteer. The soul contemplates pure beauty (and other *eide*) in its pre-incarnate state. *Eide* here nourish the soul and allow it to join the celestial parade. Thus, 'beauty, wisdom, goodness, and the like' are the source of nourishment for the wings of the soul. However, the elements of the soul represented by the horses are quite heterogeneous and cause a great disturbance and unbalance in the soul as 'one of them is noble and of noble breed, and the other is ignoble and of ignoble breed; and the driving of them of necessity gives a great deal of trouble to him [the charioteer]' [246b].

If the charioteer is incapable of balancing the houses and gives way to its 'ignoble horse', the soul falls away from the celestial

---

[41] R.E Allen. *Plato, The Symposium.* Yale University Press. New Haven. 1991. 85.

realm due to its incapacity to behold the true being as it becomes deprived of *thea*. Thus, 'fed upon evil and foulness and the opposite of good, [the soul] wastes and falls away' [246d-e]. The fall leads the soul to the incarnation, a state of existence where the soul suffers amnesia, forgets its 'vision' of *eide*. Thus, when the soul is 'unable to follow, and fails to behold the truth, and through some ill-hap sinks beneath the double load of forgetfulness and vice, and her wings fall from her and she drops to the ground, then the law ordains that this soul shall at her first birth pass…into man.' [248c-d]

Fortunately enough, we also learn from the *Phaedrus*, that what distinguishes the *eidos* of beauty from some other highest *eide* (such as wisdom or goodness) is that it has visual counterparts. Thus, the *eidos* of beauty is given to us in communion with bodies and motions.

> But of beauty, I repeat again that we saw her there shining in company with the celestial forms; and coming to earth we find her here too, shining in clearness through the clearest aperture of sense. For sight is the most piercing of our bodily senses; though not by that is wisdom seen; her loveliness would have been transporting if there had been a visible image of her, and the other ideas, if they had visible counterparts, would be equally lovely. But this is the privilege of beauty, that being the loveliest she is also the most palpable to sight [250c-d].

The *eidos* of beauty, as we can see, is transparent to the *aesthesis* and thus manifests itself to a greater extent in the world of things (comparing to wisdom, goodness, and other virtues that are not transparent to the *aesthesis*). Thus, an intellectual object, the *eidos* of beauty, becomes accessible in its impure form to sense perception of the incarnate soul. It is interesting that Plato accentuates this transparence which is so significant because it provokes a deep emotional response as a reminder of the celestial beauty once contemplated by the soul. Moreover, all souls, no matter how educated and spiritually elevated they are seem to have an equal access to beauty through the *aesthesis*. The emotional response to beauty, in turn, seems to be facilitating the recollection of the knowledge of *eide* acquired during the soul's pre-incarnate state.

Thus, another important notion, that of recollection (*anamnesis*), is introduced in the *Phaedrus*. The incarnate soul can recollect the content of *thea* by the recognition of the *eidos* of beauty trough the particulars. Visual counterparts of the *eidos* of beauty, beautiful things (be that a body, or an act, or an institution), provoke an emotional response, draw the soul to themselves and facilitate recollection. The particular beautiful things thus facilitate or trigger, so to say, the recollection of knowledge of *eide*. It indicates the capacity to recognize *eidos* through the particulars.

> Man must needs understand the language of forms, passing from a plurality of perceptions to a unity gathered together by reasoning – and such understanding is a recollection of those things which our souls beheld aforetime as they journeyed with their god, looking down upon the things which now we suppose to be, and gazing up to that which truly is [249c].

Nevertheless, the recognition of the *eidos* of beauty, its recollection, is facilitated by discursive reasoning. Here again both discursive and non-discursive stages of knowledge proper (*episteme*) go in conjunction in the process of recollection. Thus, the transition from recollecting to giving an account (*logos*) is again necessitated; recollection thus runs through *logoi*.

Thus, beauty along with goodness (and wisdom), in the middle period dialogues, represents the highest regulative principle of the soul, its 'final end' that allows soul to rejoin the celestial parade after suffering centuries of amnesia. It helps the incarnate soul to recollect its memories from the pre-incarnate state as it facilitates the recollection by shining out through images in the terrestrial world. This, in turn, facilitates the re-ascent of the soul to the celestial realm. Beauty, goodness, and wisdom (sometimes spoken of interchangeably) thus ultimately lead the soul to the state of happiness, immortality, and divinity (the road to deification in Christian theology). They manifest order (*taxis*) and rationality

44

(*noesis*) of the celestial realm. By contemplating beauty soul partakes (participates of) beauty, becomes beautiful and divine. Moreover, it is through the contemplation of beauty that many other virtues are acquired. This is the way some early church theologians approached the subject.

There is no definition of beauty in the middle period dialogues due to its simplicity and uniformity. The question that the late middle dialogues (i.e. the *Parmenides*) posited, however, was whether *eide* are really simple and uniform. The answer to the question was negative as the demonstration of a certain level of complexity of *eide* was provided (the second deduction of the second part of the *Parmenides* demonstrated such complexity). As a result, *eide* lost their purity and uniformity, become metaphysically complex, interconnected entities characterized by the compresence of opposites. The *Parmenides* thus signified a cancelation of the middle period paradigmatism and the move toward a relational account of *eide* where a certain extensional identity between *eide* was introduced. Moreover, one can clearly see an epistemic shift from non-propositional to propositional account of knowledge in the late period dialogues. An emphasis on the propositional aspect of knowledge, in turn, reintroduced the issue of defining. In addition, the method of collection and division of the late period dialogues will eventually allow for *eide* to be structured into genus-differentiae schema and will thus substantiate the possibility of defining now polyform and complex *eide*, characterized by the compresence of opposites.

Now the question to ask is whether Plato ever moved in this direction with the notion of virtues in general and of beauty in particular. The answer will be negative. Plato never re-formulated the notion of beauty based on the late period metaphysics and epistemology. He has not tried to define beauty again. Thus, the notion of beauty in Plato is associated with the middle period dialogues. It is precisely from those dialogues that the generations of Christian philosophers, theologians, and historians accessed Plato's notion and successfully internalized it.

It is precisely this understanding of beauty that we can find in the Fathers of 4th century as well as those of the 20th century (say, in Florensky's *The Pillar and Ground of the Truth*) who hypostasized the intellectual triad of Goodness, Beauty, and Truth/Wisdom and presented it as the ultimate manifestation of the ineffable deity (Goodness here is a mark of the Father; Truth/Wisdom, of the Son; and Beauty, of the Spirit). It is this understanding of the beauty of the Divine that one can find in Orthodox churches in America. It is this understanding of beauty that makes representtational arts capable of revealing the very nature of the Deity (rather than manifesting idolatry) and speaks of beauty as the ladder that allows the soul to ascent to God. It is precisely this understanding that laid down ground for mystical union with God through *theoria*.

Further Reading.
Primary Texts:

J Burnet	*Platonis Opera*. Vols. 1-5. Clarendon Press. Oxford. 1900-1907.
P Henry & H Schwyzer	*Plotini Opera*. Vols. 1-3. Clarendon Press. Oxford. 1951-67.
E. Hamilton & H. Cairns	*Plato. The Collected Dialogues*. Princeton University Press. Princeton. NJ. 1989.
B. Jowett	*Plato. The Dialogues*. 4 vols. Clarendon Press. Oxford. 1953.
J Barnes (ed)	*Aristotle. The Complete Works*. Princeton University Press. Princeton. NJ. 1984.

Studies:

R E Allen	*Plato, the Symposium*. Yale University Press. New Haven. 1991.
J Beversluis	'Socratic Definition.' *American Philosophical Quarterly*. 2.4. October 1974. (VIII).
L Chen	*Acquiring Knowledge of the Ideas*. Steiner. Stuttgart. 1992.
G Fine	*On Ideas; Aristotle's Criticism of Plato's Theory of Forms*. Clarendon Press. Oxford. 1995.
S Menn	*Plato on God as Nous*. Southern Illinois University Press. Carbondale. 1995.

M Meyer	'Dialectic and Questioning: Socrates and Plato.' *American Philosophical Quarterly*. 17.4 .Oct.1980. 281-9.
J Sallis	*Being and Logos*. Humanities Press International. Atlantic Highlands. NJ. 1986.
A Silverman	*The Dialectic of Essence: A Study of Plato's Metaphysics*, Princeton University Press. Princeton. 2002.
R Sharvy	'Euthyphro 9d-11b: Analysis and Definition in Plato and Others.' *Noûs*. 6. 2. May.1972. 119-137.
H Teloh	*The Development of Plato's Metaphysics*. Pennsylvania State University Press. University Park. 1981.
G Vlastos	'The Socratic Elenchus.' in: G. Fine. (ed). *Plato 1. Metaphysics and Epistemology*. Oxford University Press. Oxford. 1999. 36-63.
Idem.	'Socrates' Disavowal of Knowledge.' in: G. Fine. (ed). *Plato 1. Metaphysics and Epistemology*. Oxford University Press. Oxford. 1999. 64-92.
D Wolfsdorf	'The Socratic Fallacy and the Epistemological Priority of Definitional Knowledge.' *Journal for Ancient Philosophy and Science*, 37.1. March. 2004).
Idem.	'Socrates' Pursuit of Definitions.' *Phronesis*, 48. 4. 2003. 271-31.

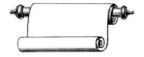

The Subversive Allegorist and the Sublime:
The Good and the Beautiful in Origen of Alexandria
Maya Machacek

Origen's scriptural commentaries have been dismissed at times for speaking to the allegorical meaning inherent within the works as opposed to the typology of these scriptural histories.[42] Origen does indeed exercise allegorical exegesis extensively in interpreting these texts as revelations of a Divinely engaged cosmos. And yet, I would argue, there is a greater or macro-typology at work in his exegeses, which addresses a constant underlying theme of the call to the individual toward moral righteousness built upon scriptural discipline. This meaning, latent in the opacity of the inscribed tome, has a purity that evokes the transformative image of the moral esoteric of divinity.[43] One might equate this change as being akin to the state of *agape*. For the Alexandrian apologist this is a call to metamorphosis, both intentional and extraordinary, that can only permeate the Christian fully over a long period of disciplined scriptural practice. In his Commentaries, his focus remains on the dynamic change present in the very *ousia* of the individual. Origen asserts that with such cultivated agency, one can access the exquisite transfigured Godhead within oneself and be illuminated with a resplendently sublime beauty.

I will begin my examination with excerpts from Origen's treatises on the *Old Testament* (derived chiefly from the *Philocalia*, that collation of his Old Testament work prepared by the Cappadocians Basil and Gregory). Then I will regard, at greater length, the matter of spiritual discipline in his seminal treatise *On First Principles*. Next I will consider that commentary wherein this relationship between scriptural discipline and spiritual perfection is most explicit, namely *On the Song of Songs*. I will conclude with

---

[42] J. O' Keefe. 'Scriptural Interpretation in Origen of Alexandria.' in: JA. McGuckin. (ed). *The Westminster Handbook to Origen*. Westminster John Knox Press. Louisville. Ky. 2004. 2.

[43] PA. Warnek. *Descent of Socrates: Self-Knowledge and the Cryptic Nature in Platonic Dialogues*. Indiana University Press. Bloomington. 2005. 5. Warnek describes this opacity as being inherent in the very capacity of human thinking.

one of his last works, his exegesis of *The Lord's Prayer*. I will argue that this, for him, is substantially his elegiac biography, an allegorical examination of his own faith as he lay waiting, racked in body in the aftermath of his torture during the persecution, for that sublime transcendence in the superlunary sphere.

To begin with, let us examine the understanding of allegorical reading as it pertains to the Hellenistic literary canon. In the 3rd century, the understanding of sacred writings (scripture or the Hellenistic *mythoi*) was largely conducted as an exegesis-of-excavation seeking the hidden truth within the written word. There was an inexorable curiosity to unearth the precise meaning held within the occlusive grasp of the physical text. This can be seen as a search for *to symbolon* or the mystical symbolic that is contained in the tight embrace of the scribed word. Thus, the only path to bring forth the hidden meaning is through a keen perception of the inner *logos*.[44] This fundamentally allegorical hermeneutic is the familiar method of philosophical and literary exegesis during the time that Origen of Alexandria was writing. Accordingly, he undertakes the work of making the 'supernatural visible' by mining the depths of mystical understanding to uncover the *hyponoia*, the substance of the text.[45] After this, this Mid-Platonic Alexandrian scholar moves through discovering the *hyponoia* to understand the *all-egoria*, the 'otherwise speaking' — the divine undertone — as it occurs in these Biblical passages.[46] Boyarin discusses Origen's move from pure Platonism to his more specific forms of delving into the depths of allegory:

> Platonism provided a framework within which Origen could think about the question of how we interpret; and Christian logos theology, the notion of Christ as the

---

[44] R. Copeland and PT. Struck. (eds). *The Cambridge Companion to Allegory*. CUP. Cambridge. 2010. 3.

[45] JK. Brown. *The Persistence of Allegory: Drama and Neo-Classicism from Shakespeare to Wagner*. University of Philadelphia Press. Philadelphia. 2007. 5

[46] G W Most. 'Hellenistic allegory and Early Imperial Rhetoric'. In *The Cambridge Companion to Allegory*, edited by R. Copeland and P. T. Struck. CUP. Cambridge. 2010. 37

incarnation of the Word, provided a solution to problems left unsolved by Platonism.[47]

To comprehend Origen's method of exegesis, therefore, we must allow that his vision is clearly set on the incarnation and the elevation of humankind through that miraculous double transfiguration, archetype and type. Boyarin is supported in this understanding by Edwards who posits that allegory in scripture is a without a doubt a 'corollary of faith'.[48] Origen has often been called a subversive exegete of the scriptures — among other colorful nomenclatures — when dealing with concepts as elusive as creation, transfiguration, salvation and other such cosmological philosophies of faith, but when reading inspired Biblical texts it is significant for us to recognize Origen's insistence that the only construct befitting scriptural interpretation is first to understand the *hyponoia* in order to discern the inherent *allegoria*.

An influential predecessor of Origen's, while not himself concerned with the issues of incarnation, was in agreement with Origen in this understanding of Scriptural reading. Philo thought that 'only prelapsarian Adam among men had had direct access to the Logos'.[49] Here Philo is speaking of the independent (hypostatic) divine Word of God, not the Christian concept of the Incarnate Word. Still, it is this same approach that becomes the foundation of Origen's exegesis of the inspired text of Christian faith. That which Philo deems the 'magic language' which the impenetrable Logos, revealed only to a few — such as Moses, who can himself only express it in a reversion to ordinary language — requires a careful unveiling of its underlying blinding light, the treasure of the Father's self-expression, always splendorous to behold, which vision then transfigures the beholder.[50] This

---

[47] D. Boyarin, 'Origen as theorist of allegory: Alexandrian Contexts.' In *The Cambridge Companion to Allegory*, edited by R. Copeland and P.T. Struck. CUP. Cambridge. 2010. 39

[48] MJ. Edwards. *Origen Against Plato*. Ashgate Press. Aldershot. 2002. 32.

[49] Boyarin. 2010. 44. See also RL. Enos. *Greek Rhetoric Before Aristotle*. Waveland Press. Prospect Heights. 1993. 73.

[50] Boyarin. 2010. 44-45

transformation, to the great Alexandrian, is beautiful. For Origen this is, in its essence, sublime beauty.

We now move to some specific works of Origen. In that exemplar of living in heavenly equanimity, in *Genesis*, God is seen as giving two specific commandments to Adam. The first, is pronounced in the singular and the other, in the plural. This singular exhortation is a positive one, to eat of every tree in the garden; and the plural is a command in the negative, namely not to eat of the tree of the knowledge of good and evil.[51] It is this singular expression of the positive command (the call to action—to go forth and do what God has said) which is of interest to Origen as exegete. He does not see here a mere gesture of largesse on the part of the Father. Instead he posits that anything that directs to a good act is a commandment of singularity because the underlying meaning, the *hyponoia*, asserts a union with the Divine, the Logos. Thus when we act as God directs, we enact a visceral metamorphosis akin to the second Adam whose spirit of divinity we hold within the cusp of our mortal being. Even if only for that prodigious instant, we are intrinsically within God the Logos, and thus encapsulated in the one. In the breath of that moment, our being is transmuted into a more beautiful form. It is an anticipation of our eschatological vocation to return to union with the Logos who made us, and from whom we have lapsed in this earthly existence.

The Alexandrian philosopher subsequently turns his attention to free will. Free will is for Origen both the gift and the pathway for achieving salvation. Since our free will is from God, and God is good, free will, according to Origen, is always captivated by that which is good.[52] However, he supposes that there is always an opposition between the creaturely instigation of instinct and the rapture of the rational. To illustrate this he regards the spider weaving its web as a creature that is acting on instinct. In fact, its very survival in terms of food and shelter depends on honoring

---

[51] George Lewis *(ed) The Philocalia of Origen*. (8.2). T&T Clark, Edinburgh. 1911. 45. (fragm. of Origen's *Commentary on Hoseah*).
[52] *First Principles*. 3.1.2. in: Lewis. 1911. 139. & (tr.). H. De Lubac. New York. 1966. 157-159.

this insistent call.[53]   In contrast we have the rational human. Origen posits that humanity possesses 'in the nature of reason possibilities of contemplating good and evil'.[54] While he concedes that the call to either action is external, he insists that the choice of response rests in our free will. Since Christian nature is united with the Logos and free will is a gift of the Divine within us, our deepest yearning is for virtue and, when we follow that nobler call, we reflect the sublime likeness of God.

Origen takes his concept of the yearning for righteousness within free will one step further. He argues that divine mercy is not akin to a denaturing of the rational man. In other words, he takes exception to those who assert that since it is mercy that saves and not our own good works, then our actions are indifferent and thus of no value in our salvation. Origen posits that exertion is not an indifferent act but rather a strong indication of inherent good.[55] In fact, he posits that the movement, or *kinesis*, toward a desired goal has the quality of the prize contained within it. Christ admonishes that the one who lusts after another in the heart has already fornicated. Origen extrapolates that thus free will makes the act of seeking an evil outcome as malicious as the evil end.   And, accordingly, the seeking of good is similarly beneficial to the ref- inement of the spirit.[56] In the context of his exegesis of the para- disial garden in Genesis, Origen is presuming his doctrine of the pre-existential fall from grace of the *Noes* directly created by the Divine Logos. But he emphatically stresses the existential aspect of humanity's post-lapsarian crisis and argues that ethically we, like our first parents, are capable of rational thought. We can use that reason to seek to be more like God or we can choose to follow the less righteous path, as did the first denizens of Eden. When we desire good in that refining pursuit we have sublimated our instinct into a quest for beauty.

Throughout his *First Principles* Origen argues most forcefully for the rational human, one who can determine right from wrong and

---

[53] *First Principles.* 3.1.2. (tr.) De Lubac. 1966.159.
[54] *First Principles.* 3.1.3. (tr.) De Lubac. 1966. 159.
[55] *First Principles.* 3.1.18. Lewis 1911. 156; De Lubac. 1966. 195-196.
[56] *First Principles.* 3.1.18. De Lubac. 1966. 196.

then, carefully, choose the good. He insists, however, that such positive choices are the result of the consistent exercise of the rational faculty. Thus he elucidates:

> The rational animal, however, has something besides its imaginative nature, namely reason, which judges the images. Some it rejects, others it approves of, the object being that the creature may be guided in accordance with these latter images. So it happens that, since there are in the nature of reason possibilities of contemplating good and evil, by following out which and contemplating them both we are led to choose good and avoid evil, we are worthy of praise when we devote ourselves to the practice of good, and of blame when we act in the opposite way. [57]

Origen contrasts animal behavior or instinctive action, with that of rational creatures, those who have access to the sublime through the transfigurative life of Christ. As humans, we share in the energy of *Logos* and are enabled to apprehend the nature of good and evil; so when we exercise the rational faculty, we choose the better path. Later in this same passage, he argues that this rationality is not possessed by the human alone. He concedes that even in the creatures created for Adam's dominion there are varying degrees of rational inclination. So he assigns some nobility to animals such as dogs and warhorses which he endows with thoughtful actions, of selective loyalty and distinctive courage respectively. However for Origen, it is only the Christian, elevated to an advantageous perception of moral action through Christ's illumination of elect humanity, who can truly choose between right and wrong. All moral human choice is built upon the premiss of the possession of reason (*logos*); but this issue of being possessed by reason involves more than a mere human capacity for ratiocination, it is an issue of no less than Union with divine Wisdom (*Logos*):

> To be subject, then, to a particular external impression which gives rise to such or such image is admittedly not one of the things lying within our power; but to decide to use what has

---

[57] *First Principles.* 3.1.3. (tr.) De Lubac. 1966. 159-160.

happened either this way or in that is the work of nothing else but the reason (*logos*) within us, which, as the alternatives appear, either influence us towards the impulses that incite to what is good (*kalon*) or seemly or else turns us aside to the reverse.[58]

The human senses thus outwardly assailed can do better than react—even with noble *instinct*—but can instead determine a course of action. In this passage the Greek word *to kalon* is used (a synonym for the good as well as the beautiful). Thus it is Origen's teaching that when we discipline our sensibilities and refine our senses to choose the good, we exemplify a divine morality that is an aesthetic of virtue. The good is the beautiful. This representation is only fractional in the Christian who is still 'on the ascent'. It is perfect in the archetype of *to kalon* who is the Divine Logos; union with whom is noetic creation's perfection.

Origen takes another moral example to elaborate his case when he puts forward the instance of the virtuous man in the face of a seductress:

> For instance, when a woman displays herself before a man who has determined to remain chaste and to abstain from sexual intercourse and invites him to act contrary to his purpose, she does not become the absolute cause of the abandonment of that purpose. The truth is that he is first entirely delighted with the sensation and lure of the pleasure and has no wish to resist it nor to strengthen his previous determination; and only then does he commit the licentious act. On the other hand, the same experiences may happen to one who has undergone more instruction and discipline; that is, the sensations and incitements are there, but his reason, having been strengthened to a higher degree and trained by practice and confirmed towards the good by right doctrines, or at any rate being near to such confirmation, repels the incitements and gradually weakens the desire.[59]

---

[58] *On First Principles*. 3.1.3. (tr.) De Lubac. 1966. 159-160.
[59] *On First Principles*. 3.1.4. (tr.) De Lubac. 1966. 161-2.

We see that for Origen, discipline and method are foremost in managing the instincts that would allow our lower, instinctive, nature to dominate our noetic capacities for transcendence. If we can extrapolate from the previous passage, no creature other than the graced human is expected to exercise moral restraint in the face of such a basic natural instinct as the sexual drive. Origen concedes that for those without ascetic discipline, the instinctive impulse will dominate all higher principles. However, when the faculties are disciplined, while the temptation may persist the desire to capitulate recedes in the face of forceful resistance in the form of a choice toward the right action, in this case chastity. Origen barely considers the seductress; in this case her endowments are to him secondary to the reaction of the man who beholds them. The metaphor here is that external reality can be subdued by the greater will of a cultivated faith. The free will to choose remains solely with the human being.[60] It is the man who is vested with the disciplined rationality that can access this spiritually beautifying action.

Origen also turns his attention towards refuting those who cite pure mercy as the plan of God's salvation.[61] Their contention is that choice has nothing to do with salvation since moral action is a human set of choices but salvation is a free gift of mercy. Origen's response to these detractors reiterates his stand on what are the principles that depict *to kalon*. Free will, he says, determines our course of action. We respond not instinctually but rather through reason to all that assaults our senses. Thus we enact choice. But this choice is determined with free will which is our gift from the transfigured incarnated *Logos*, who himself was tempted but sublimated his instinctual desire (e.g. to release himself from the cross) for the greater cause of being the moral exemplar of salvation for humankind. Since we are made in the image of that God, Origen implies, we too can choose the more arduous path of the disciplined nature (*Nous*) eschewing fleshly weakness for another step on the ascentive path to reunion with the Father

---

[60] *On First Principles.* 3.1.5. 'Reason therefore shows that external things do not lie within our power; but to use them in this way in which we ought to deal with each of them is our task.' De Lubac. 1966.163.

[61] *On First Principles.* 3.1.18. De Lubac. 1966. 194-195.

through the *Logos*. Thus, once again, the choice to act is not an indifferent quality with reference to good and evil. For Origen, the transfigurative sublime is a determined movement, a *kinesis*, within our spiritual and corporeal natures, to see and sense our God in whose image we are made, and in whose presence we ache to be once more.

This iconic movement of poignantly reaching for the Divine is most apparent in his commentary on *The Song of Songs*.[62] For Origen, assuming that the drift within the rhythm of this evocative poesy is mere sexual yearning, is the mark of an unenlightened mind. That vision of physicality, he asserts, is the metaphorical darkness which plagues the bride and isolates her from her kins-women and delays her prize, the groom. The sexual metaphor refers to the opacity of the inviolable word which will reveal its *symbolon* only to a mind adroit in penetrating the Scriptural mysteries. When we mature in our faith, according to Origen, we begin to sense and refine the enlightened divine capacity with us. With that cultivated faculty we can begin to anticipate the spiritual vision that will let us part the scriptural veil. Lawson considers this hermeneutic in Origen's method:

> The study called inspective is that by which we go beyond things seen and contemplate somewhat of things divine and heavenly, beholding them with the mind alone, for they are beyond the range of bodily sight . . . in this he (God) instills into the soul the love of things divine and heavenly, using for his purpose the figure of the Bride and the Bridegroom, and teaches us that communion with God must be attained by the paths of charity and love.[63]

Karen Jo Torjesen [64] echoes this understanding. She posits that we must first inspect the methodology behind Origen's assertion that this Old Testament work is a dramatic poem. She reasons that, for him, in this canticle the scriptural typologies reside within those

[62] *Song of Songs Commentary. Prologue. 1.* RP. Lawson. (tr.) London. 1957. 22.
[63] *Song of Songs Commentary. Prologue. 3.* Lawson. 1957. 40-41.
[64] Karen Jo Torjesen. *Hermeneutical Procedure and Theological Method in Origen's Exegesis.* Walter de Gruyter. Berlin. 1985. 8

rhetorical constructs that are most immediately accessible to our earthbound forms. These are the vehicles that deliver the mystical message of the incarnation into an apprehensible matter suitable for human consumption. Here Origen foreshadows the premise that later in this treatise he will more fully develop: that this is the very reason God was incarnated as man, since it was the only incontrovertible principle that could illuminate our path to salvation. She then elucidates how, for Origen, this typology is applied to the written word:

> Scripture, like the Incarnation itself, is a form of the *Kenosis* of the Logos through which he accommodates himself to the human need for sensible forms of knowledge . . . Exegesis as the movement from the letter to the spirit is then equivalent to the process of the discovery of, and the encounter with, the Logos through the means of the visible symbols in which he has incarnated himself. [65]

Thus, the *Song of Songs* is a dramatic wedding song since that expectant yearning of the alluring virginal bride for the enthrallment of her vigorous noble groom is a form that will systematize meaning for a reader familiar with courtship rituals. Once the reader is enchanted into the lyrical *poiesis*, [66] they can begin to discern the spiritual *hyponoia* represented by the metaphor of the dramatists within their allegorical play. [67]

Origen begins by examining the bridal party, where we encounter several familiar yet enigmatic paradigms. First, we hear from the bride who extols her sultry beauty and then, uncharacteristically, immediately laments the hue of her skin which she mourns is scorched by the sun[68]. Later, she lauds her labor in preparing for

---

[65] Torjesen. 1985. 8

[66] *Plato. Symposium.* (ed) C.J. Rowe. Aris & Phillips. Warminster. 1998. 85

[67] According to Warnek. 2005. xiii: 'Socrates suggests . . . skilful and competent knowledge, with regard to anything notable becomes possible only through a prior relation to this nature that exceeds its own proper domain and that, for this reason, a worthy *logos* of the nature of the soul or body is not possible without [relating to] the whole of nature.' (*Phaedrus.* 270).

[68] c.f. MSM.Scott. 'Shades of Grace: Origen and Gregory of Nyssa's Soteriological Exegesis of the "Black and Beautiful" Bride in Song of Songs 1:5.' *Harvard*

her bridegroom while simultaneously issuing a complaint against her servile toil, laid on her by her kinsmen, which has darkened her complexion from exposure.[69] So there is a discordant strain of expectant effort intertwined with a forlorn undertone of lament which she directs at an obscuring gloom characterized as the clouding of her visage. In his exegesis, Origen interprets her preparatory labor as distinct from her manual exertions in the fields. He deciphers the latter as the work of her unformed spirituality while her expectant work, the work of her maturity, is assessed as a metaphor for her scrutiny of the law and the prophets in anticipation of her Savior. Her dusky complexion, for Origen, is an allegory for her ignoble birth. She does not possess patriarchal lineage.[70] Origen however exegetes the value of her tone as representative of her tincture of sin which is the natural hue of a fallen nature. She has, however, through long preparation, in the examination of the law and the prophets, symbolically cleansed herself so that while the outward aspect remains indelible for those who can only behold her physicality, she is within, for those who can distinguish it, a vessel that is purified and thus excellent. For Origen, her 'penitence and faith' have recast her swarthy vestige into an illumined beauty.[71]

Origen believes that such a transformative humility (keenly to regard one's own failings and then purposefully employ restoration) can only be the result of a burgeoning self-awakening.[72] This self-knowledge is an essential characteristic of the Platonic ideal of beauty eloquently described by the priestess Diotima in the *Symposium*. Once this realization begins, the journey leads to a perfection of form. [73] It is this ideal vessel, recr-

---

Theological Review 99.1. January. 2006. 65-83. Scott's study advances that the 'innovative use of allegory' enables Origen to 'transcend racial categories and thus to obviate what might appear to modern readers as racist rhetoric.' He further expounds that, in this commentary, Origen 'utilizes black imagery to convey soteriological truth rather than racial stereotypes or anti-black sentiments', to consider 'ultimately not . . . race but . . . the doctrine of salvation.'

[69] *Song of Solomon.* 1.5-6. Lawson. 1957. 84-90, 106-113.

[70] *Song of Songs Commentary.* 2.1. Lawson. 1957.92.

[71] *Song of Songs Commentary.* 2.1. Lawson. 1957.93.

[72] *Song of Songs Commentary.* 2.1. Lawson. 1957.130.

[73] *Plato. Symposium.* (ed). Rowe. 1998. 97.

afted by such a transubstantiation and cleansed by the full apprehension of that legacy— nothing less than a humanity reborn in
the New Adam - that can accommodate the groom, the
transfigured Christ.

When examined in this way, in terms of a human vessel
enlightened by the knowledge of an imminent salvation, Origen's
exegesis clearly focuses on clarifying this underlying narrative of
a plaintive rhapsody to be completely conquered by Christ. The
bride's initial work in the fields which yields naught but a
darkening, is a labor unenlightened by faith. Thus it produces no
discernible good fruit. In fact these exertions have instead
brought forth a psychic darkness which, metaphorically, clouds
her physiognomy. Unschooled in her divine birthright, her
misdirected labors, fueled by a misunderstood legacy, leads her
into a corruptibility which disfigures her form. At this moment,
she sees herself as a mere earthen vessel, as yet unprepared to be
filled with good gifts.[74] Aware of her Creator, she does not yet
know of her integral relationship with His image. However,
when she comes to discern herself and her lineage (the truth that
her election is not of the prophets but instead of the Divine Logos
himself) she finally beholds her true form, which is but a sheer
veil concealing the transfiguration.[75] Captivated by faith, she
begins a new labor that begins to clarify her countenance. It is
this silhouette, recreated in a seraphic purity which, being now
unveiled, enchants the groom and draws him near.

This journey is unique in that her new labors of refining her form
with the study of the law and the prophets do not fill her but
rather cleanse her. This clarifying action which flushes her
corruption, simultaneously chisels her nature into one that is a
perfectly shaped vessel for Christ.[76] In other words, for Origen,
this song is a template for our journey to reclaim our gracious

---

[74] 2 Corinthians 4.7

[75] *Plato. Symposium.* Rowe. 1998. 128

[76] *Plato. Symposium.* Rowe. 1998. 91. Diotima schools the inquisitive Socrates into an understanding of this transmigration of form by stating that: 'The process of coming-into-being . . . always leaves behind something else that is new in place of the old.'

form that is incorruptible, through the complete assumption of our Being into the transfigured new nature purchased by Christ's sacrifice. This is the *kinesis* (a theme running through the Song of Songs) which senses our Savior and moves in an insistent rhythm toward an exquisitely transcendent convergence of being. In that consummate synthesis we rest in a state of splendorous beauty. In this journey we imitate our Savior who, converted the treachery of His Crucifixion, by willingly emptying Himself through death in order to fulfill the reclamation all of humankind into that state of eternal grace.

Accordingly, our Savior's time on earth was not merely defined by his vocation of teaching but also stood as the archetype that would call forth Salvation. It is for this reason that, in Origen's exegesis of this dramatic allegory, the bride is the figure who recognizes the echo of her true arrangement and recomposes herself to harmonize with the transubstantiated Christ, so that she can be united with her God. This is an act of complete submission of the natural self so that it can be reformed into a vessel that can merge with the new Adam.

This passage to being conformed to the divine is a journey so arduous that even Christ himself, in absolute realization of the terrible culminating sacrifice, hesitated, and asked if perhaps there was another way.[77] But, then, he capitulated entirely to the divine will. For the true disciple of God, this mystical journey demands unconditional surrender. It is a journey of a complete rendering to be viscerally begotten anew in full consummation of the salvific grace of Christ transfigured. This supreme sublimation to achieve the euphonic pitch of transcendental unity with the divine is the final perfection of humanity; it is sublime beauty. It is no wonder that Origen cautions us to reach carefully and in full maturity of faith, for the text of the *Song of Songs*.

Origen's commentary on *The Lord's Prayer*, begun in his early time as a presbyter at Caesarea, expounds at length on this most simple and yet profound of exclamations to the Father taught to us by the

---

[77] Matthew 26.39. Origen considered the Great Soul Jesus as a distinct *hypostasis* to the Divine Logos; a path down which the later Church Fathers did not follow.

Son. He considers it as a most perfect exhortation in so far as it was the invocation first uttered by the Son in private before being revealed to His followers. His primary focus is on the formula recorded in the *Gospel of Matthew*. In this context, Jesus has been teaching at considerable length: presenting ethical rules and new instructions, including the *Beatitudes*. Finally, He expounds on prayer culminating in that iconic exposition that has become the *Lord's Prayer*. Origen considers seriously the context of this prayer. He determines that it was necessary for our Lord first to instruct His followers on the cleansing effects of humility, mercy and righteousness. According to Origen the corporeal is, by definition, corruptible. Prayer, in contrast, is purity in essence. And yet, it too can become defiled and even impotent when humans import vain, earthbound, desires into it. So while we can dignify our fallen human form through prayer, we can also drag it further into corruptibility if we debase our prayer with our own vanity.[78] The inescapable cloak of humanity seems to be our potential for degradation. Thus it is only when Christ penetrates the corruptible that he subdues and subjugates human depravity. Then, through that sublimation He elevates humanity into divine communion. That ennobling ascent reflects resplendent sublime beauty. It is this that Origen interprets as the *allegoria*; namely the true purpose of the *Lord's Prayer*.

Origen opens his exposition on the correct mode of prayer as follows:

> But the man who is no mere actor, but has rid himself of everything that is not his very own, and sets out to make himself accepted in a theatre incomparably greater than any mentioned, enters into his chamber to his stored up wealth where he has shut away for himself the treasure of wisdom and knowledge. He pays no attention to nor does he desire anything outside, but closes all doors of sensation so that he may not be drawn away by the senses, nor any sensory image come into his mind. He prays to the Father who does not

---

[78] *On Prayer*. 19.2. (tr.) J O'Meara. London. 1954. 67-68.

shun nor abandon such secrecy, but abides there, and with Him, His Only-Begotten Son.[79]

Origen suggests that, in the depths of prayer, we should put off every part of the natural man, even the parts capable of refinement on which he expostulated in *On First Principles*. Within the interior prayer chamber there is no room for the carnal. To conceive the beauty of that cohesion with the Divine, all nature, even a refined sense of knowledge and wisdom, must be muted. Fallen beings that we are, we must empty every form of our corruption which we take in through our senses. The *symbolon*, the metaphor, he uses here is of an emptied chamber that can now be filled. Then that space is pierced with the beauty of the Father. It is the transfigured Son, the groom who is the Christ who will enter and redeem. For Origen, this happens in a melodious duet, in the perfection of the call and response of prayer.

As we have seen in Origen's exegesis of the *Song of* Songs, the purification of the earthbound form is a necessary part of the intake of the refining spirit. For Origen this process encapsulates the journey of prayer that culminates in a perfect union with the divine inhabiting the material form.[80] Origen expounds further on the matter of knowledge and wisdom which, in *On First Principles*, were exalted as exemplars of the human capacity for rationality, a quality which draws us closer to a God-like persona. Extrapolating from Paul's *First Letter to the Corinthians* he says:

> The kingdom of God will be fully established in us if we advance with ceaseless effort, when the word of the Apostle will be fulfilled, namely that Christ, when all enemies shall be subdued unto Him, shall deliver up the Kingdom to God and

---

[79] *On Prayer*. 20.2. O'Meara. 1954. 70.
[80] See also: K & E Corrigan. *Plato's Dialectic at Play: Argument, Structure and Myth in the Symposium*. The Pennsylvania State University Press. PA. 2004. 235. There are many similarities with Plato's understanding of the purification necessary for the Soul in its return to the Ideal Form.

the Father, so that God may be all in all. Therefore (pray) without ceasing with a disposition made divine by the Word.[81]

Here he draws upon the initial fall of Adam who made corrupted that which was pure and then the redemption by Christ, the second and final Adam, who took on sin without becoming sinful in order to destroy corruption and save mankind.[82] Origen expects that the rationality of this progression will be perceived as true beauty as he asserts that those who have refined and thus magnified their Divine capacities will be drawn inexorably to the veracity of this perfect paradigm of redemption.[83]

After setting these large-scale soteriological horizons, Origen's commentary then turns to an exegesis of our request for daily bread.[84] Origen argues that rather than a substantive feeding, this is instead a request for a 'super-substantial', an *epiousios* sustenance.[85] Once we are cleansed, we seek to be filled by the indivisible *ousia*, which mystery (like bread remaining unbroken in itself – where he recalls the miracle of the feeding of the multitudes), can nonetheless fill, refresh, and sustain our mortal shell by its purified essence. He notes that, even momentarily, when we are perfected in such a spiritually refined prayer, we share in the divine immortality.[86] In its Aristotelian sense, this is for Origen the symmetrical beauty of the soul.[87]

A gradual ascent to sublime beauty is not without its snares. Thus Origen finds it necessary to refute critics who claim that any God who would 'test' his followers is not a good god.[88] The supplication to be delivered from testing, in the Lord's Prayer is,

---

[81] *First Principles*. 25.2. O'Meara. 1954. 86. See also 1 Corinthians 15.24-28 and K. & E Corrigan. 2004. 170-2, who allude to the Platonic influence on Origen as he evaluates the condition of a fallen humanity with a capacious flair for the Divine.
[82] 1 Corinthians 15. 20-25
[83] *On Prayer*. 27.2-4. O'Meara. 1954. 92-95.
[84] Matthew 6.1; *On Prayer*. 27.2. O'Meara. 1954. 92.
[85] *On Prayer*. 27.7. O'Meara. 1954. 96.
[86] *On Prayer*. 27. 7-11. O'Meara. 1954. 96-99.
[87] K. & E. Corrigan. 2004. 234
[88] *On Prayer*. 29.13. O'Meara. 1954. 120.

according to Origen, a result of our own fallen natures. [89] The corporeal form will succumb to evil. God's didactic and therapeutic method, on our behalf, is then to intensify the experience of that evil. And so, all suffering is indeed a consequence of our fall. When we are sufficiently chastised so that we no longer even wish for carnal pleasures, because of the pains they inevitably bring upon us, God will deliver us from our sins.[90] Thus in a strange correlation, our own failings become the stairway back to the ascent to beauty.

The argument that our sinful natures are the very catalytic paradigm for our salvation is not problematic for Origen. He asserts that it is only when we have experienced the true depravity of sin that we can elect the good. The development of a discerning mentality is, for Origen, a first premise of the corporeal form moving away from a sensory state to one that begins to mimic the nature of God. Thus a righteous Divine vengeance in the purposeful drowning of the senses in depravity as a result of our instinct-led assent to debauchery, is like the allegory of gold that is tested in fire.[91] Thus chastised, our rational faculties, in subdued humility, and emptied of the wicked impulses, will yearn with more intensity for the face of God.[92] Then the indivisible good will gather us into that capacious engulfing of salvation; and, so transformed, we will become sublime in the countenance of our spirit.[93]

---

[89] Matthew 5.12; *On Prayer*.29.13. O'Meara. 1954. 120.

[90] RPC. Hanson,. *Allegory and Event: A Study of the Sources and Significance of Origen's Interpretation of Scripture*. SCM Press. London. 1959. 214. 'The Word is a physician of souls, and as physicians often deliberately aggravate and worsen their patients states, that they may eventually cure them, so God often deliberately leaves people in sin or hardens them that he may lead them more surely to final repentance . . .'

[91] See the notion expressed by John Donne in: 'A Valediction Forbidding Mourning.' *John Donne: The Complete English Poems*. C.A. Patrides (ed). Everyman's Library. New York. 1991. 97

[92] JA. McGuckin. *At the Lighting of the Lamps: Hymns of the Ancient Church*. SLG Press. Oxford. 1995.

[93] *On Prayer*. 29.15; ibid. 27.2. O'Meara. 1954. 124.

We can see the motif of progression into the fulfillment of salvation by transfigured communion (an abiding theme for Origen), in the commentaries we have regarded here. We began this essay by observing Origen's scrutiny of the commandments given to our pre-lapsarian parents by the Logos; and then we turned to his insistence that discipline was the proper way to rediscover our potential for participation in divine communion, through an immortal transubstantiation. That formidable discipline was further exemplified in his treatise on the *Song of Songs*. Christ's admonition on the right manner of prayer, addressed in his *Commentary on the Lord's Prayer* is, in a manner of speaking, Origen's final admonition on the subject, as this exemplary devotion becomes his own evocation of the promise of healing redemption. Origen has journeyed from his foundational Platonism to redefine the Christian principle of conjoining with the One, the Logos Incarnate. In doing so, he has defined for other generations, a deeply Christian path towards the ascent to Beauty as it is revealed in the Incarnation.

Origen's Commentary on the *Our Father*:
A Prayer of Love, Forgiveness, and Beauty.

Pr. Dr. Nicu Dumitraşcu

The Bread of the soul

Prayer is the *Anaphora*, the lifting up, of our mind, and heart and will to God. It is the means by which we speak to our heavenly Father of our heart's desire for redemption and happiness. To put it another way, prayer is the loving and trustful conversation of the soul with God. Even as children talk to their parents, so Christians address God in prayer. He is the origin and final destination of everything. For a true Christian, prayer is the nourishment of the soul; only by feeding the soul with prayer can a Christian achieve life and happiness in the divine Kingdom.

Prayer does not consist simply of the movement of the lips, for they are merely the means of the voice of the heart; but it must be done with perseverance, trust and hope. In Church as well as in the privacy of the home, the believer can pray, and not only by means of contemplative meditation, but also vocally in song.[94] Irrespective of the way in which it is performed, prayer is graciously received by God if it is made with considerately and attentively, with mind and heart unified in a single cry to God.

Nevertheless, in order that our prayer can become a 'column of fire' rising from earth to heaven and be received by God day and night under all of life's circumstances, then prayer must be made with tears of repentance, a humble spirit, and with contrite heart (with *Penthos*). As the prophet David said in Psalm 50: 'a troubled spirit, a broken and contrite heart, O God, you will not despise'. Jesus assured us that 'Whatever you ask for in prayer, believe that you have received it, and it will be yours' (Mark 11:24) and Paul exhorts us: Pray unceasingly (Colossians 4:2).

---

[94] Orthodox spirituality envisages three types of prayer: *Laudatory*, through which we praise and glorify God, *Thanksgiving*, when we offer thanks for all that we have received from God and *Intercessory (petitionary)*, by means of which we ask our heavenly Father to forgive us and show forth his mercy.

Throughout the two thousand year history of the Church many of the Fathers, hermits, and laity composed prayers addressed to the Father, the Son, and the Holy Spirit, to the Holy Trinity, the Ever Virgin Mary, the angels and the saints. Yet none of these prayers ever reached the heights of that which was given to us by Jesus Christ Himself in his Sermon on the Mountain, namely *The Lord's Prayer*.

The Lord's Prayer is the synthesis of all Christian teachings on salvation. There was not, and there is not in the heritage of Christian spirituality, in public or individual worship, in the catechetical or homiletic *corpus*, ever such a complex and perfect prayer. It basically sums up all the elements of the *thesaurus* of Christian faith. In terms of its origin and content, the Lord's Prayer is divine, the gift of the Saviour Christ Himself. It is simple and understandable for all Christians, regardless of their level of education, and is short, being a true digest of all our requests. In terms of its structure and shape, the Lord's Prayer is a masterpiece in form; showing forth a perfect harmony, an articulated structure and impeccable internal logic. In respect to its nature, it is a prayer of universal brotherhood, evoking unity and peace between people.[95] In short, it summarizes the entire Christian faith as it has been taught out of the Holy Scripture and Church tradition.[96]

For such reasons, it has been a perennial concern of the Church Fathers, and the interpreters of the Holy Scriptures, to interpret it the prayer exegetically and make it known to all. One of the

---

[95] M. Neamțu. 'Rugăciunea domnească în tâlcuirile Sfinților Părinți (The Lord's Prayer in the Interpretation of the Holy Fathers)'. *Mitropolia Olteniei*. 7-8. 1973. 571-574.

[96] In this regard we can also note the opinion of Saint Maximus the Confessor according to which through the 'Our Father' we ask from God to give us all the goods that arose from the work of the embodied Word of God. In other words, the petition is not made in relation to quotidian needs and requests, but refers to the fullness of the goods of salvation [T.Zisis. 'Rugăciunea domnească în tâlcuirea Sfântului Maxim Mărturisitorul (*The Lord's Prayer in the Interpretation of Saint Maxim the Confessor*), translated by Grigorie Benea from the Greek to Romanian: *Tabor*. 8. November 2010. 6.]

earliest of the interpreters was Origen, the most important exponent of the Alexandrian school of exegesis. The Lords' Prayer consists of the opening address and seven petitions following after it. Origen builds his commentary around that list, and we shall follow his structural progress in what follows.

Filial relationship

For the Fathers, the opening phrase 'Our Father who art in heaven' has a deep *Trinitarian* and *filial* character. The *Trinitarian* character lies in the fact that once the Father is addressed, automatically the Son and the Holy Spirit are invoked in trinitarian *taxis*. Moreover, we are led to address the Father as 'our' Father in the revelation that we are all brothers and sisters in Christ. This is the *filial* character. One of Origen's primary notes is the way he thinks attention must be paid to the form of address. Why God is named 'Father'? And who has the right to address God as Father?

He explains the difference between the ways of thinking about God in the worlds of the Old Testament texts and those of the New. In the Old Testament the idea of 'Father' is associated with that of Master, inspiring awe, and the term 'son' is very close to that of slave.[97] Things have changed so dramatically through the coming of Christ, for Origen, that in the New Testament the very notion of *son* has been redefined. All can become *sons* of God on these terms: believe in His Son (*Pistis*) and receive Him in our hearts (*Agape*).[98]   Moreover, Origen shows that in the New Testament there is a filial relationship between God and Mankind.

---

[97] *Patrologia Graeca*. (PG). 11. 231C (ed. J.P. Migne. 1857: reprint, Athens: Centre for Patristic Publications. 2002). Clement, his former teacher states that that the person who utters the words 'Our Father' passes from the state of slave to that of Son, governed by love and not by fear. (*Eclogues on the Prophets*; PG. 9. 362A). His teaching seems to be at one with the Pauline doctrine as far as the external meaning is concerned, but there are differences of essence. While the Apostle Paul considers *love* especially in its spiritual aspect (*agape*), Clement refers to its intellectual side, the love of the man of science for the object of his research, his feelings when his purpose has been attained and he has gained the knowledge he had been longing for. In this respect God can be called our Father because he helps us to achieve knowledge of the divine through communion with Him.
[98] PG. 11. 231A.

Christians have become sons of God through their adoption by Christ the Savior, in whose Person all the expectations of the world have been fulfilled.[99] A process of inner renewal takes place. Through liberation from the grip of evil and a total acceptance of Christ, human beings can become similar to Him. And since the Logos is in the image of God the Father (*kat' eikona*), through likeness to Jesus man may reach likeness (*homoiosis*) with God Himself.

This soteriological process how we become sons of God is due to the fact that His Son transformed us into brothers similar to Him.[100] This state of likeness (*homoiosis*) is generated by a thorough change in human individuals as they make their way towards moral perfection, towards sinlessness. In other words, for Origen, God is our Father because we have been made sinless brothers of His Son.[101] Having established this base principle of transform-ation to likeness, Origen raises the next question: Who has the right to call God by the name of Father? His answer to this is quite clear: it is only the Son of God, the sinless One. Everybody else claiming divine filiation incurs the risk of being a liar, or sacrilegious, for they would be calling themselves sons of

---

[99] S. Petcu. 'Rugăciunea domnească în cultul creştin şi explicarea ei în literatura patristică din primele trei seole creştine (*The Lord's Prayer in Christian Cult and its Interpretation in the First Three Centuries of Patristic Literature*), *Studii Teologice*. 1-2. 1974. 74.

[100] By the incarnation of God's Son human beings have been elevated to the dignity of sons, sharing the the heritage of His Kingdom. Divine paternity and adoption are in this earthly life in a genuine (primary) state, perfection but the radical fulfillment is still to come in Heaven, in the Kingdom perfected. (C. Corniţescu, A Review of 'Rugăciunea domnească. Studiu filologic, istorico-teologic şi exegetic' (*The Lord's Prayer. Philological, Historic-theological and Exegetical Study*), by D. Coravu. Athens. 1979; in *Ortodoxia*. 4. 1980. 635.

[101] Centuries later another great interpreter of the 'Our Father', St. Maximus the Confessor, said that we call God 'Father', not because He is by nature Maker (Creator), but because by grace He is the Begetter, so becoming our Father. In other words we are children of God, we have the grace of adoption and we call Him Father, not because He created us, but because we are reborn through the redemptive work of His Incarnated Son, Jesus Christ. He is the one who made us children of His Father through grace. Our sonship always refers to adoption by grace. c.f. Zisis. 2010. 7.

God while still living in sin.[102]   Now this position seems to contradict what he says in other writings where he establishes three distinct categories of people who can address God with the name Father, by right of being 'sinless ones'. This primarily refers to Jesus Himself (though Origen sometimes infers that some other great spirits such as John the Baptist were incarnated on earth without prior sin having necessitated their birth here); those who have been reborn through baptism and who no long sin; and those who have been baptized.[103]

Origen's rhetorical point in this threefold distinction is really to make a clear division between the baptized whose lives were changed afterwards into moral rectitude, and those who follow Christianity with more of a lip service. Only those Christians from the second category are entitled to call God 'Father', he argues, namely the Saints and the faithful who lead an outstandingly virtuous life. Eventually though, he also admits a chance for the third category as well: for they also can say the 'Our Father' without it being counted as an impiety on their part, provided they are conscious of its importance for their souls and make an effort not to sin any longer.

The second part of Origen's address turning around the phrase: 'Who art in heaven' gives the theologian the opportunity to express his doctrine on the relationship between God, the Creator of the world, and heaven, which is part of His creation. For Origen, Heaven is not a material reality[104] but it does exist as a place apart; the best that can be, the 'place' where the angels and the souls of the righteous dwell.[105] God is everywhere, both in heaven where He fills with His own Spirit and strength the beings that live there, and on earth, in the souls of true believers who have opened themselves to Him.[106] Origen contends that God is more in heaven than on earth, and distinguishes different degrees of His presence in angels, saints, and the souls of the faithful who are still here on

---

[102] PG. 11. 233 D.
[103] *Contra Celsum*.PG.11. 799.
[104] PG. 11. 233D.
[105] PG. 11. 235 C.
[106] PG. 11. 234 C.

earth.[107] Therefore, to say the prayer: 'Our Father who art in heaven', means that God is in heaven, but He is not circumscribed within the narrow limits of a particular place, but transcends any spatial boundaries, expressing the omnipresence and universality of His being.[108] His presence in the same time, both in heaven and among the faithful, is not to be understood as a spatial transition of the Father and the Son toward the one who loves the word of Christ, but rather as an assumption by the Son of a humanity which He raises to the rank of deification. Or, more specifically: the Word of God came down to us and was humble in his dignity. Now He goes from this world to the Father, so that we are able to contemplate Him in his perfect condition, as He came out from the state of humility and entered again in His perfection; we share in his perfection, in a mystical way, through a spiritual ascension of our soul.[109]

Sanctification and Hope

Origen considers the phrase '*Hallowed be Thy name*' to be an ardent prayer asking God to help us better understand Him and know Him, in his attributes as the absolute divine being.[110] The phrase brings with it at least two major concerns. The first is related to the significance of the invocation of holiness. It is about an actual request, or rather a wish. Why should we ask that God's name be hallowed? He is holy in His very nature. In the opinion of many Fathers of the Church the expression can be taken as an inducement to increase praise outside, in the world through worship, learning, preaching, blessing and praise.[111] But Origen presents a somewhat different interpretation. He sees it as an expression of Christian desire to deepen more and more the secrets of the absolute Being. He says that he who prays must meditate and ask that God's name be hallowed as in the word of the psalms. The Psalmist asks us to agree with the same spirit in

---

[107] PG. 11. 236 B.
[108] Petcu. 1974. 74.
[109] PG. 11. 235 A.
[110] PG. 11. 236 A-B.
[111] C. Zavoianu. 'Rugăciunea Domnească după Sfântul Grigorie de Nyssa.' (*The Lord's Prayer according to St. Gregory of Nyssa*). *Glasul Bisericii*. 9-10. 1981. 889.

order to encourage us to deepen a truer and more sublime consciousness of God.[112]

The second concern of his analysis, is related to the relationship between the name of God and His person. In other words, does the sanctification of the name refer only to the Name or to the Heavenly Father Himself? Origen says that God's name is nothing more than what is God.[113] What is God is His name, and *vice versa*. By God's name, in scripture, is understood God in person, and thus to invoke His name means to invoke His presence.[114] And so, when we invoke the sanctification of the name of the Father, we pray for ourselves, the people of God, for our increased dedication through prayer, worship and a virtuous life that should reflect in itself God's holiness.[115] We are aware however, that we are not capable of obtaining virtue by our own power without God's help and support. That is why we ask our heavenly Father, since He is Holy, to sanctify us too by His Name. In other words, we ask Him to help us, who bear the Christian name, to be holy so that we can lead a virtuous life, full of good deeds, worthy of the name and holiness of God, whose sons we are. It would be illogical to believe that this is tantamount to a request that God's name might be rendered holy, sanctified in an attributed sense, since He is holy in and of Himself. The name of a being summarizes and expresses the essential features of the person who is being named. There is a strong identification of the name with the person that owns it, and this is very much supported by evidence from the Scriptures, Origen argues.

---

[112] Neamtu. 1973. 958.

[113] *Commentary on Ps. 24.2.*

[114] This interpretation is in total agreement with our normal usage. Calling someone's name is a sign of closeness and spiritual communion, a sign of intimacy.

[115] This idea is taken up and developed later, in a particular manner, by Saint Maximus the Confessor. In his opinion, the Father's name is hallowed when we kill earthly desires and we are purged of the passions that sicken the soul. Once the passions are killed, outbursts of anger stop, which creates suitable conditions for the man to be changed into 'Church', in order to be worthy to say 'Thy kingdom come'. Zisis. 2010. 7.

The clause of the prayer *Thy Kingdom come* expresses hope. This request is closely connected with the first, because the name of God cannot be hallowed as appropriate in all the earth until the Kingdom fully comes. It means that we must pray that God should give us His blessings on earth and in heaven. Origen believes that the kingdom of God is a state of the soul.[116] It is a kingdom that comes in direct co-operation with our own efforts to achieve it. It is something dynamic, active, and can only be won by a continuous fight against sin. It is spiritual. Our knowledge of God and the virtue that must necessarily grow in our hearts go hand in hand, leading us towards perfection until ultimately we pass from this transitory life into eternity.[117] This transformation can only be achieved together with and through Christ, who unified in Himself the material and spiritual worlds. He is the Light of the world, the Master of the Universe, who has defeated once and forever the master of the kingdom of sin and death.[118] Each person is called to decide for himself. He who wants to obtain the kingdom of God must fight for it, and the first step is to break away from sin, with the help of Christ. Origen also has in view an earthly or material kingdom. The Apostle Paul refers to it as the kingdom the Son will establish in the name of the Father at the end of time. We also pray for this when we say: 'Thy kingdom come'. We pray that God will give His blessings on earth to us, and to others too, his children by adoption.

The clause of the prayer *Thy will be done on earth as it is in heaven* is seen by Origen as a request to God to help us to fulfill His will. The will of God was revealed to us by our Lord Jesus Christ in His Gospel which He has already fulfilled, namely, that 'All should be saved and come to the knowledge of the truth' (1 Tim 2. 4). God's will is for His children, those who are believers, to be perfect both in terms of knowledge of the evangelical truth, as well as from the moral point of view.[119] This petition is given special treatment in

---

[116] PG. 11. 238 B-C.
[117] PG. 11. 238 D.
[118] PG. 11. 239 C-D.
[119] N. Petrescu. 'Rugăciunea Domnească: Tatăl Nostru.' (*The Lord's Prayer: Our Father*). *Mitropolia Olteniei* 1-3. 1977. 193.

Origen's thought. He offers two interpretations: allegorical and literary.

The allegorical interpretation relies on the way Origen identifies 'heaven' with Jesus Christ because He is himself 'the throne of God' and there is no better or more suitable one. Christ is totally penetrated by, and filled with, God. The 'Earth' for Origen stands for the Church because it is called 'God's footstool'. Nothing else is more fitting for this office.[120] In conclusion, the meaning of this part of the prayer is, for Origen: 'Let your will be done as Christ Himself fulfilled it in the Church.'[121]

The Alexandrian also has a literary, less allegorical, interpretation of the same phrase to offer, based on the heaven-earth antithesis, and on that between the inhabitants of heaven and those of the earth. If we believe that the will of God is entirely fulfilled in heaven, we must also find an answer to the following question: What happened to the evil angels whose fall comes about precisely because of their disobedience? To what extent does this thought shatter one's belief that if one prays to God for the fulfillment of His will on earth it will ever be fully carried out?[122] Origen thinks it is important to provide an answer to this issue. The evil angels can no longer be considered inhabitants of heaven because they are in hell and sporadically on earth. In conclusion, God's will shall be fully carried out in heaven,[123] and shall increasingly be done on earth; since earth is the footstool paired with the throne. Even so, the two aforementioned interpretations stand closely connected to his overarching moral conclusion, namely: heaven is divine, therefore good and eternal whereas the earth is full of sin and is transient. In consequence, those who live according to God's will are good (or heavenly) people, but those

---

[120] Clement says the Church is the place within which the will of God is fulfilled on earth. The *earthly* Church is a copy of the *heavenly* Church. It is the blessed territory where the Paradise we lost through the Fall is recreated. It is a state whose ruler does not belong to this world. He is invisible because He transcends it, because He is the very Word of God, the Son of God Himself. He is the guarantee that the will of God will be fulfilled. *Stromateis.* 4.7. P.G. 8. 214.

[121] PG. 11. 241 A.

[122] PG. 11. 242 D.

[123] PG. 11.242 A.

who do not abide by the divine commandments are bad (earthly).[124] Each member of the Church, therefore, must pray that the Father's will should be fulfilled through Christ, who has 'All power in heaven and on earth' (Mt.28, 18), and if God's will is fulfilled on earth as it is in heaven, then the earth will no longer be the earth, but will in fact become like heaven.[125]   From this perspective the third petition of the prayer can thus be interpreted holistically in this way: 'Let God's will be fulfilled by evil people as it is by good people; let evil souls become good and may God forgive them all through His infinite loving kindness, so that after a due period of repentance he may make them partakers of eternal bliss.'[126]

Communion and inter-communion

According to Christian teaching the human being is composed of body and soul, each having its own needs. The body needs material food while the soul needs spiritual food. But the body is the home of the soul, and the soul takes its life only in the body, and so between them is an inter-communion, and thus the demand is appropriate: *Give us today our daily bread'*, which has a double meaning, both material and spiritual.[127] Bodily food alone can not fill a man, no matter how rich he might be, because he also has a soul upon which God's very likeness is imprinted. Through the term *bodily bread* Origen understands everything our body asks of us to live, and through the term *spiritual bread*, he recognizes reference to the Eucharist. That is why, the 'spiritual

---

[124] PG. 11. 242 C-D.

[125] Petcu. 1974. 75.

[126] PG. 11. 242 C-D.

[127] Saint Maximus the Confessor   gives a great importance especially to the anagogic or spiritual meaning according to which the *bread* is the divine food, the bread of life and of knowledge or wisdom which the first man lacked the first man because of sin. If he had not sinned, man would not have been touched by death. Maxim prefers this interpretation because Jesus Christ himself urged His disciples not to worry about the material bread (and all the necessities of life), but first of all to seek God's kingdom. And even if He taught us to ask for the daily bread, the one that is ephemeral, we must not exceed the temporal limits that are fixed by the prayer. In other words, we should not collect wealth, but we have to ask, without any worry, just the daily bread to prepare for the transition from this life to the eternal, immortal. Zisis. 2010. 8.

bread' is also 'the bread of life', or 'the heavenly bread', which Christians eat to gain immortality (Jn. 6.51)[128]. Moreover, he notes, the demand stands in the text in the plural. We do not say 'my bread', but 'our bread', which shows that we have a moral duty to pray God, to give what is necessary for all human life, on this earth, for the purpose of intercommunion, because we are all brothers and sons of Him Who is above.[129]

The request 'Give us today our daily bread' is basically centered around three words: bread (*artos*), hyper-essential (*epiousion*) and today (*simeron*). For Origen *Artos* is not ordinary bread, something that emerges in several teachings of Jesus on the theme. Although, in the Gospels the word 'bread' - and by extension 'food' - has a variety of meanings [130], Origen focuses his analysis on one chief among them. He shows that even as ordinary food differs according to the age or health of the person who eats it, so too heavenly food (the Word) also comes in many forms (*Epinoiai*). For children it is milk, for the sick it is vegetables and for the strong it is meat.[131] But the Holy Eucharist is the governing form of food and the power which holds together the body of Christ, the Church.[132]

Origen says that the word *epiousios* (which he carefully does not render as 'daily' (*ephemerinos*) might well be a creation of the Evangelist Mathew from whom Luke took it over because we do not find this word anywhere else in the Bible.[133] It derives, he

---

[128] At the time of Moses, God sent material bread from heaven, namely the *heavenly manna*, symbolizing the spiritual bread, namely Christ, known by various names, such as for example *bread of angels* (Ps.77. 29).

[129] Petrescu. 1977. 608.

[130] Jesus Christ calls *bread* or *food* the faith in Him (Jn. 6.27) and Himself (Jn. 6.32) and His body (Jn. 6.51).

[131] PG. 11. 247 C.

[132] PG. 11. 244 B-C.

[133] It seems that it has one close etymological parallel, namely *periousios* (Ex. 19.15). Both are derived from *ousia*, which is what remains of a thing (or phenomenon) after what was left out everything is in it by chance, it means the essence. In other words *epiousios* is the adjective of *ousia* and translates into 'essential' or 'existential'. The essence or essential core of the human is represented by *nous* or *psyche*. Therefore, the bread can use the predicate *epiousios* only if it refers to what is essential in it. And then we can say *Artos epiousios* can

76

argues, most probably from *ousia* (essence) and it could be translated as 'hyper-essential'. Origen's spiritual interpretation here goes very well with the idea of the Logos who is characteristic to our rational being and may thus be considered as the foundation of our *nous*. Therefore, 'bread' is given to us in the Holy Eucharist for everlasting life.

The word today (*simeron*) has a dual meaning, Origen notes. On the one hand, it tells us we must ask food for today, not for a week or a month or a year, to keep us away from the sin of greed and on the other hand it urges us to pray daily to God, not only from time to time, or only when we have trouble or distress. There must be no gaps in our program of prayer, because we do not know what gives us our earthly life, and have to pray to stand in dependence.[134] The word 'today, for Origen, primarily denotes eternity in the context of the prayer. It means the time now; because while yesterday may mean the past, in general, and tomorrow connotes the future, the truth is that with God there is no time. He is the eternal Today. For us the words today, yesterday and tomorrow are all temporal (Heb. 13:8). To pray daily shows us the Christian duty to believe in the perennial Divine Providence, and in God's continuous help and assistance, who gives us every single day what we need and what we ask for in prayer.[135] Origen gives to the word *simeron* (this day) a correspondingly cosmic spiritual analysis. He evolves a theory according to which the Holy Scriptures speaks about an 'infinite number of cosmic periods' (*aiones*, Ages) which are called 'days'. Whenever we ask for our daily bread from our Father we ask it for 'each of the ensuing cosmic periods'.[136] Thus we pray 'From Age to Age.'

---

be the bread which supplies the essential part of the human being or which nourishes it (PG. 11. 244 B-C. 508).

[134] Only this is certainly ours, because the hope of the future is a mystery. Or in other words, bodily life belongs only to the present, and a life with hope belongs only to the soul. Human incompetence does not know how to use them both naturally, and while hope in future is assigned to bodily life, to the spiritual life is assigned the bounded pleasures of the present. c.f. Zavoianu. 1981. 894-896.

[135] Petrescu. 1977. 609.

[136] PG. 11. 251 C.

Mutual forgiveness and destruction of temptation

As Origen discusses the Lord's Prayer he sees how strongly the problem of *brotherly forgiveness* is highlighted. It is an enduring factor in the life of any Christian community. We are all sinners and subject to mistakes. We often stand wrongly before God, before our brothers and sisters, and even before ourselves; meaning that we delude and deceive ourselves with unimportant things or those that are spiritually harmful. This is why forgiveness is essential for the Christian; so as to be reconciled with himself, with his fellows, and with God. Without forgiveness we can not even take the first step in the path of salvation. For Origen, the petition *And forgive us our trespasses as we forgive those who trespass against us* refers to both material and spiritual life. Christians have duties not only towards other people, but also to God; as Father, Son and the Holy Spirit. These they rarely fulfill.[137]

Accordingly, Origen takes time at this instance of his commentary to analyze what is involved in the concept of 'mistake'. Whether it refers to the Matthaean *ophelimata* (mistakes/debts), or to the Lukan *amartias* (sins), he says, makes little difference; the meaning is identical in both versions. *A mistake* is an unfulfilled duty, therefore it *is a sin* and he who has committed a mistake is to be punished.[138] Yet, nobody is able to fulfill all duties at once, but it is possible to do all things gradually.[139]

With this we come to the words of the fifth request (the petition for forgiveness). Origen argues that for some who recite the prayer: they receive their forgiveness at this very moment. On his way towards perfection, he explains, a Christian passes through many 'stages'. God forgives the trespasses of those who have set their faces towards the upward journey, and helps them not to commit sin any more. They are thus manifested as being counted worthy to utter the words of the prayer and to call God Father. The rest of us who do not fulfill our duties, or only fulfill them partially, are not granted forgiveness of sins through this request

137 Petcu. 1974. 75.
138 PG. 11. 252 A.
139 PG. 11. 252 C.

alone. The condition of our being forgiven relies on the following clause: namely that we have to learn and start to forgive all those who have wronged us up to the very moment of our prayer.[140]

Temptation is an active force that arises in the soul of man, urging him directly to do bad things. It comes from the sinful desires of man and also arises from the devil. Temptation never comes from God because God does not tempt anyone (James 1. 13), that is, He never urges anyone to sin [141]. If, however, we admit that God does allow us to be tempted, then we have to confess that He never allows it to overpower us. Its purpose is only to investigate the strength of our faith. By this request of the prayer, therefore, we fundamentally ask God not to allow temptation to overcome us. In this petition 'And lead us not into temptation' Origen explains that our entire life is a temptation; so temptation cannot be totally avoided.[142] Its source is the continuous natural conflict we experience between soul and body, which has a great influence upon our relationship with God. At the same time, temptation is also nourished by the presence of the evil spirits within this world; and last, but not least, by the very tests (trials) that come to us from God.[143]

Origen offers examples from Holy Scripture and the lives of the apostles and saints.[144] He knows that the omnipotent God can conceivably remove all temptation from our life, but we cannot ask Him to do that because it would not profit us from a spiritual point of view. On the one hand, temptation is an inseparable part of life, a personal and inner struggle with the body and with the evil spirits. On the other hand temptation is necessary because it

---

[140] P.G. 11. 256 B. Clement of Alexandria discuss this request just once and in the same way. Our being forgiven by God is directly dependent upon our readiness to forgive those who have wronged us. Nobody can address God unless he is able to address his neighbor. Only after we have forgiven are we entitled to humbly ask this from Him who is the source of all good things. Only then can we hope that our sins will be forgiven. See *Stromateis*. 7. PG. 9. 13 D.

[141] The concept of 'leading into temptation' in the final part of the Lord's prayer refers to 'being tested' i.e. by trials and tribulations.

[142] PG. 11.256 A.

[143] PG. 11. 256 B.

[144] PG. 11. 256 C.

trains and strengthens us; it is only by means of it that we can find the way towards our Creator.[145]   It is, in a way, a method of familial 'rearing' by means of which God makes us worthy to be called His children.   What we can do, however, is to ask God to make us victorious in this unceasing fight with sin.   Origen explains that often God brings trials (temptations as tests) upon believers in order to help them work out their salvation and shed the sins which draw them from heavenly to earthly things. Among several examples he provides, he highlights the scriptural example of the flock of fowl which God sent to the hungry people of Israel in the desert; a typological explanation of God's ways of exorcising the evil that exists within mankind.[146]   In brief, therefore, his exegesis of the sixth clause of the Prayer can be summarized as follows: 'Do not let us fall into many sins or into serious sins so that you, O God, should not be compelled as a watchful Physician to use the bitterest medicine upon us in order to cure us.'

The last petition reads: *But deliver us from the evil one*. The evil one (*poniros*) is the Devil, who works at evil consciously. For Origen, he is the personal embodiment of evil and sin, and manages to lure mankind towards all kinds of delusions. Two of his most effective methods, Origen argues, are to present bad things as being good, and to use people as media, whom he has turned (or intends to turn) into his servants.[147] In spite of all these devices, however, he can not tempt us without God's permission, since God is almighty. The classic example in this respect is the tempting of the very Son of God (Lk. 4. 1-12). The fight to resist temptation is thus the fight to resist the devil, and consequently victory in this battle means victory over the devil himself; it is an eschatological view of morality.

Origen sees The Devil as responsible not only for the sickness of the soul, but also for physical sickness. Physical sickness is often brought on by moral sickness (sin) and by its schemer (the Devil). We must pray to be protected from diseases, earthquakes, starv-

---

145 PG. 11. 263 B.
146 PG.11. 261 B.
147 PG. 11. 265 C.

ation, and so on. On the other hand, often we support our fellow men (who can be the tools of the devil) in terms of their wickedness and slackness. Our divine teaching urges us not to take revenge on them,[148] but to look at them with understanding and love so that their hatred [149] may turn into amazement, their wonder to curiosity, and their curiosity to peace and understanding; for in this tolerant way the Church will be able to correct them and morally improve itself. This is the path, he argues, that the Church in the face of persecution ought to follow in the hope that it will gain eternal life. This fight against evil is unceasing and we can only win with the help of God. In the Lord's Prayer, therefore, we basically ask for strength and permanent help in this confrontation with the apocalyptic 'enemy'. Origen does not talk here about the possibility of getting rid of the Devil once and for all, neither does he mention the idea of achieving a life devoid of temptation. The aim is ever a moral one: to withstand temptation and defeat the Devil.[150]

The Prayer of Love

In concluding this review of Origen's exegesis of the Lord's Prayer, we see that he has made a veritable exegesis of 'the Prayer of Love'. The requests of the Lord's Prayer are made for all, in all times and places. Although usually this prayer is recited individually, it is, in essence, a collective prayer; a prayer of the community and a prayer of deep communion. It teaches us to pray for one another, it makes us into brothers and sisters; children of the heavenly Father, because it evokes in and among us all the deepest springs of forgiveness and love.

In Origen's perspective we see that when we pray to the Father, we pray to the Holy Trinity, because the Father is never separated from the Son and the Holy Spirit. The Lord's Prayer is thus a prayer of unity among people, and between people and God, between heaven and earth. We might add that it is also an ecumenical prayer because it is a prayer of the great family of all

---

[148] Petrescu. 1977. 627-628.
[149] He writes out of the context of violent Roman persecutions of the Church.
[150] PG. 11.266 C-D.

Christians, regardless of denomination.[151] But above all else, as Origen insists, it is a prayer suited to the depths of the soul. It is a symbol of moral perfection, a call for us to pray in order to be exorcised by God's holiness from our sins and rise higher in the light of virtue. This most beautiful prayer, in the hands of a beautiful and spiritual commentator, emerges radiantly as a prayer of forgiveness and love. Such is the vision of how God's will to unite heaven and earth may be fulfilled.

---

[151] Zăvoianu. 1981. 899.

An Ascetic Aesthetic: St. John Chrysostom
On the Discernment Of Beauty in Music

Kristen Leigh Southworth

In the field of classical theological aesthetics, considerations of Beauty as a transcendental quality of existence abound. Meanwhile, the question of how Beauty with a capital 'B' might relate to any discernment of beauty in the actual artistic expressions and forms which we encounter in our world, remains subject to much neglect. Yet, if we ever hope to return Beauty to its proper place in our transcendent theological discourse, we will ultimately have to face the question of its relationship to our present experience of the beautiful in the daily world. This will require the development of a means for identifying and interpreting the beautiful as it manifests in actual artistic, as well as cosmic, creation.

This paper seeks to contribute to such a cause by outlining and identifying St. John Chrysostom's discernment of the beautiful in the musical expressions of his own day. Chrysostom is an ideal candidate among the early church fathers for such an analysis precisely because he seems, at least at face value, to be particularly hostile to an aesthetic perspective. Nowhere does he address the subject of Beauty in the transcendental sense, and as a committed ascetic, he is not surprisingly lacking in an affinity for, or interest in, worldly notions of aesthetic beauty.

Furthermore, Chrysostom has often been cited as having one of the most stringent polemics against what is variously labeled 'pagan' or 'secular' music. In one sermon, he chastises his fourth-century congregation for their familiarity with this kind of music as compared to their lack of familiarity with psalms and Scripture:

> Who of you that stand here, if he were required, could repeat one Psalm, or any other portion of the divine Scriptures? There is not one...[but] should anyone be minded to ask of you songs of devils and impure

effeminate melodies, he will find many that know these perfectly, and repeat them with much pleasure. [152]

Understanding these kinds of warnings in such a way that they might contribute to a discernment of the beautiful in the diverse musical expressions of our own time requires a close examination of Chrysostom's musical context. Many of the available historical accounts presume distinct, oversimplified stylistic and functional boundaries between 'secular' music, often characterized as pagan and non-liturgical, and 'sacred' music, usually regarded as Christian and liturgical. But these categories of sacred and secular, particularly as they have come to be applied to contemporary music, fail to offer a truly adequate means for identifying the spiritual and sometimes sacramental qualities of music as it manifests in a variety of contexts. This brief look at some of Chrysostom's statements regarding music hopes to provide a more nuanced approach to our understanding of how and where we might identify musical beauty from an Orthodox Christian perspective.

In spite of Chrysostom's obvious interest in the liturgy, he is clear in his assertion that the musical practices of Christians were intended not simply for liturgical worship, but to envelop and penetrate the whole of a person's everyday life. Chrysostom therefore urges his hearers not only to sing hymns of praise at their meals, but also to teach their children and wives to sing them at the looms and during their other work. [153] Let us, then, begin the task of identifying the music that Chrysostom regards as worthy of enveloping the lives of Christians with a consideration of music outside of the liturgy. Chrysostom appears to have a particular interest in the symposium; that is, at the meals and post-supper drinking parties rooted in the common ritual practices of voluntary religious and other associations in the early centuries of Christianity[154]. He says this:

---

[152] Stapert. 2007. 127-128.
[153] Wellesz. 1961. 95.
[154] Alikin. 2010. 211.

It is mostly at meals that the devil lurks. There he has as allies drunkenness and gluttony, laughter and disorder, and dissipation of soul. Therefore it is particularly necessary at meals and after meals to build a stronghold against him through the security which comes from the psalms, and to sing sacred hymns in praise of the Lord, by standing up with one's wife and children after the *symposia*...Just as these invite mimes, dancers, and indecent women to their meals and call up demons and the devil, and fill their houses with innumerable brawls, so those invite Christ into their houses, and call upon David with the zither....These people make their house a theatre; you shall make your dwelling a church. For nobody would fail to call a gathering a church, where there are psalms, and prayers and dances of the prophets, and God-loving thoughts in the singers.[155]

Given the common assumption of a taboo on dancing and a ban on instruments in the early church, it is perhaps surprising that Chrysostom seems to endorse dancing in the tradition of the prophets, and recognize a Christian use of the zither to call upon David. While we might be tempted to interpret this passage in a metaphorical sense, in his *Homilies on the Psalms* [156] Chrysostom openly concedes that God permits the use of instruments among His people because He wants 'to temper them in love and harmony' by 'blending the sweetness of melody in with the effort of paying attention.'[157] Though he had a clear preference for the use of the vocal instrument alone, even Chrysostom understood that participation in instrumental music and dancing, in addition to singing psalms and hymns, were appropriately reverent expressions of praise within the Christian community, as long as they inspired 'God-loving thoughts' and stood in contrast to other forms of musical and artistic expressions in the cultural milieu.

In what way did the music of the early Christians seek to differentiate itself from the kinds of music that Chrysostom criticizes?

[155] Wellesz. 1961. 95.
[156] JP. Migne. *Patrologia Graeca*. vol. 55.
[157] cited in McKinnon. 1987. 83.

Traditional scholarship has typically regarded the music of the early church as generally not rhythmic, in contrast to the secular music of the time.[158] However, Chrysostom's following statement calls this assumption into question:

> Wishing to make the task more agreeable and to relieve the sense of laboriousness, [God] mixed melody with prophecy, so that enticed by the rhythm and melody, all might raise sacred hymns to him with great eagerness. For nothing so arouses the soul, gives it wing, sets it free from the earth, releases it from the prison of the body, teaches it to love wisdom, and to condemn all the things of this life, as concordant melody and sacred song composed in rhythm.[159]

Moreover, much of early Christian music is cited as being highly improvisational, and from its improvisational character, scholars deduce that melodic choices would have been influenced by the Hellenized-Syrian folk music of the taverns and markets.[160] Furthermore, because hymnic worship was the bedrock of all ancient Greek religion and hymns did not belong to any particular section of society – Christian or otherwise – throughout Christian antiquity the influence of pagan and secular songs was absorbed by church hymnographers.[161]

For all his dire warnings against the demonic nature and dangers of certain kinds of 'pagan' music, Chrysostom still has praise for the lullabies and work songs of everyday people:

> Not only travelers, but also peasants often sing as they tread the grapes in the wine press, gather the vintage, tend the vine, and perform their other tasks. Sailors do likewise, pulling at the oars. Women, too, weaving and parting the tangled threads with the shuttle, often sing a certain melody, some-times individually and to themselves, sometimes in concert. This they do, the women, travelers, peasants, and sailors,

---

[158] Stanley. 1980. 365.
[159] McKinnon. 1987. 80.
[160] Stanley 1980. 365
[161] McGuckin. 2008. 644-645.

striving to lighten with a chant the labor endured for working, for the mind suffers hardships and difficulties more easily when it hears songs and chants. [162]

Here, Chrysostom is not specifically referencing the work songs and lullabies of Christian peasants, but is showing a much broader respect for the music of common working people. In it he seems to admire those musical qualities that assist the mind in suffering hardships and difficulties more easily. In light of this, perhaps the aesthetic distinctions between secular and sacred music in the early centuries of Christianity are not as neatly delineated as many earlier scholars have tended to assume.

Likewise, perhaps the labels pagan or secular are not the most accurate means of characterizing the music that Chrysostom was really cautioning against. It is clear that he addresses the question of music as an ethical problem,[163] yet as it turns out, this evaluative assessment is one that he shared with many of his non-Christian contemporaries. Already in the fifth century BCE, Plato had developed a theory that applied gender constructions and ethical associations to certain modes of music. Those that were considered 'effeminate' were seen as morally degenerating due to their association with various forms of stage life in which pimping and prostitution were a common part of the entertainment experience.[164] Clement of Alexandria's arguments in the second century against instrumental complexity, polyphony, and chromatic modes have been shown to be a reapplication (and even a somewhat wooden regurgitation) of Plato's theory.[165] This is what Chrysostom is reiterating as well in his own characterization of 'demonic' music when he warns his congregations that 'effeminate songs…weaken the tension of our soul.'[166]

An overview of the cultural-musical landscape of the late Roman Empire sheds even further light on the nature of the criticisms

---

[162] Stapert. 2007. 127.
[163] Wellesz. 1961. 96.
[164] Cosgrove. 2006. 270-271.
[165] Cosgrove. 2006. 270-282.
[166] St. John Chrysostom. *On Wealth and Poverty*. SVS Press. New York. 1981. 59.

Chrysostom makes with regard to certain types of music. Evidence reveals that during this time a highly sensual quality had come to pervade both vocal and instrumental music in private feasts and public shows alike. When Chrysostom claims that 'where the *aulos* [Pan-flute] is, there Christ is not,'[167] we have no reason to assume that this is because he identified something inherently wrong with the instrument itself. Rather, this is a reference to the fact that the *aulos* was usually performed by prostitutes or otherwise sexually provocative and available girls while dancing in a flagrantly erotic manner.[168]

The early Christians were certainly not the only ones to abhor these kinds of musical practices and developments. As early as Cicero in the first century BCE there were complaints of decline, and Quintilian and Seneca saw 'in the newfangled music signs of moral as well as artistic degeneration' and looked back to a time when music was 'more serious and more sacred.'[169] Thus we find that Chrysostom's grievances correspond with the sophistic critiques regarding popular music that had already been circulating among non-Christians in the Mediterranean world for quite some time.

Moreover, the late Roman Empire saw a great proliferation of music in the theaters and arenas where Christians had been mocked and persecuted. Minstrels entertained at baths and in the streets, highly trained slaves made music in the houses of the wealthy, and acclaimed virtuosi (including the emperor Nero) competed in musical contests that valued technique over artistic quality, creating wealthy, insolent, and arrogant stars in a spectacle that sounds strikingly similar to today's TV show *American Idol*.[170]

It was in contrast to this kind of prevailing musical culture that the songs created and sung by the Christians of the early church

---

[167] Bowersock (et al. edd). 1999. 598.
[168] Cosgrove. 2006. 263.
[169] Stapert. 2007. 137.
[170] Stapert. 2007.137-139.

attempted to find expression for the ideal of a universal brotherhood in a universally practicable form.[171] As such, the hymn was characterized and defended as a kind of music that all people could participate in without competition or judgment. Chrysostom therefore says with regard to Christian singing that:

> No charge will be made against anybody for the way he sings, whether he be old or young, hoarse, or even lacking rhythm. What is required here is an uplifted soul, a watchful mind, a contrite heart, a powerful reasoning, a purified conscience. If you enter the holy choir of God possessing these, you will be able to stand next to David. There is no need of zithers, or taut strings, or a plectrum, or skill, or any instruments. [172]

Again, there is no reason to interpret Chrysostom's statement regarding the lack of *need* for instruments as signifying support for an all-out ban. The thrust of his argument is against the need for technical skill, a reference to the prestige so often associated with being a skillful instrumentalist. He certainly never condemns anyone for actually having talent either in singing or playing an instrument. But Chrysostom argues that such talent should not be *required* in order for Christians to participate fully in the making of music. Instead, he supports a kind of musical expression that, regardless of style, setting, or technical complexity, uplifts the spirit and builds up the community through the values of love, gratitude, and radical equality. In so doing, he encourages and supports the musical self-expression of all Christians equally and communally.

St. Ambrose of Milan, a contemporary of St. John Chrysostom, both echoes and beautifully elaborates on his understanding of the underlying values, function, and stylistic character of Christian music in the fourth century:

> A psalm is the blessing of the people, the praise of God…the joy of liberty, the noise of good cheer, and the echo of

[171] Runes & Schrickel. 1946. 655.
[172] Wellesz . 1961. 95-96.

gladness. It softens anger, it gives release from anxiety, it alleviates sorrow; it is protection at night, instruction by day, a shield in time of fear, a feast of holiness, the image of tranquility, a pledge of peace and harmony, which produces one song from various and sundry voices in the manner of a cithara...It is a kind of play, productive of more learning than that which is dispensed with stern discipline...A psalm is sung at home and repeated outdoors; it is learned without effort and retained with delight. A psalm joins those with diff-erences, unites those at odds and reconciles those who have been offended, for who will not concede to him with whom one sings to God in one voice? It is after all a great bond of unity for the full number of people to join in one chorus.[173]

Through this brief investigation we can already begin to identify a particular kind of aesthetic that St. John Chrysostom discerns in the music he reveres and encourages among his fellow Christians. But it is an aesthetic that in many ways challenges our typical notions of how we seek to identify beauty in artistic forms. While he criticizes certain musical characteristics, modes, instruments, and technical abilities associated with sexual promiscuity, wealth, and prestige in the musical culture of his day, in the final contextual analysis, these surface-level aesthetic qualities do not ultimately concern him. The deeper aesthetic that he discerns and reveres in musical expression is the presence of humble authenticity. This is what makes music beautiful for Chrysostom, regardless of its context. His deepest respect and recognition of the spiritual value in music are in those songs that are sung by and for the common people, both within and outside of Christian ritual contexts, which manifest attentiveness, humility, and sincerity of heart before God.

This kind of aesthetic discernment should give us pause for thought. Applying it to our own context might cause us radically to reconsider some of our most dearly held notions about what constitutes a Christian manifestation of beauty in the musical

---

[173] Stapert. 2007. 103-104.

forms and expressions we encounter both inside and outside of liturgical settings. It might force us, for example, to take a second look at the value of folk musical forms, which are rooted in an accessible style, are easily remembered, and are readily participated in by the majority of people. Musical styles that are marked by this kind of simplicity may even offer a higher spiritual value than some of the more prestigious pursuits in classical operatic-style music that still commonly abound in church music today. It seems that St. John Chrysostom is asking us to reconsider where we identify songs that demonstrate an aesthetic capacity to effectively lead people to consider and experience more deeply the love of God, to perform their work and other tasks with greater joy, to suffer hardships and difficulties more easily, and perhaps most importantly, to bring people together in a spirit of unity, radical equality, and love.

Further Reading

Alikin, V. A.   *The Earliest History of the Christian Gathering: Origin, Development and Content of the Christian Gathering in the First to Third Centuries.* Brill. Netherlands, 2010.

G Bowersock.   'Music.' *Late Antiquity: A Guide to the Postclassical*
et al. edd.   *World.* Belknap Press. Massachusetts. 1999.

St. John Chrysostom   *On Wealth & Poverty..* St. Vladimir's Seminary Press. (*Popular Patristics Series*). New York. 1981.

C. H Cosgrove.   'Clement of Alexandria and Early Christian Music.' Journal of Early Christian Studies 14, 3, 2006, 255-282.

J A McGuckin.   'Poetry and Hymnography (2): The Greek World.' in: Harvey & Hunter, eds. *The Oxford Handbook of Early Christian Studies.* Oxford University Press. Oxford. 2008.

J McKinnon (ed).   *Music in Early Christian Literature.* Cambridge University Press. Cambridge. 1987.

D Runes &   'Musical History: Periods In.'
H Schrickel.(eds).   *The Encyclopedia of the Arts.* Philosophical Library. New York. 1946.

S Stanley (ed).	'[Music of the] Early Christian Church.' *The New Grove Dictionary of Music and Musicians* . vol. 4. Macmillan. London. 1980.
CR Stapert	*A New Song for an Old World: Musical Thought in the Early Church.* Eerdmans. Grand Rapids. 2007.
EA Wellesz	*A History of Byzantine Music and Hymnography.* Clarendon Press. Oxford. 1961.

The Beauty of Reflection in St. Gregory of Nyssa

Zachary Ugolnik

For now we see in a mirror, dimly, but then we will see face to face. For I know only in part; then I will know fully, even as I have been fully known. 1 Corinthians 13:12

And all of us, with unveiled faces, seeing the glory of Lord as though reflected in a mirror, are being transformed into the same image from one degree of glory to another. 2 Corinthians 3:18

From Narcissus of Greek legend to the dark Queen in *Snow White*, we have identified with those who seek consolation in their own reflection. 'Mirror, mirror, on the wall, who is the fairest of them all? the Queen famously asks. We use reflections to acquire knowledge of our own beauty. We also use them to become more beautiful. A reflection can lead to delusion and self-obsession, but it can also lead to self-knowledge and transcendence. The *Bhagavad-Gita*, the Buddhist *Platform Sutra*, and the 15th century Persian Poet Jami, among others, all compare the human psyche to a mirror that must be polished in order know oneself. This self-knowledge is linked to the knowledge of the divine. Theophilus of Antioch, in the second century, writes: 'As a burnished mirror, so ought man to have his soul pure...when there is sin in a man, such a man cannot behold God.'[174] Origen refers to the wisdom of God as 'stainless mirror'[175] and to the Son of God as a reflection of the Father.[176] Ephrem the Syrian (306–373) also describes the Holy Gospel as a mirror, and in another poem describes a scene where:

> A person who is teaching a parrot to speak, hides behind a mirror and teaches it in this way: when the bird turns in the direction of the voice speaking, it finds in front of its eyes it own resemblance reflected.[177]

---

[174] Theophilus of Antioch. *To Autolycus.* 1.2. *The Ante-Nicene Fathers.* Vol. 2. A. Roberts & J Donaldson (edd). Eerdmans. Grand Rapids. MI. 89.

[175] Origen. *De Principiis.* 5. in *Ante-Nicene Fathers.* Vol. 3. 247.

[176] Origen. *De Principiis.* 12. in *Ante-Nicene Fathers.* Vol. 3. 251.

[177] S. Brock and G. Kiraz. (trs). *Ephrem the Syrian: Select Poems.* Brigham Young University Press. 2007. 23.

In all these cases, through the mirror we comprehend something that otherwise would be incomprehensible. But it is in Gregory of Nyssa (335-395) that the mirror becomes more than a metaphor. David Hart in his essay, 'The Mirror of the Infinite: Gregory of Nyssa on the *Vestigia Trinitatis'*, to which this work is indebted, writes if we 'were to attempt to isolate the one motif that pervades Gregory's thought most thoroughly, and that might capture in a single figure the rationality that unifies it throughout, it would that of a mirror.'[178]

This essay will attempt to further articulate Gregory's understanding of reflection in regard to beauty, and will argue, not surprisingly, that Gregory's notion of the beautiful and his notion of the mirror are intrinsically linked. Gregory finds in the image of a mirror a medium through which the transcendence of divine beauty can be preserved, and yet the immanence of divine beauty can be made visible through the transfiguration of our own world. Beauty, as an act of reflection, is an encounter between the divine and the divine in us. I will with conclude with a brief discussion of how this conception of reflexivity runs throughout Eastern Orthodox representations of beauty.

The Eye of Reflection

Vision, for Gregory, is a meeting of two separate sources of light: 'the eye enjoys the light by virtue of having light within itself to seize its kindred light.'[179] In both Plato and Plotinus, we find a similar treatment of the mechanics of the eye, corresponding to a general 'emission theory' of vision, associated with the writings of Euclid and Ptolemy. For Plato, the 'pure fire which is within us' is 'made to flow through the eyes' and 'when the light of day surrounds the stream of vision, then like falls upon like.'[180]

---

[178] D. Hart. 'The Mirror of the Infinite: Gregory of Nyssa on the *Vestigia Trinitatis'* in: S. Coakley. (ed). *Re-Thinking Gregory of Nyssa*. Blackwell. Oxford. 2003. 117.

[179] Gregory of Nyssa. *On Infants*. (W.Moore and HA. Wilson. trs.) in: P Schaff & H Wace (edd). *Nicene and Post-Nicene Fathers of the Christian Church: Second Series.* Vol. 5. 375-376.

[180] B. Jowett (tr) *The Dialogues of Plato*. Vol. 2. (*Timaeus*). OUP. Oxford. 1871. 538-539.

Plotinus, in the second century CE, parallels the rules of vision with the same rules that determine the soul's ability to comprehend beauty: 'Never did eye see the sun unless it had first become sunlike, and never can the Soul have vision of the First Beauty unless itself be beautiful.'[181] And we find the same philosophy of *mimesis*, or imitation, in the Nyssen's understanding of vision. In *The Great Catechism*, we read:

> For as the eye, by virtue of the bright ray which is by nature wrapped up in it, is in fellowship with the light, and by its innate capacity draws to itself that which is akin to it, so was it needful that a certain affinity with the Divine should be mingled with the nature of man.[182]

For Gregory, vision is an act of magnetism between the light within in the eye and the light in the world, where like attracts like. Though the exterior object occupies the privileged position, vision, in this sense, is binary, where neither subject nor object have singularly passive roles but each emits light, participating in 'fellowship' (*koinonia*). The same forces rule the perception of beauty, in that our nature as made in the image and likeness of the divine is continually attracted to the archetypal beauty of God that we reflect.

Beauty As Procession

The deified soul is the supreme reflection of the divine, endowed with the image of God, and, to quote Gregory, a 'dignified royalty.'[183] But divine presence, and thus beauty, is also found throughout creation. 'For who,' Gregory asks, 'when he takes a survey of the universe, is so simple as not to believe that there is Deity in everything, penetrating it, embracing it, and seated in

---

[181] Plotinus. *Enneads* 1.6.9. in: S. MacKenna. (tr). *The Enneads*. Faber & Faber. London. 1969. I am indebted to Nicoletta Isar's article: 'The Vision and Its 'Exceedingly Blessed Behold': Of Desire and Participation in the Icon.' *Anthropology and Aesthetics*' 38. 2000. 56-72, for bringing my attention to this text in Plotinus.

[182] *The Great Catechism*. 5. in: *Nicene and Post-Nicene Fathers of the Christian Church*. Vol. 5. 478.

[183] *On the Making of Man*.4. in *Nicene and Post-Nicene Fathers of the Christian Church*. Vol. 5. 391.

it?'[184] Gregory's writings, following Plotinus in a similar fashion (and continued later in pseudo-Dionysius) demonstrate a procession of beauty in the natural world. In an elegant passage that warrants extended citation Gregory, in his treatise *On The Making of Man*, illustrates how this procession applies to both the universe and to humanity:

> When the rain falls from the clouds or the overflow from the river channels causes the land beneath it to be saturated with moisture…the same substance becomes bitter in wormwood, and is changed into a deadly juice in hemlock, and becomes different in other plants, in saffron, in balsam, in the poppy: for in one it becomes hot, in another cold, in another it obtains the middle quality: and in laurel and mastic it is scented, and in the fig and the pear it is sweetened, and by passing through the vine it is turned into the grape and into wine; while the juice of the apple, the redness of the rose, the radiance of the lily, the blue of the violet, the purple of the hyacinthine dye, and all that we behold in the earth, arise from one and the same moisture…the same sort of wonder is wrought in the animated soil of our being by Nature, or rather by Nature's Lord. Bones, cartilages, veins, arteries, nerves, ligatures, flesh, skin, fat, hair, glands, nails, eyes, nostrils, ears — all such things as these, and countless others in addition, while separated from one another by various peculiarities, are nourished by the one form of nourishment in ways proper to their own nature, in the sense that the nourishment, when it is brought into close relation with any of the subjects, is also changed according to that to which it approaches …[185]

This is a more a 'showing' moment than a 'telling' moment. Gregory does not necessarily explain the presence of beauty in the natural world in this passage, but he clearly demonstrates its existence. To use the rhetoric of Gregory: who would be 'simple'

---

[184] *The Great Catechism 26.* in *Nicene and Post-Nicene Fathers of the Christian Church*, Vol. 5. 495.

[185] *On the Making of Man.* 4. in *Nicene and Post-Nicene Fathers of the Christian Church*, Vol. 5. 426.

enough to read 'the juice of the apple, the redness of the rose, the radiance of the lily,' and not be reminded of beauty? Each of these examples is a manifestation of 'moisture'(and can be understood as a metaphor for the archetypal beauty of the divine) throughout creation, one in nature yet infinite in form. The diversity of the natural world is then mirrored in the physiology of humanity. All of our parts, our 'bones, cartilages, veins,' and so forth, participate in the reception of the same 'moisture.' Gregory's parallel language suggests an anthropology in which man is a macrocosm of the universe, a concept he articulates in other writings. Humanity mirrors the universe. Each reflects the other, in the sense that both participate in the reception of 'moisture,' or a substance of the same source. Gregory elaborates, in another passage, of how this procession operates in human nature:

> As we said that the mind was adorned by the likeness of the archetypal beauty, being formed as though it were a mirror to receive the figure of that which it expresses, we consider that the nature which is governed by it is attached to the mind in the same relation, and that it too is adorned by the beauty that the mind gives, being, so to say, a mirror of the mirror. [186]

The *nous*, or mind, is a mirror of God, in the sense that we are governed by a divine nature, and in turn, that 'nature which is governed by' the mind, that is, the body, also acts a mirror. Gregory continues in this passage: 'So long as one keeps in touch with the other, the communication of the true beauty extends proportionally through the whole series, beautifying by the superior nature that which comes next to it.'[187] Beauty by its very nature is a procession of divine reality through a series of reflections. If at any time this connection is interrupted and 'the superior follows the inferior' the 'misshapen character of matter' is revealed. 'For in itself,' writes Gregory, 'matter is a thing without form or structure.' This procession, then, can also act inversely, in the sense that when the mind follows the body, the

---

[186] *On the Making of Man.* 12. in *Nicene and Post-Nicene Fathers of the Christian Church*, Vol. 5. 398-399.
[187] All the citations in this paragraph are from Gregory's: *On the Making of Man, Nicene and Post-Nicene Fathers of the Christian Church*, Vol. 5. 398-399.

'transmission of ugliness' can flow from the body to the mind, sullying its image as made in the likeness of God. The genesis of evil occurs in this withdrawal from what is beautiful.

The Soul as a Mirror

Gregory marks a fine distinction between beauty that appeals to the senses and 'intellectual beauty.'[188] Beauty in matter, however, can act as a catalyst for the desire to comprehend the beauty that transcends all form and shape. In his treatise *On Virginity*, Gregory acknowledges that it can be difficult to distinguish between 'the material vehicle and the immanent beauty.'[189] But he offers an interesting solution: 'There is but one vehicle on which man's soul can mount into the heavens, namely the self-made likeness in himself to the descending Dove.'[190] This reference marks Gregory's use of self-knowledge as a conduit for the knowledge of God. We cannot know God, but we can to a better degree know ourselves. The reflection of God in our souls, for Gregory, therefore, acts as the lens through which we can distinguish beauty's immanent source. The purer our choices in life, the better position we are in to comprehend beauty.

We can turn to Gregory's *Commentary on the Song of Songs,* for an elaboration of this quality of the soul. This treatise is replete with imagery of divine reflection, from the first sentences of the first homily addressing those who have wrapped themselves in the 'bright garments...displayed upon the mount of trans-figuration,'[191] to the last homily where Gregory refers to the soul as a 'living mirror possessing free will.'[192] Throughout the narrative of the bride and bridegroom, the beauty of the groom (representing Christ) is demonstrated through his reflection in the bride. Gregory writes in the voice of bridegroom: 'By approaching my archetypal beauty, you have yourself become beautiful', and

---

[188] *On Virginity.* 11. *Nicene and Post-Nicene Fathers of the Christian Church*, Vol. 5. 356.
[189] ibid. *On Virginity.* 11. 356.
[190] ibid. *On Virginity.* 11. 356.
[191] *Commentary on the Song of Songs.* (Jaeger. edn. 43). C. McCambley. (tr). Hellenic College Press. Brookline. 1987. 264.
[192] *Comm. Song of Songs.* (Jaeger. 44). McCambley. 1987. 264.

he explains: 'human nature is in fact like a mirror, and it takes on different appearances according to the impressions of free will.'[193] He continues with a metaphor that not all life-scientists might agree with any longer: 'If anything abominable is held up, its ugliness is impressed on the mirror—for example a frog, toad, centipede, or anything unpleasant to behold.'[194]

It is this same quality of the soul, however, that allows it to be transfigured by the divine. The vision of God, reflected in our souls, as achieved by the bride, is the apogee of all vision. However, even in those cases when a person becomes, as Gregory writes, 'perfect in every way, such a person would not have it in his nature to look steadily upon the Word of God as upon the sun; rather he sees it within himself as in a mirror.'[195] Even in perfection we cannot gaze directly at God, but can only see his beauty in our transfigured soul. Thus God's ineffability remains intact while his vision is revealed in us. The question remains whether Gregory's notion of the soul as a mirror of the divine can only be applied to the context of a heightened mystical state, or those 'perfect in every way'? As imperfect humans, for whom the purity he describes in his treatise *On Virginity* or the ecstatic union he describes in his *Songs of Songs* seems out of reach, are there other means through which we can gaze upon a reflection of the divine?

Gregory speaks of two other mirrors of the divine, which can perhaps be thought of as more accessible: the vision of others who have achieved deification and the vision of the church. Gregory interprets the line from the bride's friends 'You have given us heart,' to mean: 'that is, you put in us a soul and mind to comprehend the light in you.'[196] The bride can be understood as a soul that has achieved the spotless reflection of deification and through her reflection demonstrates the beauty of the divine. She is beautiful, in so far as she is able to impart to her friends the beauty of the bridegroom, for: 'by contemplating the

---

[193] *Comm. Song of Songs.* (Jaeger.104). McCambley. 1987. 92.
[194] *Comm. Song of Songs.* (Jaeger.104). McCambley. 1987. 92.
[195] *Comm. Song of Songs.* (Jaeger. 90). McCambley. 1987. 84.
[196] *Comm. Song of Songs.* (Jaeger. 256). McCambley. 1987. 166.

bridegroom's beauty in his spouse, they are marveling at his invisible, incomprehensible presence in all creatures.'[197] No one can see God, Gregory reminds us, but we can gaze upon truly reflective souls that have achieved deification.

We can also go to church. Through the incarnation 'the invisible in manifested in flesh,'[198] and Christ thereby 'made the Church his own Body.'[199] The Church takes on the attributes of the incarnate Logos, as a visible reflection of the unknowable God. Gregory puts it simply: 'Thus persons looking into the Church's face, as if it were a clean mirror, see the Sun of Righteousness who is comprehended by that which is visible.'[200]

Beauty is that which makes us aware of God's image within us, which could perhaps be described as a sensation, however fleeting, of eternity, or a taste of Christ's resurrection. The image within us is a 'vehicle' in the sense that it facilities movement towards to the divine. Beauty 'moves' us in ways which non-beauty does not. This is the paradox of Gregory's thought: the interplay of interiority and exteriority. The comprehension of beauty is an inward turning, but unlike vanity, this turning within finds in its depths a mirror which reflects the infinite beauty present in all things.

In A Mirror Dimly

Unlike Narcissus, who fell in love with his own reflection, those who contemplate the beautiful do not see themselves; they see God. But how is this reflection an actual depiction of divine beauty and not another delusion of material reality? At first glance, a mirror's reflection could be seen as a secondary truth to that which it reflects; an understanding found in Plato's *Republic*. Socrates in Plato's *Republic* divides 'visible things' into two categories: first, 'images,' that is 'shadows, then reflections in water and in all close-packed, smooth, and shiny materials, and

---

[197] *Comm. Song of Songs.* (Jaeger. 256). McCambley. 1987. 166
[198] *Comm. Song of Songs.* (Jaeger. 256). McCambley. 1987.166
[199] *Comm. Song of Songs.* (Jaeger. 257). McCambley. 1987.166.
[200] *Comm. Song of Songs.* (Jaeger. 257). McCambley. 1987.166.

everything of that sort'; and, second, 'originals of these images.'[201] Describing the works of a carpenter, Plato writes 'imitation is far removed from the truth, for it touches only a small part of each thing and a part that is itself only an image.'[202] Thus, a reflection is a considerable step away from the original.

In Paul's *First letter to the Corinthians*, we could perhaps read a similar association of a mirror and obscurity. The beginning of chapter thirteen, verse twelve is translated in the New Revised Standard Version as: 'For now we see in a mirror, dimly, but then we will see face to face.' The Greek *ainigmati*, from which the English term 'enigma' derives, is translated, here, 'dimly.' This term shares its root with the verb 'to speak in riddles,' thus connoting a shadow, or darkness. The mirror in this verse, perhaps then, is contrasted by a real encounter. The dark mirror gives way to an actual meeting. We can extrapolate then, a similar treatment of *mimesis* here to that of Plato, where the copy, 'the mirror,' is depicted as inferior to the actual thing.

But if God is incomprehensible and as we read in Exodus [203] we can never gaze upon his face and live, then the medium through which we see him can never be removed, and cannot thus be regarded as such an inferior thing, being so quintessential. We are always limited by human nature, perhaps even in the life to come. But this nature, through its capacity for the indwelling of God, also allows us to know God by being known by him. Paul continues the verse: 'For I know only in part; then I will know fully, even as I have been fully known.' Thus already in Paul, in the last phrase of this verse, we have a reciprocal action of knowing. Gregory provides the following reading of this verse in his *Commentary on the Song of Songs*: 'Our understanding of the divine resembles what we seek. It does not show its form which no one has seen or can see, but through a mirror and a riddle, it provides a reflection of the thing sought; that is, a reflection

---

[201] GMA. Grube. (tr). *Plato's Republic*. 6.510. (C.D.C. Reeve's revision). Hackett. Indianapolis. 1992. 183.
[202] *Republic*. 10. 598. Grube & Reeve. 1992. 268.
[203] Exodus 33. 20.

present in the soul by a certain likeness.'[204] Indeed, Gregory understands the beatitude: 'Blessed are the pure in heart; for they shall see God'[205] to refer 'not [to] the vision of God face to face,' but rather as an expression of how 'the kingdom of God is within you.'[206]

With this in mind, Paul's verse can be thought of as less a progression from a mirror to a lack of a mirror, than as a progression from a dirty mirror to an ever-clearer mirror. Through grace and virtue, the medium through which we see the divine becomes infinitely less and less obscure. We find such an image in Paul's *Second Letter to the Corinthians*, where through 'Seeing the glory of Lord as though reflected in a mirror,' the reflection allows for emulation, suggesting that even in the *eschaton* in our assimilation to God, we can proceed from 'glory to glory.'[207] Gregory's many references to mirror imagery in his corpus are essentially extrapolations on this understanding of Paul's verses in the Corinthians.

Apophatic Reflection

Interestingly, when explaining the reflection of the divine, which can be likened to an act of imitation, or *mimesis*, Gregory often uses the image of a sculptor. The beatification of the soul, then, is not a process of constructing an imitation, as is the case in the carpenter described in Plato's *Republic*, but is rather a process of unveiling a shared substance. Hans Urs von Balthasar describes Gregory's spiritual movement as: 'a successive elimination of all that 'we have', to constitute what 'we are.' '[208] Gregory does not (as Origen so famously did) mark a radical distinction between the 'image' we were endowed with in Genesis and the 'likeness' we seek in the life to come, thus the image that we perpetually strive to achieve is one we already possess. The Church, too, as

---

[204] Gregory of Nyssa. *Comm. Song of Songs.* (Jaeger. 87). McCambley. 1987. 82.

[205] Mathew 5.8.

[206] Gregory of Nyssa. *6th Homily on the Beatitudes*, as cited in: V. Lossky. *The Vision of God* . SVS Press. Crestwood. 1983. 85.

[207] 2 Cor. 3.18.

[208] H. Balthasar *Presence and Thought: An Essay on the Religious Philosophy of Gregory of Nyssa.* Ignatius Press. San Francisco. 1995.121.

endowed with the Holy Spirit as the Body of Christ can only be tarnished by imperfect human action. In Gregory's commentary in *The Song of Songs* on the mirror of the Church, he links this quality of reflection with sculpting:

> In the case of chiseling a certain form in marble, sculptors chisel and remove material to represent the mode's form. Thus the many hands of the Church's body must be fashioned into something beautiful by the chiseling effected through much reflection so that their hands may be pure gold.'[209]

Reflection, here, is described in apophatic terms. It is a taking away by means of light, like a laser cutting a stone. The passions and sin 'must be removed by the instruments of reflection so that the pure, unadulterated gold of free will might alone remain.'[210] Gregory also compares sculpting to the perfecting of the soul in the concluding chapters of *On The Making of Man*, where the sculptor creates an image 'not by the change of the material into the figure, but by the figure being wrought upon the material.'[211] The soul through its possession of a divine substance, or stamp, is already an original depiction of the divine; it is already there, merely requiring revelation. Thus, in these deliberate resonances of Paul, Gregory describes the soul as 'appearing at first somewhat obscurely, but afterwards increasing in radiance concurrently with the perfecting of the work.'[212] This perfection, or revelation of the soul occurs through removing our passions, that is by acquiring *apatheia*: 'For the rays of that true and divine virtue shine forth in a pure life by the outflow of detachment (*apatheia*) and make the invisible visible to us.'[213] Through the emanation of divine energy in our souls, impurities are removed. The perception of beauty, by its very nature, therefore, requires this reciprocal act of seeing light and becoming purified by the light.

---

[209] *Comm. Song of Songs.* (Jaeger. 408). McCambley. 1987. 248.
[210] *Comm. Song of Songs.* (Jaeger 408). McCambley. 1987. 248-249.
[211] *On the Making of Man.* 29.
[212] *On the Making of Man.* 29.
[213] *Comm. Song of Songs.* (Jaeger.90). McCambley. 1987. 84.

In Eastern Orthodox thought, we can turn to the act of encountering an icon, to better understand this paradoxical quality of beauty as introspection. To see an icon is to be seen. The Saint's deified face looks at our face, revealing the depths of our being. This conception of an image as a mirror or mediator of the divine, whether in ourselves or portrayed in a painting, has come to play a very important role in Eastern Orthodox culture. From the perspective of historical theology, we might want a further account of how this aspect of Gregory's thought influenced Eastern Christianity's notion of an image. On a conceptual level, however, we can point to Gregory as an exemplar of a mode of thought in Eastern Christianity where reflexivity is an inherent characteristic of beauty.

Unlike suspicious views of *mimesis* (such as those sponsored by Plato), the 'reflection' comes to be an ideal representation of the beautiful through its suggestion of participation and encounter. John Hayward, in his essay *Mimesis and Symbol in the Arts* explains: 'Artistic *mimesis* under Christian influence records the involvement of all persons, however humble, in a divine drama. The artist, unlike the philosopher, is not a removed observer aiming at neutral and rarified high levels of abstraction. He is the conveyer of a sacred reality by which he has been grasped.'[214] Two examples in Eastern Orthodox visual culture will suffice: the legend of the *Mandylion* and the development of 'inverse perspective' in iconography.

In the Legend of the Image of Edessa, or *Mandylion*, Christ impresses his own likeness on a cloth, which comes to be regarded as the prototypical icon.[215] According to the version included in

---

[214] JF. Hayward. 'Mimesis & Symbol in the Arts.' *Chicago Review*. 15.1. 1961. 96.
[215] We find the same association of cloth and mirror in the *Hymn of the Pearl* where the robe of glory becomes an icon of reflection: 'But when suddenly I saw my garment reflected as in a mirror/ I perceived in it my whole self as well/ And through it I recognized and saw myself/ For though we derived from one and the same we were partially divided and then again we were one, with a single form.' B. Layton (tr). *The Hymn of the Pearl*. in: *The Gnostic Scriptures: A New Translation with Annotations and Introductions*. SCM Press. London. 1987. 374.

the tenth century text *Narratio de Edessena,* Ananias could not paint a portrait of Christ due the brilliance of the Lord's face, and so: 'The Savior washed his face with water, wiped off the moisture with the towel that was given him, and in some divine and inexpressible manner his own likeness was impressed on it.'[216] This *Mandylion* is viewed, we can assume, on the same side on which Christ's imprinted his face, thus it is akin to a negative image, similar to a reflection. The Greek *Letters of the Three Patriarchs,* composed in 836, describes King Abgar viewing the image of Edessa 'as if he was actually seeing the sender in a mirror.'[217]

Turning to fourteenth century Russia, we see the development in iconography of what has come to be known as 'inverse perspective,' which can be understood as an attempt to represent the reflexive qualities of an icon. Unlike the linear perspective taken to such pitch in Renaissance art, where all space is rendered according to a unique perspective, the eye drawn into a vanishing point on the horizon, iconic space moves outwards towards the viewer. Mountains bend backwards producing S-curves with jagged edges. The back of thrones appear spherical, the right arm set apart from the curve of the left side, demonstrating multiple perspectives.

Indeed, as Ouspensky points out, the *poddllinki,* or Russian pattern books for copying icons, describe the left and right of icons from a viewpoint inside the picture looking out, akin to the terms 'stage left' or 'stage right.'[218] We do not stand side by side with these saints and look into an unknown void, but we look at each other. An Icon depicts an encounter of love. Like the Hindu notion of *Darshan,* we see in order to be seen; the eye, though it may not emit light, depicts a reflection of what it sees.

---

[216]As cited in H L Kessler. *Spiritual Seeing: Picturing God's Invisibility in Medieval Art.* University of Pennsylvania Press. Philadelphia. 2000. 71.

[217] *The Letter of the Three Patriarchs to Emperor Theophilus and Related Texts.* Translated by Joseph A. Munitiz. *Porphyrogenitus.* Camberley. Surrey. 1997. 34.

[218] B.Uspenski . 'Semiotics of the Icon: An Interview with Boris Uspenksi.' *PTL: A Journal for Descriptive Poetics and Theory of Literature.* 3. 1978. 540. [cited in Isar, 2000. 67].

St. John of Damascus describes icons as windows to heaven, but when we find ourselves in a position to gaze at these icons, we find a reflection of our world transfigured. We do not gaze at the back of God, like Moses on Sinai, but through the incarnation, we look upon a human face as, authentically, the face of the divine, inviting us to find beauty in all of our encounters. St. Gregory of Nyssa may have been the first Christian Father of the Church to fully articulate this notion of beauty as a reflection.

Beauty and the Unceasing Movement of Desire in
St. Gregory of Nyssa's *On the Life of Moses*

Lisa Radakovich Holsberg

St. Gregory of Nyssa's *On the Life of Moses or Concerning Perfection in Virtue* has been described as both a mystical and a moral treatise.[219] The *Life* was most probably written in the early 390's during the last years of Gregory's lifetime.[220] Although certainly intended for a wide audience, the work is addressed to one 'Caesarius' to assist him in living the Christian life.[221] Bookended by a prologue and conclusion, the *Life* is divided into two unequal parts: a History (*Historia*) of the biblical account of Moses' life derived from Exodus, Numbers, and Deuteronomy; and an allegorical Contemplation (*Theoria*) of this history according to Gregory's spiritual interpretation. Gregory's main concern is the *Theoria*, which presents Moses as a spiritual exemplar worthy of imitation. Moses' three theophanies and his responses to them comprise the architecture for the Patriarch's spiritual ascent, an ascent that culminates in Moses becoming a friend of God – which is, for Gregory, the 'only thing worthy of honor and desire' and is 'the perfection of life' (II.320). All images and interpretations in the *Life* are oriented toward this conclusion; a conclusion which is not an 'end,' so to speak, but rather the establishment of a never-ending and ever-growing relationship.

But the *Life* is not only a mystical and moral work. In addition to its spiritual wisdom and admonishments toward moral excel-

---

[219] NV. Harrison. 'Gregory of Nyssa (c. 335-c.395): The Life of Moses.' *Christian Spirituality: The Classics.* Ed. A. Holder. Routledge. London. 2010. 25-26, 29. Also A. Meredith. *Gregory of Nyssa.* Routledge. London. 1999. 99-100.

[220] c.335-c.395 AD. Gregory of Nyssa. *The Life of Moses.* Translated by A.J. Malherbe and E. Ferguson. Paulist Press. New York. 1978 - the text used for citations of the *Life* in this essay, unless otherwise noted.

[221] The addressee is named as Caesarius in some manuscripts; Olympios or Peter in others. Recent scholars agree that the treatise was meant for the monastic communities founded by Gregory's brother Basil; perhaps to be read aloud to the monks. (see Harrison. 2010. 27).

ence, the philosophical category of beauty, and indeed the very qualities of beauty itself, also permeate the treatise. Gregory's descriptive language is rich in vitality, liveliness, and visual imagery emphasizing the elements of beauty that comprise the story of Moses' life. His spiritual pedagogy explores the beauty of the virtuous and divinized human soul. And, above all, the literary structure of the *Life* draws on the rich Platonic tradition of the spiritual ascent to ultimate beauty – the ascent so famously articulated by Diotima, the priestess of Mantinea, in the *Symposium*.[222] The idea of Beauty works throughout the treatise to call, quicken, guide and sustain the spiritual seeker. Desire and the movement of unending progress (*epektasis*) work together with beauty in the pursuit of the virtuous spiritual life and the union comprised in friendship with God.

Before exploring the moral, mystical and aesthetic elements in the *Life*, it is important to remember that the overriding purpose of the treatise is to encourage and enlighten the reader. Gregory firmly establishes the intent and tenor of the treatise in the prologue's opening paragraph:

> At horse races the spectators intent on victory shout to their favorites in the contest, even though the horses are eager to run. From the stands they participate in the race with their eyes, thinking to incite the charioteer to keener effort, at the same time urging the horses on while leaning forward and flailing the air with their outstretched hands instead of with a whip (I.1).

The reader is immediately gripped with a sense of something happening. Promptly catapulted into the scene, the reader is a simultaneous participant in the excitement of the race. Heightening the suspense of anticipation, Gregory continues:

> While you are competing admirably in the divine race along the course of virtue, light-footedly leaping and straining constantly for the prize of the heavenly calling, I exhort, urge and encourage you vigorously to increase your speed. I do

---

[222] Meredith. 1999. 85-86.

this, not moved to it by some unconsidered impulse, but to humor the delights of a beloved child (I.1).

The race is on, the cheering commences – and the reader is hooked. The burst of heightened engagement that is the opening chariot race sets the image for the spiritual journey that will follow. In opening the treatise with this vividly dynamic trope, Gregory provides the metaphor and the motivation for his reader's spiritual growth. Every educator knows that the most essential, and often elusive, element of good pedagogy is inspiring in the pupil the motivation to learn and to stay the course of instruction until she has achieved mastery. In his gripping opening, and in the pedagogical concerns for the spiritual welfare of his reader throughout the treatise, Gregory situates himself easily among the company of gifted educators. Motivated by the prize and sustained by enthusiastic support accompanied with delight, the reader of the *Life* sets off on the course of virtue in the divine race.

Eternal Progress

In his pedagogical task, Gregory establishes in his opening paragraphs another primary theme: his famous doctrine of *epektasis*. The doctrine of *epektasis*, otherwise known as eternal progress, is the distinctive engine humming throughout the *Life*, urging the reader on (from the cheering opening chariot race until the conclusion of the treatise) to leap and strain ahead in the spiritual race without pause for the *prize of the heavenly calling*. Throughout Gregory's interpretation, the great Patriarch Moses is depicted as recognizing and following the heavenly calling to greater and greater heights; in a journey without end.

This stretching out (*prokope*) of eternal progress takes place over natural creaturely limits; limits that are not negative in themselves but are rather marks of perfection. Gregory explains that the perfection of any sensible (perceived by the senses) thing is marked by boundaries that both describe and complete (or perfect) the thing itself. These boundaries are right and fitting and are not in any way to be deplored as an imperfection. In created things that are perceivable by the senses, their boundaries are precisely their perfection. Yet the spiritual seeker is called not to remain within the boundaries of created perfection, but rather to stretch beyond limits. This is possible by participation in virtue, which has no limit. Gregory begins his discussion of limit and virtue this way:

> The person who looks at a cubit or at the number ten knows that its perfection consists in the fact that it has both a beginning and an end. But in the case of virtue we have learned from the Apostle that its one limit of perfection is the fact that it has no limit. For that divine Apostle, great and lofty in understanding, ever running the course of virtue, never *ceased straining toward* those things *that are still to come* (I.5).

The scriptural inspiration for Gregory's doctrine of *epektasis* is Philippians 3.13. This verse contains St. Paul's testimony of *ceaselessly straining ahead for what is to come*. Virtue is the limitless field for this effort, for virtues are not only characteristics of human moral excellence, but they are also attributes of the divine. As such, they are constitutive in some way of God – and as divine attributes, are therefore limitless and absolute.[223] And so, the one who pursues virtue pursues nothing less than participation in God (*metousia theou*):

> Certainly whoever pursues true virtue participates in nothing other than God, because He is himself absolute virtue (I.7).

The unceasing quality of the movement of *epektasis* is operative in, and essential to, the transcending of boundaries and thus participation in divine life. Gregory will not admit of any stopping in the race of virtue:

> Since, then, those who know what is good by nature desire participation in it, and since this good has no limit, the

---

[223] One of Gregory's theological accomplishments, developed in his confrontations with the Neo-Arian Eunomius, is his position on the absolute infinity of God the Creator. Meredith. 1999. 18.

participant's desire itself necessarily has no stopping place but stretches out with the limitless (I.7).

Stopping in the pursuit of virtue goes against natural desire. But even more, the choice of stopping or continuing the pursuit is crucial to Gregory's understanding of the exercise of human freedom. For Gregory, there is no such thing as a neutral pause in this race. Stopping means effectively a turn in the opposite direction. Stopping marks a boundary that is inadmissible for the infinite; and as such, indicates the start of the race of evil:

> Just as the end of life is the beginning of death, so also stopping in the race of virtue marks the beginning of the race of evil. Thus our statement that grasping perfection with reference to virtue is impossible was not false, for it has been pointed out that what is marked off by boundaries is not virtue (I.6).

There is no such thing as merely 'stopping' – rather, we must and *do* in fact move and pursue. In our movement and pursuit, we exercise our human freedom in the choice to orient ourselves to either virtue or evil.

In the light of the vast ontological separation between creation and the Creator, inherent in the Christian doctrine of *creatio ex nihilo*,[224] Gregory's doctrine of *epektasis* describes the pull of the created soul, via the currents of desire for God, across that unbridgeable separation towards an experience of the presence of the incomprehensible and unreachable God. [225] *Epektasis*, as Andrew Louth remarks:

> ...expresses the fact that God cannot be comprehended, that the soul can come to no final knowledge of God, [and] that its longing for God will never be finally satisfied: the soul

[224] A. Louth. *The Origins of the Christian Mystical Tradition: From Plato to Denys.* OUP. Oxford. 2007. For the early Christian theologians coming to terms with elements of inherited Platonism and the doctrine of *creatio ex nihilo* see Louth. op. cit. xii-xiii, 73-76, 78-9, 87, 192.
[225] Louth. 2007. 79, 87.

will always be inspired by its experience of God to long for more.[226]

The movement of *epektasis* is both satisfaction and the desire for more. Each step in spiritual progress satisfies, yet each step reveals a new vista as enticement for further progress. Not only does the soul progress in the ascent, but one's capacity for the ascent also increases. Desire moves through satisfaction but not satiety, continually strengthening one in the good – which is the condition of possibility for further ascent – and provoking additional desire. Nonna Verna Harrison describes the unceasing movement of desire and change in *epektasis* in this way:

> For change to become good, people must go forward continually; if they stand still they will slide backward. Desire for God is what impels them forward. In eternal growth, one is inspired by what one can see of God to look beyond it toward what one cannot see. Though God is unknowable, one strives to go further toward God, even into God. Then, by God's grace, one receives more of the divine life. Then desire is rekindled, so one is continually moved to go onward. As the desire increases, the gift increases, and with it the capacity to receive expands too. Because God is infinite, and humans are finite at every point in time, unending growth in God always remains a possibility. Once they are engaged in this dynamic of growth, people are filled to capacity at each moment but can always receive more of God. They are always satisfied, yet never satiated, always desirous of more. So those who are making progress are in a paradoxical situation. They are always at rest, since they are firmly fixed in the good, and they are always in motion, ever moving upward into the divine.[227]

This is a provocative idea. The living of the virtuous life becomes truly that: the *living*. It is not a commodity, or a static achievement, or a moment demarcating a finishing line. Instead, the

---

[226] Louth. 2007. 88.
[227] Harrison. 2010. 31-32.

living of the virtuous life is a *verb* – an ongoing verb grounded in the continual promise of the love and presence of God.

It is important to understand that this unceasing movement toward God is not, however, an exercise in frustration.[228] The human person is not set upon a Sisyphean path of futility, condemned to continual striving without attainment merely for the sake of being in perpetual motion. In Gregory's spiritual striving, one most certainly does freely attain – and is then beckoned on to the next horizon. There is progress.

In his pedagogical intent to enlighten and encourage his reader, his emphasis on the critical orientation of human freedom, and the unleashing of the movement of desire and change in *epektasis*, Gregory sets up in the opening paragraphs of the *Life* significant themes that bear on the moral, mystical, and aesthetic identity of the treatise. Let us return to virtue to examine in more detail the moral and mystical elements of the *Life*, with a specific look at the role of beauty in virtue.

The Moral, Mystical and Beautiful in Virtue

In contemporary virtue ethics, the practice of virtue is frequently referred to as forming a 'disposition' of virtue in the human being.[229] One is not virtuous by value of committing one virtuous act; rather, one is virtuous because one has formed a disposition of

---

[228] Kathryn Rombs notes that Hans Urs von Balthasar asked: 'Whether this doctrine did not amount to one of eternal frustration?' K. Rombs. 'Gregory of Nyssa's Doctrine of Epektasis: Some Logical Implications.' *Studia Patristica*, Vol. 37: *Cappadocian Writers and Other Greek Writers*. M.F. Wiles, & EJ. Yarnold. (edd). Peeters. Leuven. 2001. 288-293. (292). Louth (2007. 92) also mentions Balthasar's view that 'the knowledge of God gained through the mirror of the soul' was given by God 'as a compensation for the impossibility of seeing the unknowable God, a compensation the soul accepts with resignation.' There is no trace, however, of a tone of resignation or frustration in the spiritual journey described by Gregory in *The Life of Moses*. If anything, there is a mounting sense of anticipation of newer and greater dimensions, along a path of eternal promise. As Meredith (1999. 22) comments, 'For Gregory there are no absolute ends in the spiritual life, either here or hereafter, only new beginnings.'

[229] J. Porter. 'Virtue Ethics.' *The Cambridge Companion to Christian Ethics*. Ed. R. Gill. Cambridge University Press. Cambridge. 2000. 96-111. (96).

virtue resulting from many virtuous acts. This disposition reflects a change in the capacities, orientations, and actions of the human being. In effect, one changes oneself through the pursuit and practice of virtue. From Aristotle to Alasdair MacIntyre, ethicists have looked to the practice of virtue as a guide for moral excellence.[230] For Christian ethicists, virtue ethics has also embraced Christ as the model of perfect virtue, and the imitation of Christ in Christian virtue as the path to moral perfection.[231]

What is compelling about Gregory's treatment of the virtues is that he views them as not only representative of human moral excellence, but also as an essential part of the spiritual path of divinization by grace (*theosis*). The pursuit of virtue in Gregory's writings is a means of divinization, for the virtues are God's way of indwelling the human being.[232] Acquiring virtue is then a path of becoming like God (*homoiosis tou theou*) and participating in God (*metousia theou*).

Further examples of divinization by virtue may be found in other Gregorian texts. Gregory states in his *De virginitate* that virtue becomes 'the outward manifestation of divinization.'[233] In *De oratione dominica* 5, the one who has ascended to the summit of virtue is, according to Martin Laird, 'almost no longer shown in terms of human nature, but, through virtue, becomes like God Himself...'[234] Moreover, in the *Commentary on the Song of Songs*, Gregory interprets the Bride as ascending up 'steps of virtue' after the Word, a luminous ascent in virtue that perpetually transforms the Bride in light and beauty.[235] The virtues then contribute to participation in further attributes of God, such as the divine

---

[230] DJ. Harrington, & JF. Keenan. *Jesus and Virtue Ethics: Building Bridges Between New Testament Studies and Moral Theology*. Sheed & Ward. Lanham. MD. 2002. 24.

[231] Porter. 2000. 99. See also Harrington and Keenan. 2002. 24.

[232] Martin Laird notes that Canevet 'reminds us that for Gregory virtue is not a set of qualities we must acquire, but is God dwelling within us.' M. Laird. *Gregory of Nyssa and the Grasp of Faith: Union, Knowledge and Divine Presence*. OUP. Oxford. 2004. 188.

[233] Laird. 2004. 197.

[234] Laird. 2004. 189.

[235] Laird. 2004. 186.

beauty; likewise divinization also implies the beautification of the human soul.

Anthony Meredith notes that a clue to Gregory's understanding of the term virtue may be found in the sixth of his *Homilies on the Beatitudes*, in Gregory's exegesis of Jesus' teaching: '*Blessed are the pure of heart, for they shall see God*'.[236] In this homily, Gregory links religious virtue to both knowledge of God as experienced in the vision of God, and in the virtuous moral purity of one's life. Meredith insists that Gregory refuses to separate mystical experience from the moral life, not even to place them beside each other sequentially with the moral life serving as a preparatory stage for mystical experience.[237] Religious virtue comprises *both* moral excellence and mystical experience, as one part is 'that which concerns right conduct,' and the other part is 'that which concerns God.'[238] In the *Life*, Gregory explains the two parts of religious virtue:

> Religious virtue may be distinguished in the following way: part deals with the divine; part deals with moral behavior; for part of religion is purity of life. To begin with we must know how we are to think of God, and that knowledge entails entertaining none of the ideas which are derived from human understanding. The second part of virtue is taught by learning by what practices the life of virtue is realised (II.166).[239]

There is a distinct aesthetic element evident in this understanding of religious virtue as both moral and mystical. 'Seeing' (a pivotal aesthetic sense) becomes for Gregory the way one 'knows' and 'possesses' the good things of God. Seeing is thus a way of 'participating in.' In his sixth *Homilies on the Beatitudes* Gregory elaborates with the following understanding of what it means 'to see':

---

[236] Meredith. 1999. 99-100.
[237] Meredith. 1999. 100.
[238] Meredith. 1999. 100.
[239] Meredith. 1999. 106.

In scriptural usage, seeing means the same as possessing. So it is that when Scripture says, 'May you see the goods of Jerusalem' [Ps. 127. 6] it means the same as 'May you find'. Similarly, when Scripture says, 'Let the wicked be removed so as not to see the glory of the Lord' [Isa. 26. 10] the prophet means by 'not seeing' the same as 'not sharing in'. Therefore, whoever has seen God has possession through that sight of whatever is contained in the list of good things, that is, life without end, everlasting freedom from corruption, immortal happiness, a kingdom that knows no end, unceasing joy, true light, the spiritual and sweet voice, unapproachable glory, perpetual rejoicing, the complete good.[240]

In this beatitude, seeing is dependent upon purity of heart.[241] But how is this purity of heart accomplished? The answer lies in the divinely graced beauty of the pure heart and its capacity to reflect the beauty of the divine image. Gregory writes further in the same *Homily*:

So, too, ought we to understand the text that lies before us, namely that the Lord is insistent that blessedness consists not so much in knowing God as in having God within. 'Blessed are pure of heart, for they shall see God'. It does not appear that God is offering a face to face vision of Himself to those who have purified the eye of the soul. Instead the nobility of the saying perhaps means, what is elsewhere stated with greater clarity, that 'the kingdom of God is within us'. By this we are to learn that whoever has cleansed his heart from every passionate disposition, perceives in his own inner beauty the image of the divine nature.[242]

The purified heart (or soul) reflects and makes its own the image of divine beauty. The contemplation of beauty by 'seeing' and 'knowing' and the 'possessing of/participating in' the divine life are all elements of theological aesthetics at play in Gregory's writing.

---

240 Meredith. 1999. 92.
241 Meredith. 1999. 93.
242 Meredith. 1999. 95.

As Harrison writes: 'To share in virtues is to participate in God.'[243] Choosing virtue is not simply a moral choice, but also a spiritual and aesthetic one. Choosing virtue (an exercise of human freedom) is a step further in the ascent toward union with God and divinization according to the likeness of God's beauty and virtue. Harrison notes that: 'A choice to act virtuously is a choice to join one's will to the divine will, and thus to become united with God.'[244] For Gregory, virtue present in the human being is indicative of the gracious indwelling of God, and the ascent in virtue leads to increasing and unceasing participation in the light and beauty of God. Gregory explicitly links the acquisition of virtue to spiritual and moral progress – and illustrates the fruit of this progress in the beauty of the divinized soul and its reflection of divine beauty.

The Unceasing Movement of Desire

Gregory understands the human being by nature as one of change and desire, and Gregory's view of change is positive. As noted earlier, change and desire are operative in the doctrine of *epektasis*. For Gregory, the fact that the human being is in movement is not a matter of moral concern, but the decision which orients the direction of that movement most assuredly is. In his *Oratio Catechetica*, Gregory remarks on the movement of change in concert with considerations of the roles of beauty, desire, and human freedom. According to Gregory, we must continually decide to direct the movement of change, spurred by attraction and sustained by desire in endless progress, toward the good and the beautiful:

> Change, you must know, is a movement which never ceases, from the condition one is in to another. There are two types of movement. There is one in the direction of the good [*to agathon*], which is always taking place, where progress is endless, because there is no boundary to that which is explored. The other is in the opposite direction, whose very reality (*hypostasis*) consists in having no reality

---

[243] Harrison. 2010. 29.
[244] Harrison. 2010. 29.

....seeing that our nature cannot remain unchanged by itself, simply because it possesses an indestructible urge towards movement, its free choice is always moving towards something, as the desire [*epithymia*] for the beautiful [*to kalon*] is ever drawing it naturally towards movement.[245]

In the *Life*, Gregory frequently employs the Greek term *to kalon* to signify the Good and/or the Beautiful. This term is also usually synonymous with God. In English translations of Gregory's works, *to kalon* is more often rendered 'the good' than 'the beautiful'; although I believe the case can be made, according to the Platonic stream in which Gregory is surely swimming, that 'the beautiful' is just as accurate a translation as, and perhaps more accurate in many instances than, 'the good.'[246] It is important to remember that in ancient Greek philosophy, the good and beautiful are frequently classed as one, and the moral and the aesthetic are not separated. [247] Gregory stands firmly in this tradition: his use of *to kalon* means the beautiful as the good and *vice versa*, although, as we saw above, Gregory also uses *to agathon* to specifically refer to the good. Using the philosophic tradition as a guide, I will insert an alternative 'beauty' in the remaining translated excerpts of *to kalon* when the cited translator has chosen 'good' over 'beauty.'

Gregory understands the human being as naturally attracted to the beautiful (*to kalon*) and desiring to participate in that beauty (*metousia theou*). From the *Life* we learn:

Certainly whoever pursues true virtue participates in nothing other than God, because he is himself absolute virtue. Since, then, those who know what is good/beautiful

---

[245] Meredith. 1999. 77-78.

[246] For discussion on *to kalon* and the good and the beautiful in Plato's philosophy, see V. Bychkov. 'The Platonic Tradition.' in: *Aesthetic Revelation: Reading Ancient and Medieval Texts after Hans Urs von Balthasar*. CUA Press. Washington. 2010. 129-175.

[247] RJ. O'Connell. '*Eros* and *Philia* in Plato's Moral Cosmos.' *Neoplatonism and Early Christian Thought: Essays in honour of A.H. Armstrong*. Eds. HJ. Blumenthal & RA. Markus. Variorum Publications. London. 1981. 3-19. (6-7).

[*to kalon*] by nature desire participation in it, and since this good/beauty has no limit, the participant's desire itself necessarily has no stopping place but stretches out with the limitless....the one limit of virtue is the absence of a limit (I.7-8).

For Gregory, 'The perfection of human nature consists perhaps in its very growth in goodness/beauty [*to kalon*]' (I.10). In our growing, we discover in ourselves a limitless capacity of participation in virtue and beauty and thus in God: continually transcending boundaries, moving forward, and with an ever-growing capacity and desire to stretch beyond boundaries as they newly present themselves and then dissolve behind us in transcendence. In this participation in transcendence, we participate in the possibility of infinity, through the infinite possibility of growth in the God who is without limit.

Intrinsic to Gregory's grasp of human nature is an understanding of the human being as a creature of passion and desire (*epithymia*). Gregory, however, does not seek the elimination of desire. Rather, his writings shepherd the seeker toward the education and training (*paideia*) of desire through ascetic practice, the acquisition of virtue and, most of all, the constant orientation of human freedom and desire toward God.[248] In the spiritual life, desire is a power within the soul. Desire, not rightly ordered, can inhibit the soul's progress; but desire is a force that can also enable the soul to achieve great heights, providing it is purified and rightly oriented.[249] Divine beauty elicits desire in the human being, which has a natural attraction toward it, and draws that desire in movement towards itself.

This human and divine dynamic of relationship is key to understanding the role of beauty and the unceasing movement of desire in the *Life of Moses*. It is through this dynamic relationship

---

[248] For an in-depth discussion of the education and training of desire in Gregory of Nyssa, see M. Laird. 'Under Solomon's Tutelage: The Education of Desire in the *Homilies on the Song of Songs*.' in: *Re-Thinking Gregory of Nyssa*. (ed). S. Coakley. Blackwell. Malden. MA. 2003. 77-96.

[249] Laird. 2004. 60.

that we witness the *Life* as not only a mystical and moral treatise, but also an aesthetic one. The fire of desire, inspired and sustained by beauty, and properly educated and trained, is the fuel of this dynamic relationship propelling the human being toward becoming a 'friend of God'.

The Ascent to God – Moses

In the *Life*, the beauty revealed in the journey of Moses' three theophanies (the beauty of virtue and the divinized soul; the beauty and sublimity of the burning bush, the heavenly tabernacle and priestly vestments; and the beauty of, and desire for, God) attests to the beauty of the call of the divine, and to the unceasing movement of desire in Moses' response to that call. The three theophanies of Moses assume symbolic significance as three cardinal stages of spiritual ascent towards apophatic union with God.

The first theophany is that of Moses' encounter with the burning bush. In this encounter, Moses observes what his senses and rational mind cannot comprehend: a bush on fire; burning, and yet not consumed by the flames. Both his sight and his hearing are illuminated by the rays of light emanating from the bush, purifying him to receive the 'undefiled teachings' (I.20). Commanded to remove his sandals, he spiritually sheds the 'dead and earthly covering of skins' placed around 'the feet of the soul' (II.22). Moses thereby acquires the 'knowledge of truth,' which, in Gregory's view, means 'not to have a mistaken apprehension of Being' (II.23). Moses realizes that 'none of those things which are apprehended by sense perception and contemplated by the reality of the understanding really subsists, but that the transcendent essence and cause of the universe, on which everything depends, alone subsists' (II.24). God is true Being, 'neither increasing nor diminishing....standing in need of nothing else, alone desirable, participated in by all but not lessened by their participation,' and Moses' apprehension of this is the 'knowledge of truth' (II.25). God is ultimate reality. God is unchanging, while all that Moses knows of the world is subject to change. Everything knowable in the world exists from God.

The second theophany is represented by Moses' first climb up Mount Sinai into the dark cloud (*nephele*). The people have shrunk back in fear. Overwhelmed by the sight of this awesome cloud with a mysterious fire shining out of its darkness, a cloud wrapped so densely around the mountain that it obscures the peak from view, the people are also terrorized by the sounds of the trumpets (I.43). The trumpets blare into the air the divine word, laying down their formidable ordinances, in the form of blasts ever increasing in volume with a great 'terribleness' of sound (I.44).

Gregory writes that the people 'as a whole were incapable of enduring what was seen and heard' (I.45). Moses will climb the mountain alone. Far from weakening him, however, his solitariness gives him strength. Gregory notes that:

…having been stripped as it were of the people's fear, he boldly approached the very darkness itself and entered the invisible things where he was no longer seen by those watching. After he entered the inner sanctuary of the divine mystical doctrine, there, while not being seen, he was in company with the Invisible. He teaches, I think, by the things that he did, that whoever is going to associate intimately with God must go beyond all that is visible and, lifting up his own mind as if to a mountaintop and to the invisible and incomprehensible, believe that the divine is there, where the understanding does not reach (I.46).

Moses has been purified of all 'sensual and irrational emotion' and preconceptions by the experience of his first theophany (II.157). From the encounter with light at the burning bush which banishes the darkness of false knowledge of God and replaces it with the rays of truth, Moses is now drawn to enter a new and different darkness, that of the incomprehensible nature of God:

For leaving behind everything that is observed, not only what sense comprehends but also what the intelligence thinks it sees, it keeps on penetrating deeper until by the intelligence's yearning for understanding it gains access to the invisible and the incomprehensible, and there it sees God. This is the true

121

knowledge of what is sought; this is the seeing that consists in not seeing, because that which is sought transcends all knowledge, being separated on all sides by incomprehensibility as by a kind of darkness (II.163).

From his penetration into this 'luminous darkness' (II.163), Moses receives the overwhelmingly splendid and beautiful visions of the heavenly and earthly tabernacles and the priestly vestments, and receives the divine Law inscribed on tablets of stone. He moves beyond what he learned from the burning bush to understand that God is not only ultimate and true Being, the source and subsistence of all existence, but that God is also incomprehensible. In the cloud, God is present yet beyond the reach of human rationality and understanding.[250]

Moses returns to the Israelites, and discovers them bowed down in worship before the idol of the golden calf. In consternation, he lets fall the stone tablets of the divine Law from his hands, and the tablets dramatically shatter on the ground. Moses exhorts the Israelites to repent. He then returns to Mt. Sinai, where he repeats another forty days in union with God. During this third theophany, Moses requests to see God face to face. The heavenly voice responds that 'what the petitioner seeks cannot be contained by human life' (II.220). Moses' request cannot be gratified; at least not in the manner in which he has posed it. Yet, the divine concession nonetheless answers Moses when God reveals

> ….there is a place with himself where there is a rock with a hole in it into which he commands Moses to enter. Then God placed his hand over the mouth of the hole and called out to Moses as he passed by. When Moses was summoned, he came out of the hole and saw the back of the One who called him (II.220).

In the *Life*, Gregory likens the hole in the rock to Christ, as the 'heavenly house not made with hands which is laid up by hope for those who have dissolved their earthly tabernacle' (II.245). He elaborates this image with many aesthetically descriptive names

---

[250] Meredith. 1999. 102.

of Christ, among them 'the crown of righteousness,' 'pleasure of paradise,' 'eternal tabernacle,' 'pillar of strength,' and 'throne of judgment' (II.246-7). Standing on 'the rock (the rock is Christ who is absolute virtue),' then one is both 'steadfast and unmovable,' and poised to set the heart flying 'upward through its stability in the good' (II.244). One recalls Nonna Verna Harrison's words regarding *epektasis* as being at rest, fixed on the good yet simultaneously always in upward motion toward the divine. The rock of Christ stabilizes one in the hope of all good things, and 'he who finds any good finds it in Christ who contains all good' (II.249). It is likely that Gregory gleaned some of this christological interpretation of the revelation of God through the hole in the rock from his predecessor Origen, whose writings bear a major influence on Gregory. One can see the similarity of approach in Origen's *Canticles Commentary*:[251]

> Like to these is the saying of God to Moses: 'Lo, I have set thee in a cleft of the rock, and thou shalt see my back parts.' That rock which is Christ is therefore not completely closed, but has clefts. But the cleft in the rock is he who reveals God to men and makes Him known to them; for no–one knoweth the Father save the Son. So no-one sees the back parts of God, that is to say, the things that are come to pass in the latter times, unless he be placed in the cleft of the rock, that is to say, when he is taught them by Christ's own revealing.[252]

Notwithstanding this christological nuance, Gregory's primary thrust of the experience of Moses' view of God's back is to establish that if one wishes to see God, one must follow God. Just as a hiker must follow her guide, since if she positions herself facing the guide she would be oriented entirely in the wrong direction, just so the one seeking God 'will not turn aside from the right way if he always keeps the back of his leader in view' (II.252). One does not go before God, nor does one face God. One follows. Gregory explains:

---

[251] Origen. *Commentary on the Song of Songs*, 4.15.
[252] Cited in: Louth. 2007. 61-62.

For he who moves to one side or brings himself to face his guide assumes another direction for himself than the one his guide shows him. Therefore, he says to the one who is led, 'My face is not to be seen', that is, 'Do not face your guide.' If he does so, his course will certainly be in the opposite direction, for good does not look good in the face, but follows it (II.253)… What is perceived to be its opposite is face to face with the good, for what looks virtue in the face is evil. But virtue is not perceived in contrast to virtue. Therefore, Moses does not look God in the face, but looks at his back; for whoever looks at him face to face shall not live, as the divine voice testifies, 'man cannot see the face of the Lord and live' (II.254).

The key to knowing God, therefore, is following God. Christ, the cleft in the rock, reveals God. Because knowledge of God comes in the form of following (an act of pursuit) it bears a direct relationship to the nature of the soul in its *epektasis* towards ever new heights and distant horizons into the unlimited potential and possibility of God. Gregory continues, describing the upward nature of the soul and drawing again upon Philippians 3.13 for support:

Once [the soul] is released from its earthly attachment, it becomes light and swift for its movement upward, soaring from below up to the heights (II.224).

If nothing comes from above to hinder its upward thrust (for the nature of the Good attracts to itself those who look to it), the soul rises ever higher and will always make its flight yet higher – by its desire of the heavenly things 'straining ahead for what is still to come', as the Apostle says (II.225).

Made to desire and not to abandon the transcendent height by the things already attained, it makes its way upward without ceasing, ever through its prior accomplishments renewing its intensity for the flight. Activity directed toward virtue causes its capacity to grow through exertion; this kind of activity alone does not slacken its intensity by the effort, but increases it (II.226).

For this reason we also say that the great Moses, as he was becoming ever greater, at no time stopped in his ascent, nor did he set a limit for himself in his upward course (II.227).

Desire, linked with beauty and virtue, thus continues to move the human soul onward unceasingly and eternally in the soul's ascent toward union with God. In the *Life*, this ascent is a journey characterized by light, darkness, and apophatic recognition of the incomprehensibility and unknowability of God. Moses' bold following of God, beyond human concepts, even to the luminous unknowing darkness on Mt. Sinai, beyond human knowing, concepts, and understanding, is one of the most famous illustrations of Gregory's apophatic spiritual theology.

The Ascent to Beauty – Diotima

Gregory's allegorical spiritual interpretation of the three theophanies of Moses corresponds to the pattern of the ascent to beauty found in the speech of Diotima, the priestess of Mantinea, in Plato's *Symposium*.[253] In this justly famous oration, Diotima sets herself the task of initiating Socrates into the mysteries of Love. She first demonstrates that one is called and drawn to ultimate Beauty initially by noticing and loving an individual beautiful body. One then considers how the beauty of that body is related to the beauty of other bodies, and realizes that the lover of beauty must love every lovely body. Following this realization, one comprehends that the beauty of bodies are as nothing in comparison to the beauties of the soul; and as a result of the encounter with a beautiful soul, one will change in noble virtue:

> …so that wherever he meets with spiritual loveliness, even in the husk of an unlovely body, he will find it beautiful enough to fall in love with and to cherish – and beautiful enough to quicken in his heart a longing for such discourse as tends toward the building of a noble nature (210b-c).

---

[253] The following excerpts of Diotima's speech in the *Symposium* (209e-212c), are taken from: E. Hamilton, & H. Cairns. (edd). *The Collected Dialogues of Plato Including the Letters.* Princeton Univ. Press. NJ. 1969. 561-563.

From contemplating the beauty of the soul, one is led to the beauty of laws and institutions, the sciences, and across 'beauty's wide horizon....toward the open sea of beauty' where one will find the

> ...most fruitful discourse and loftiest thought, and reap a golden harvest of philosophy, until, confirmed and strengthened, he will come upon one single form of knowledge, the knowledge of the beauty I am about to speak of (210d).

Then, the next revelation of the beautiful

> ...bursts upon him that wondrous vision which is the very soul of the beauty he has toiled so long for. It is an everlasting loveliness which neither comes nor goes, which neither flowers nor fades; for such beauty is the same on every hand, the same then as now....

> Nor will his vision of the beautiful take the form of a face, or of hands, or of anything that is of the flesh. It will be neither words, nor knowledge, nor a something that exists in something else, such as a living creature, or the earth, or the heavens, or anything that is, but subsisting of itself and by itself in an eternal oneness, while every lovely thing partakes of it in such sort that, however much the parts may wax and wane, it will be neither more nor less, but still the same inviolable whole (210e-211b).

When the pursuer of beauty has managed to move past his initial devotions to this contemplation of beauty in eternal oneness, he must then:

> ... approach, or be led toward, the sanctuary of Love. Starting from individual beauties, the quest for the universal beauty must find him ever mounting the heavenly ladder, stepping from rung to rung, that is, from one to two, and from two to every lovely body, from bodily beauty to the beauty of institutions, from institutions to learning, and from learning in general to the special lore that pertains to

nothing but the beautiful itself, until at last he comes to know what beauty is …. And if….man's life is ever worth the living, it is when he has attained this vision of the very soul of beauty. And once you have seen it….you will care nothing for the beauties that used to take your breath away and kindle such a longing in you ……. only then will a man be quickened with the true (and not specious) virtue, for it will be virtue's self that quickens him, not virtue's semblance (211b-e).

Pausing here for a moment, let us consider how Diotima's speech contains elements found in Gregory's doctrine of *epektasis*, including a progressive spiritual illumination evident in Moses' three theophanies in Gregory's *Life of Moses*. According to Diotima, the pursuer of beauty finds beauty first in the senses in the appreciation of the first individual beautiful body. However, after further knowledge, he realizes that beauty is not confined nor defined by that particular beautiful body, but is actually something beyond the senses as a quality that is shared by many different beautiful things. This quality cannot really be known except as something that subsists in itself in an eternal oneness. The pursuer of beauty, with each new discovery of beauty, is continually spurred on by the desire for beauty to each new stage of the ascent, satisfied at each stage but not satiated. Through the toil and effort of the pursuer of beauty, the virtue of love grows in his soul as more and more beauty is revealed for him to love; and the virtue of nobility is accordingly formed into his nature. He is led to the sanctuary of Love where he will attain not a semblance of virtue found in lesser manifestations, but rather the vision of the soul of beauty itself. In this union, virtue's true self will quicken him.

Gregory's structure of the theophanies in the *Life* neatly aligns with the details of the spiritual ascent described in Diotima's speech. From observable phenomena such as the burning bush to the unknowable God in the cloud of darkness and on to his request to see God face to face, Moses travels from stage to stage in increasing knowledge, illumination, and love. The eternal climb, the progress in the development of virtue through the effort

127

of the ascent, and the increasing revelation of truth and being, all parallel the ideational structure of the oration of Diotima.

In the following passages from the *Life*, Gregory attests powerfully to the dynamic of the unceasing movement of desire in response to the call of beauty. One can hear clearly the echoes of Diotima's voice in these words:

> When the soul is moved towards what is naturally lovely, it seems to me that this is the sort of passionate desire with which it is moved. Beginning with the loveliness it sees, it is drawn upwards to what is transcendent. The soul is forever inflaming its desire for what is hidden, by means of what it has already grasped. For this reason, the ardent lover of beauty understands what is seen as an image of what he desires, and yearns to be filled with the actual substance of the archetype. This is what underlines the bold and excessive desire of him who desires to see no longer 'through mirrors and reflections, but instead to enjoy beauty face to face.' The divine voice concedes what is demanded by actually refusing it, and in a few words displays the immeasurable depths of its ideas. On the one hand, the divine generosity grants the fulfillment of his desire; on the other hand, it promises no end to desire, nor satiety of it (II.231-232).[254]

The similarity between the two ascents is striking, from the structures of the ascents to the very words used to describe them. The similarity is, however, significantly not a complete one. At the end of the ascents, particularly in the experience of the vision 'face to face' with the object of desire, we see a compelling difference in Gregory's Christian account. In Diotima's speech, the fulfillment of the ascent is realized with the vision face to face of the very soul of beauty. There is a final achievement of the soul's desire. Moses, however, is refused his request to see God face to face. He is instead granted the vision of seeing the back parts of God through the hole in the rock that is Christ, the revealer of God. Moses' desire is obliquely realized through the divine rejection of the

---

[254] Meredith. (1999). 106.

requested face to face encounter. What could be the meaning of this decided difference in the description of Moses' ascent?

Gregory no doubt resonated strongly with Diotima's ascent to beauty, sounding her rising melody yet again, but this time in the key of holy scripture and a Christian spiritual interpretation of Moses' story in the *Life*. The climax of the two ascents is resolved by different material, as noted above. Yet there is another similarity following the climax: the resulting relationship between the soul and the soul's object of desire bears a similar name in both works. For following the vision of beauty's very self, Diotima's pursuer of beauty achieves immortality in earning this title: being called *the friend of god* (212a). Likewise, Gregory exhorts Caesarius to the life of perfection in virtue following Moses' example, with the aim of being *known by God and becoming God's friend* (II.320). The climax of both ascents is friendship with God: a divine-human relationship (*philia*) resulting from a journey in virtue and illumination.

But Gregory outdoes Diotima here. It is precisely at this point that the meaning of the different climax in Moses' ascent becomes clear. Moses is known by God and becomes God's friend, but he does not see God face to face. He sees God by following the back of God. The relationship exists dynamically in continual pursuit. In the divine concession of granting Moses' request by refusing it, Gregory's God ensures that in effect, the relationship of God with God's friend never ends. By placing the fulfillment of the soul's desire in the unending, eternal, flow of *epektasis*, the spiritual ascent depicted in the *Life* continues unceasingly. The relationship between God and the human soul in Gregory's work carries on into eternity. The Christian theologian here marks off a necessary differentiation between the Creator and the created, yet at the same time resolves the philosophical problem of the separation of the creaturely from the divine, by the doctrine of mystical union through eternal pursuit.

The Language of Beauty

A last remark must be made in honor of the beauty of Gregory's lavish use of descriptive language. The aesthetic language of beauty presents itself, frequently and vividly, throughout the *Life*. Moses is portrayed as a baby 'already appearing beautiful in swaddling clothes'; so beautiful that 'he caused his parents to draw back from having such a child destroyed by death' (I.16). The Egyptian princess who discovers Moses floating on the Nile 'saw the outward grace evident in him' and took him as her own son (I.17). Moses receives the beauty of the three theophanies; particularly the intricately detailed vision of the beauty of the tabernacle and priestly vestments. The face of the Patriarch is transfigured luminously after his encounter with God. Moses responds to the call of beauty in the theophanies and changes his life. Each new stage in his ascent brings Moses not only knowledge and faith, but also provokes action that includes bringing beauty and justice into his world.

At the end of Part 1, the *historia*, Gregory describes Moses' death in this manner:

> Time had not harmed his beauty, neither dimmed his brightness of eye nor diminished the graciousness of his appearance. Always remaining the same, he preserved in the changeableness of nature an unchangeable beauty (I.76).

Moses' spiritual greatness and relationship with God sustain him in beauty throughout his life. Further on, the conclusion of the *Life* captures once again the attraction of beauty in stimulating desire, and the power of beauty to provide a worthy model of imitation:

> These things concerning the perfection of the virtuous life, O Caesarius, man of God, we have briefly written for you, tracing in outline like a pattern of beauty the life of the great Moses so that each one of us might copy the image of the beauty which has been shown to us by imitating his way of life (II.319).

Gregory's final words in the treatise reveal the outcome of the imitation of such a model of beauty, the outcome that is declared by Diotima and realized by Moses himself:

It is time for you, noble friend, to look to that example and, by transferring to your own life what is contemplated through spiritual interpretation ....to be known by God and to become his friend. (II.320).

Coda

Gregory illumines, through the dynamic of desire, the human and divine relationship inherent in the doctrine of God. The human being is continually called, deeper and deeper, into an apophatic knowledge of God and to participation in God, yet a full knowledge and participation is of course impossible, for one 'cannot see God and live.' At the same time, Gregory says, one 'steps on the rock' that supports (II.244) and achieves progress, continuing to climb to new vistas of desire. Moses is granted a vision of God's back through the hole in the rock, the rock Gregory names as Christ, the revealer of God (II.244); and one orients to the revealed God by following God's back, as the hiker follows the guide. To see God face-to-face is to be turned in the wrong direction. For Gregory, then, to follow is to behold.

The desire for God, for the beauty of God, never ends; and God's response in infinite wisdom withholds the face-to-face encounter. In the eliciting of desire, God grants the fulfillment of desire by ensuring there will be no end nor satiety of it, and thus no cessation in the following of God. There is a dynamic interplay of relationship here between humanity and God, each one desiring the other.

Beauty, the unending movement of desire, and the participation in divine life by the following of God are all themes developed extensively throughout the Orthodox theological and mystical tradition, in particular in the works of Ps. Dionysius (c. late 5th century), St. Maximus the Confessor (580-662), and St. Gregory Palamas (1296-1359); all of whom are indebted to Gregory's thought.[255] St. Gregory of Nyssa's doctrine of *epektasis* will continue through the centuries influencing subsequent Christian teaching on God, identifying the dynamic currents of the beauty

---

[255] Meredith. 1999. 138-139.

of both human and divine desire operative in the ongoing relations of divine and human friendship.

It is quite clear that Gregory's *Life of Moses* attempts, from its vivid visual detail and down to its underlying formal structure, to trace an outline of the beauty of Moses' life in order that others may imitate and follow. The treatise is a spiritual manual; it is a teaching guide for the believer seeking perfection in the Christian life. Beauty as well as human and divine desire are inseparably linked in Gregory's allegorical and spiritual exploration of the life of the great Moses. Gregory examines, in this work, the pursuit of virtue, the exercise of human freedom, and the response to the call of beauty: all of which are depicted as part of a heavenly calling which elicits, directs, and sustains the unceasing movement of desire toward becoming God's friend. Making ample use of the language of beauty, the Platonic model of ascent to beauty depicted in the *Symposium*, and thrumming with desire and unceasing movement in the doctrine of *epektasis*, Gregory renders the *Life of Moses* as not only a treatise of mystical wisdom and moral excellence, but assuredly one of the finest early Christian examples of aesthetic writing as well.

Eternal Pilgrimage of Beauty:
The Pattern of Perfection According to St. Gregory of Nyssa.

Rebecca Thekla Raney

*You are more beautiful than the Sons of men...Listen, O daughter, and see,
and incline your ear; and forget your own people, and your father's house;
and the King shall greatly desire your beauty. (Psalm 45: 2, 10-11)*

Prelude

These profound words from Psalm 45 capture the essence, motivation, and goal of the spiritual life. Here, the Psalmist, in a
theophanic revelation, acknowledges the God-Man Christ as the
most beautiful among the sons of men and then kindles the desire
of the Daughter to incline her ear, and embark on an exodus from
her own familiar earthly attractions in order to really become
beautiful and participate in the King's glorious Beauty. St Gregory
of Nyssa, in his *Commentary on the Song of Songs,* as well as his
theological interpretation of the *Life of Moses,* expands on this
mystery, encapsulating the whole of the spiritual ascent of the
soul in terms of an ecstatic pattern, sparked by the desire to
encounter and partake of true Beauty. As the soul conforms to this
pattern it journeys on an eternal quest of ever-deepening
communion with the Beloved, which we may call a 'Pilgrimage of
Beauty.' This pattern emerges in St. Gregory, not so much in terms
of visual shapes, but more as living, non-linear, patterns of action.

The process of *Theosis* and conforming to the likeness of God has
been well understood as a matter of growing in love and virtue in
imitation of the Lord. We have the commands, for instance, to
Love God, love the neighbor, to become meek, merciful, holy,
pure in heart, and even to become 'perfect' (*teleios*) as our Father
in Heaven is perfect.[256] St. Gregory, in these two related texts,
prompts us also to consider that God's unlimited virtuous
attributes are not only 'Good' and 'True,' but harmoniously also
Beautiful. Accordingly, those who seek to conform to His likeness
are in effect, simultaneously on a quest of Beauty as they 'Seek

---

[256] Matthew 5.48

first the Kingdom.'[257] In the Gospel of Matthew 13:45-46, the Kingdom of Heaven is represented as a 'beautiful pearl.' Metropolitan Kallistos Ware has also remarked, that when St. Peter, at the site of the Transfiguration exclaims that: 'It is good for us to be here,'[258] the Greek word (*kalos*) for good, literally translated means: 'It is beautiful for us to be here.' In the same way, when Christ calls Himself the 'Good Shepherd' the phrase can equally mean 'Beautiful Shepherd.'[259] It follows, then, that the evangelical exhortation for us to pursue perfection could equally be parsed: 'Become beautiful as your heavenly Father is beautiful,' since the Kingdom of God, and the process of salvation, are so unequivocally linked with the vital aspect of Divine Beauty.

Metropolitan Kallistos notes how the term *kalos*, the most commonly used adjective to communicate the ancient Greek philosophical notion of beauty, can also be translated as 'good', but in the sophistic understanding of the triad in which the 'One' was understood as being both true, good, and beautiful, a different word for good was normally used, namely: *agathos*.[260] In order etymologically to understand the meaning of the beautiful, he suggests that we should look at the verb *kaleo*, which means 'I call or summon, invoke or evoke.'[261] Intrinsic to the nature of the Beauty then, there he finds an implicit invitation. Metropolitan Kallistos writes:

> This is the special characteristic of beauty: it calls out to us, it beckons to us and draws us to itself, igniting our God-given desire for Him. It takes us out of ourselves in an ecstatic way and brings us into relationship with the 'Other.' It awakens within us a feeling of *Eros*, a sense of longing and yearning.[262]

In this way, the notion of Divine Beauty can be understood in its wholeness as embodying qualities of its adjective, noun and verb,

---

[257] Matthew 6.33
[258] Met. Kallistos. 2008. 10.
[259] *Ibid.* 10
[260] *Ibid.* 9.
[261] *Ibid.* 9.
[262] *Ibid.* 9.

bridging and uniting the aesthetic and the practical life in the dynamic motion of salvation.

In the Jewish tradition, both of Gregory's foundational texts in his theology of beauty (the biblical narratives of the life of Moses and the *Song of Songs*) are read during the liturgical calendar celebration of the Passover services, as narratives commemorating the salvation of the people of Israel. St. Gregory also follows this tradition, understanding these paralleled passages as comm.-unicating the life of perfection or salvation. In his approach, Gregory focuses his attention on their mutual 'pattern of beauty,'[263] for communicating this mystery. This paper will similarly argue, from a more pastoral, theological, perspective that according to St. Gregory, the 'pattern of Beauty' described in our two texts also provides the foundation upon which the whole life of salvation can, and should, be grounded or envisioned. Using his imagery from the *Life of Moses* and the *Commentary on the Song of Songs*, this paper will argue that the path of salvation can appropriately be imagined as more of a Pilgrimage of Beauty, where one (to use the traditional language) does 'acquire the Holy Spirit', 'climb the ladder,' 'embody the Beatitudes', 'die to the old man and live to the new', 'become perfect and imitate Christ'; but where we may also, most appropriately see the entire organic process of *Theosis* as made sense within the context of this quest for eternal Beauty.

If the full power of the Gospel message and reality is to be uniquely incarnated and differentiated in each person and in the entire cosmos, then the vital role that Beauty plays in this process must never be ignored or forgotten. St Gregory, in his *Life of Moses*, evokes the 'climbing' of the patriarch to Sinai's summit as paralleling his inner pilgrimage to Beauty. He says this:

> What Moses was experiencing, I think, was a longing which filled his soul for the Supreme Good; and this longing was constantly being intensified by his hope in the Transcendent, arising from the beauty which he had already glimpsed; and this hope constantly inflamed his desire to see what was

[263] St. Gregory of Nyssa. *The Life of Moses*. 1978. 136

hidden because of all that he had attained at each stage. Thus it is that the ardent lover of beauty, constantly receiving an image, as it were, of what he longs for, wants to be filled with the very impression of the archetype. The bold demand of the soul that climbs the hills of desire tends towards the direct enjoyment of Beauty, and not merely through mirrors or reflections.[264]

In this short paper I wish to outline briefly the essentials of this pilgrimage of beauty as described by St. Gregory, using examples from these two classic and profound works, highlighting the three key components in the process: *Ekstasis, Epektasis,* and *Re-entry.* This *Re-Entry* of the soul from contemplation (*Theoria*) to the community (*koinonia*) will be explained utilizing insights taken from the classical pilgrim literature of Greek antiquity with which St. Gregory would have been familiar, and which illustrates the personal transformation and social impact that this mystical pilgrimage generates. The spiritual mechanics of this pursuit and the great mystery of this pilgrimage of Beauty will be explored, using a more pastoral approach, as we investigate the interrelationship of the theological elements of *Ekstasis, Epektasis* and *Re-Entry.*

St. Gregory's Basic Theological Framework

St Gregory's ascetic treatises and commentaries on Scripture, particularly his *Commentary on the Song of Songs,* as well as his theological interpretation of the *Life of Moses,* represent the height of his mystical theology which can be more appropriately understood simply as his pastoral call to transform Christian life. Both works mirror the soul's ascent to God, and highlight complementary aspects of this path. The noted Jewish Scholar John Levenson has remarked that these two biblical foundational stories have been closely related even from ancient times. He explains: 'The *Song of Songs* eroticizes the *Exodus* account while the *Exodus* story desexualizes the *Song of Songs.*'[265] According to St. Gregory, they are in fact two tales telling of the same spiritual

---

[264] *The Life of Moses.* 1978. 114
[265] 2010 Lecture: Harvard Divinity School. *The Jewish Liturgical Year.* 1667A /13.

journey, and this is why he thinks they can be treated together to accentuate the life-giving patterns of Beauty that are woven through their respective stories of salvation.

Upon the initial investigation of St. Gregory' texts, the intentional focus on very intimate and dynamic spiritual processes rather than static prescriptions for predicted salvific results, jumps out at the reader. At this point, the imagery of 'pilgrimage' becomes useful in order to understand the patterns of perfection more contextually. The metaphor of movement from place to place has frequently been used to describe the supernatural reality of the spiritual journey. The Lord proclaims 'I am the Way, the Truth and the Life'[266] and Christianity itself was initially referred to as 'the Way'.[267] St Paul also describes the ascetical, spiritual struggle of following Christ in terms of running a race.[268] The term pilgrimage, therefore, can help us to understand the spirit behind St. Gregory's expositions on the life of perfection, because unless believers acknowledge that this journey is actually one of 'devotional travel,'[269] then they will be disappointed when desires and longings remain unmet, or when they never seem to 'arrive' at the place where they have imagined God to be dwelling and waiting to meet them.

In each act of physical pilgrimage to a specific place, the motivations seem the same: the pilgrim came to pray. Pilgrimage specialist Pierre Maraval posits that the pilgrim believes in some way that, 'his prayer would be fortified by all that the place itself could bring and contribute, which is essentially to say by all that could be seen and touched.'[270] The literature of pilgrimage seems to show that the essence of a traditional pilgrimage was related to this issue of prayer. This implies an unceasing holy desire, either for enlightenment, healing, intercession, or an intimate encounter with a living God which implied contact with a Transcendent and

---

[266] Jn. 14.6.
[267] Acts. 22.4
[268] Gal. 2.2.
[269] AM. Talbot. 2003. 59-61.
[270] P. Maraval. 2003. 71.

transforming reality.[271] This participation in the holiness of a place or the veneration of a sacred relic involved all of the senses, whether sight, sound, or touch; but always there was a reaching out through the visible media to the invisible transcendent. It was as if it were an image of communion where the Uncreated and the Created could seek to connect.

Maraval puts it this way: 'The first objective of the pilgrim was not to be better informed, but rather to nourish his or her personal prayer. If the sight of these places led the pilgrim to that end, it was because they were places of memory where one could see, hear, and even touch that which would direct one's attention to a higher reality brought to life through contemplation.'[272] It was the same with those seeking a blessing or wisdom from saintly hermits or elders. Maraval cites St. Theodoret of Cyr who said (concerning visitors to St. Symeon the Stylite): 'Those coming for the spectacle return instructed in things divine.'[273] For all pilgrims the consequence was the same: a divine theophany had been lodged in that particular place, or person, and it was that hoped-for inspiration, consolation, and rejuvenation from the energies of God, which motivated and sustained the pilgrims' travels. Maraval notes also that there was a belief in the 'living force' contained within the relics or holy places. The pilgrims did not come solely to worship in a holy place, 'but rather to adore or venerate the place itself as a means of participating in its holiness. It was also important for the pilgrim to bring away some part of this holiness and appropriate through some form of physical contact part of the holiness of the place they had come from near or far to venerate.'[274]

This image of the person on pilgrimage, captures the essence of this eternal journey of union with God and that quest which is ever seeking deeper communion with Him. It is clear from the historical records about pilgrimage in the Byzantine era that often 'such journeys were difficult, even perilous, and on occasion

---

[271] Maraval. 2003. 63, 71.
[272] ibid. 72.
[273] ibid. 72.
[274] ibid. 73

forbidden.'[275] Nevertheless, there have always been those few who have voyaged on the long and 'narrow path' that leads to true and abundant life. St. Gregory of Nyssa was one of those pilgrims and he leaves us pieces of a map, which is really 'The Way,' so that we too may have our hearts set aflame by heroic journeys into the unknown, the hope of encountering fountains of wisdom, adventures in uncharted territory, and the promise of personal wholeness in the most intimate communion with Divine Beauty after having embraced the threatening obscurity seeking to find God in the present darkness of our em-passioned existence.

For St. Gregory, one participates in the True, the Good and Beautiful, by harnessing one's own desire for the Holy by embarking on a personal Exodus away from entanglements in the world's deceptive and imperfect wisdom. Only then is the soul prepared to pursue God, the only true Goodness and Beauty, who is completely 'Other'. This, he sees, necessitates an ecstatic relationship where one must literally die to oneself in order to emerge, embracing an unknown and unfamiliar reality of which one has no prior experience.[276] It is then that a person may come to an awakening sense that God can never be known through the customary human means of inquiry and sense perception.[277] The crisis happens when a person approaches the chasm between the created and uncreated realities and arrives at a moment where despair and hope converge; where one simultaneously realizes that the only reliable vehicle of departure for such a journey is one's faith in the unseen.[278]

Gregory notes that throughout the soul's quest it will experience both the tension of annihilation and fulfillment, where its insatiable desire for the Beloved will be its only guide and map on this expedition of real becoming.[279] This is the ecstatic journey out of one's own soul towards the eternal Good and the Beautiful,

---

[275] Talbot. 2003. 60
[276] *Commentary on Ecclesiastes* (Hom. 7). Text in: J. Daniélou. (ed). *From Glory to Glory*. SVS Press. Crestwood. 2001.122-129.
[277] *Commentary on Ecclesiastes*. (Hom. 7). Daniélou. 2001. 120
[278] *Against Eunomius* 12; Daniélou. 2001. 119-122.
[279] *On Perfection*. Daniélou. 2001. 83-84.

whose inherent virtue is also limitless, and thus permeates the soul with grace, satisfying every level of its desire, while never exhausting or quenching the desire itself. The soul then learns a most crucial thing if it is to succeed on its quest: as it journeys with, towards, and in God, the abiding communion that it seeks to find in an encounter with the Beloved can only be fulfilled as it dynamically embraces and harnesses the perpetual presence of desire, freeing it from its earthly preoccupations and channeling it towards the direction of the unseen God.

This apparent paradox proves to be the greatest temptation for the believer sent from the devil, but is in fact precisely how St. Gregory explains the dynamics of stability and motion in the spiritual life.[280] Since, God never wants to violate humanity's most precious asset, moral freedom, St. Gregory writes, He allows disciples to 'experience the pain of the pleasures of the carnal and worldly life so that then he can use their freedom to put to death the deeds of incorruption' so that they should 'willingly desire to return to their former blessedness.'[281] Through human freedom then, we can willingly choose the Good and the Beautiful and once again become good and beautiful in the self, without incorporating necessity into the path towards perfection. This position flew in the face of most of what the ancient, pre-Christian world, had thought of as the 'defective' nature of change. St. Gregory, on the contrary, defines this reality as the 'positive idea of the process of change'[282] essentially confirming that God is changeless (*atreptos*); He is infinite and transcendent, but we change. We have movement (*kinesis*) and God correlates this process to be that which joins us to Him, rather than that which separates us as the ancient world formerly believed. For the Platonists, change was seen as an evil and a defect of the cosmos, where pure intelligence was far superior because it was immutable (*atreptos*). St. Gregory shatters this notion by denying the concept that change was inherently evil. He revolutionized the

[280] *Life of Moses*. 1978. 116-118
[281] *On the Dead*. Daniélou. 2001. 13.
[282] Daniélou. *Introduction*. 2001. 47

term of the idea by equating it with the biblical sense of 'being born again'.[283]

St. Gregory describes two types of change: the first he sees extensively in the biological world where change is seen as merely cyclical and repetitious, characterized by the constant succession of 'filling' and 'emptying'. For example, he writes, 'The pleasure of drinking ceases when one's thirst is quenched; and similarly in eating, satiety extinguishes our appetite. So every desire ceases with the possession of its object, and if it comes again, it also goes away again.'[284] If man lives merely on this plain then he lives for the satisfaction of his desires alone. Because these things were never meant to satisfy completely, Man must continually replenish his reserves, caught in a vicious cycle of emptying and filling his appetites, only to be trapped in the endless cycles of the demands of the natural pleasures. This is in fact 'motion (*kinesis*) without progress (*prokope*)[285].

The second type of change for St. Gregory is growth in the good. This capacity for improvement transforms the soul, changing it successively into the divine, moving us 'from glory to glory' in the famous phrase he borrows from St. Paul.[286] St. Gregory writes: 'Thus we are always improving and ever becoming more perfect by daily growth, and never arriving at any limit of perfection, for that perfection consists in our never stopping in our growth in good, never circumscribing our perfection by any limitation.'[287]

St. Gregory explains too that: 'The Devil whispers that the spiritual journey is in fact too arduous, or he convinces us that the Beauty of the transitory is in fact substantive and worthy of our attention and pursuit. For this is the way that evil diverts our most precious guide, compass and sustenance for the trip: that is, our desire.'[288] The devil delights in seducing man to be consumed

---

[283] Daniélou. *Introduction*. 2001. 48
[284] ibid. 49
[285] ibid. 50
[286] 2 Cor. 3.18.
[287] Daniélou. *Introduction*. 2001. 52
[288] *Commentary on Ecclesiastes*. (Hom.1). Daniélou. 2001. 45.

with material things so that he will restrict his gaze from ever looking heavenward. But it is precisely through this process of transformation, by going out of oneself in faith towards the Beloved, while never fully possessing the heart's desire, that the soul is fulfilled at every stage, and even so mysteriously 'grows' in order to allow for deeper communion, finding that in this relationship it is actually being 'born again.'

Ekstasis

For St. Gregory, Abraham embodied the necessity of departure that each soul must experience in order to launch out towards the Divine. He writes: 'Abraham, at the divine command went forth from his own country and from his own kind, but his migration was such as befitted a prophet in quest of the knowledge of God.'[289] This pilgrimage happened in the Spirit and Abraham walked by faith and not by sight. Gregory continues: 'And so, the Lord of all creation is called the God of Abraham, almost as though He had been discovered by the Patriarch himself, and this was because he went out not knowing where he was going.'[290] St. Gregory explains that it is at such a juncture that Faith takes the place of that which escapes our knowledge.[291] He describes the quest of Abraham in these terms: 'He went far beyond that which can be perceived by the senses; and from the beauty that he saw around him, and from the harmony of the heavenly phenomena, he gained a yearning to gaze upon the archetypal Beauty.'[292]

We note in his theology how the soul's holy desire, once it has been freed from the shackles of materialistic devotion, sparks this initial changing of the mind and this purification of the heart, because it has been captivated by 'ecstatic love.'[293] In using the language of love and desire to explain this theological ecstasy, St Gregory stresses the point, using yet another paradox: that Love and Desire are purely 'passionless passion':

---

289 *Against Eunomius.*12. Daniélou. 2001. 119.
290 Heb. 11.8.
291 *Against Eunomius.* 12 Daniélou. 2001. 121.
292 *Against Eunomius.* 12 Daniélou. 2001. 120
293 *Commentary on the Song of Songs.* Daniélou. 2001. 44

In order to have us understand its most profound doctrine, the Scriptures use as a symbol that which is the most violent of all our pleasurable inclinations; I mean the passion of love. Thus we are meant to understand that the soul that contemplates the inaccessible beauty of the divine nature falls in love with it in much the same way as the body is attracted towards things that are connatural with it. But here the entire disturbance of the soul has been transformed into impassibility, all carnal passion is extinguished in us and the soul burns with love by the sole flame of the Spirit.[294]

Using a wonderful image, St. Gregory writes: 'The ecstasy of the soul in the spiritual pilgrimage is symbolized by the series of the events in the Exodus account: the momentous pilgrimage out of Egypt by the Jews and their crossing of the Red Sea into their new life, the guide in this new existence being the cloud, which is more appropriately defined as the grace of the Holy Spirit.'[295] The soul on its own journey, like the Israelites has to flee from the Egyptian army of the passions and worldly pleasures that torment and enslave it.[296] In the *Song of Songs* it is written: 'Arise, come my love, my beautiful one, my dove.'[297] Gregory takes this as primarily indicative of God's invitation to the Soul to rise to communion with the Absolute. There is a wonderful sequence here: 'The bride hears the command, she is empowered by the Word, she arises, advances, come close, becomes beautiful, and is then called a dove.' Ultimately, 'human nature cannot become beautiful until it draws near to the Beautiful itself and becomes transformed by the image of the divine Beauty.'[298]

These ecstatic movements by themselves, although intense, are not enough to sustain the soul on its pilgrimage of beauty from glory to glory. The ecstatic motion of the soul which frees it from the bonds of the senses and the self, is intimately connected with the severance from the passions of the old self which like Adam

---

[294] *Commentary on the Song of Songs.* Daniélou. 2001. 44.
[295] *The Life of Moses.* Daniélou. 2001. 82-85.
[296] *Ibid.*
[297] *Commentary on the Song of Songs.* Daniélou. 2001. 97-98.
[298] *Ibid.*

and Eve's 'garments of skin' in Eden, distort its own natural beauty and its ability to manifest the print of divine beauty in its essential being. St. Gregory illustrates this point by commenting on the parable in Luke 15, writing: 'When the great image of the King is discovered and shines forth again, just as it was stamped on our drachma in the beginning by the Creator, stamped on the hearts of everyone, then do all our faculties unite in that divine joy and gladness as they gaze upon the ineffable beauty of what they have found.'[299] Accordingly: 'The man who has purified all the powers of his soul from every form of sin will be able to see that essential Beauty which is the source of everything else which is beautiful and good.'[300] It is in their purity of heart, that human beings are enabled truly to 'see God,'[301] because the 'Kingdom of God is within.'[302] St. Gregory beautifully describes this phenomenon of purification in terms of the soul being like a mirror that reflects the beauty of the Lord. He notes: 'Such a man who has purified himself, will look at himself and he will see within himself the object of his desire; and thus he will become blessed, for gazing upon his own purity he will see the archetype within the image.'[303]

The importance of purification is vividly symbolized in St. Gregory's account from the Exodus account in *The Life of Moses* where before Moses can converse with God at the Burning Bush he must remove his sandals.[304] St. Gregory interprets this to symbolize the importance of purification before an encounter with God. Similarly, before Moses ascends the Mountain in Sinai to receive the Law he records Moses commanding that 'the herd of animals must driven back as far away from the mountain as possible.'[305] This St. Gregory exegetes as conveying the truth that only by purification can one traverse the mountain of spiritual knowledge to contemplate transcendent being. In the account of

---

[299] *On Virginity*. Daniélou. 2001. 113-115
[300] On Virginity. Daniélou. 2001. 111
[301] Matthew. 5.8
[302] Luke. 17.21
[303] *On the Beatitudes*. (Hom.6). Daniélou. 2001. 102
[304] *The Life of Moses*. Daniélou. 2001. 93-97.
[305] *Ibid.*

the Bride, there is also the dramatic symbolism of the myrrh conveying the meaning of death: death to the old self and the death of the passions. The Bride speaks of this personal sacrifice in the Canticle saying: 'I rose up to open to my beloved: my hands dropped with myrrh, and my fingers were full of myrrh.'[306] St. Gregory explains this mystery by reminding the readers that when the concept of myrrh is mentioned in scripture it most certainly conveys the image of death.[307] 'The Word simply cannot be united to us,' he exclaims, 'unless by the mortification of our bodies on earth when we transform the veil of the flesh.'[308] The bride has fulfilled this requirement for intimate relationship, entering into this reality by, 'Being buried with Him unto death by Baptism.' St. Gregory writes, that in her case: 'There was also a free and spontaneous mortification of all her bodily passions.'[309] Hence, she received the power of the Resurrection. In St. Gregory's commentary the Bride's voice witnesses to this powerful truth when it says: 'Mortifying my members on earth; I undertook this mortification willingly; the myrrh was not put into my hands by someone else, but flowed from my own free will.'[310] This signifies how, I believe, no one can complete this pilgrimage for anyone else. Each one of us must make their own experiential journey themselves.

St. Gregory explains the enormity of this ecstatic movement of the soul through a vivid example where he says it is like someone being asked to step out from a 'craggy cliff overlooking a bottomless cavern where we experience no sensory support for our outstretched foot.'[311] In this vertigo, the soul is entering a completely unfamiliar territory. It is this precise movement that most resembles the notion of *Eros*. This ecstatic movement of the soul

---

[306] *Song of Songs*. 5.5
[307] *Commentary on the Song of Songs*. (Hom. 12). Daniélou. 2001. 213-214.
[308] Daniélou. 2001. 213-214.
[309] Daniélou. 2001. 213-214.
[310] Daniélou. 2001. 213-214.
[311] *On The Beatitudes*. (Hom.6). Daniélou. 2001. 43.

towards God, Gregory argues: 'Is not a longing for possession in a self-centered way, but a truly ecstatic love.'[312]

Epektasis

When the ecstatic soul inevitably reaches out for what it desires, it soon comes to the realization that it can never possess the Good and the Beautiful which by nature has no limits , being infinite and outside time and space. St. Gregory relies heavily on Philippians 3:13 to expand on his argument where it reads: 'Pressing on towards the goal of Jesus Christ forgetting what lies behind and stretching forward (*epekteinomenos*) to what lies ahead.'[313] It is this movement of going out towards God which St Gregory focuses on with the term *epektasis*. He explains this passage by explaining that God always creates ever new and expanding spaces within the soul to perpetually increase its desire and capability to participate in Him (Man's archetypal first principle) even more fully. In the same vein, St. Gregory notes that the soul is both initially affirmed to be beautiful, but then called to 'become beautiful,' just as the soul is referred to as a 'dove,' and even so subsequently invited to become a dove.[314] Jean Daniélou explains: 'In bidding the bride to become beautiful even though she is beautiful, He reminds us of the words of the Apostle who bids the same image to be transformed from glory to glory.'[315]

St. Gregory also notes how the Lord himself exhorts his spiritual children to embrace this *epektasis* when he said: 'Be perfect (*teleios*), as your heavenly Father is perfect.'[316] St. Gregory explains that this perfection is never to be understood as a stagnant or stationary state, rather the essence of the perfection lies not in 'being' but in continuously 'becoming' perfect. There is a double aspect of the soul's progress in that it has a real participation (*metousia, methexis*) in God's beauty and goodness as it ascends, but the soul's desire always remains 'Other' demanding,

---

[312] *Commentary on the Song of Songs.* Daniélou. 2001. 44
[313] Phil. 3.13
[314] *Commentary on the Song of Songs.* (Homily. 5). C. McCambley.(tr). 1987. 118-120
[315] 2 Cor. 3.18.
[316] Matthew. 5.48

therefore, that the soul must continually 'go out' from itself seeking what is beyond itself. This is how we have the ascent from glory to glory, where each stage has its own unique brilliance, but where the new glory constantly overshadows the old, encouraging the soul to continue to climb.[317] As St. Gregory notes: 'Sin is ultimately the refusal to grow.'[318] 'The real meaning of seeing God;, he continues, 'Is never to have this desire satisfied. No limit can be set to our progress towards God: first of all, because no limitation can be put on the beautiful, and secondly because the increase in our desire for the beautiful cannot be stopped by any sense of satiety.'[319]

This continual *epektasis* is exemplified in St. Gregory's observation in the *Life of Moses* that the patriarch: 'Although he had even seen God from the rear and received the utterance of the Divine Name, 'I am who I am,' still desired to see more!' Gregory writes: 'The man who thinks that God can be known does not really have life; for he has been falsely diverted from true Being to something devised by his own imagination. ... So it is that Moses' desire was filled by the very fact that it remained unfulfilled... and this is the real meaning of seeing God: never to have this desire satisfied.'[320] The same point is illustrated by St Gregory in his *Commentary on the Song of Songs* where he states: 'The Bride will always discover more and more of the incomprehensible and unhoped-for beauty of her Spouse throughout all eternity. It is at this point that she has received within her God's special dart; she has been wounded in the heart by the sting of faith; she has been mortally wounded by the arrow of love.'[321]

This is a fractal reality of unfolding ontology. It is this creative tension between being and becoming that the Neo-Platonists described using the key terms of 'procession'(*ekporeusis*), 'reversion' (*strophe*), and 'rest' (*anapausis*). The Platonic comm-entator Eric Perl writes that both procession and reversion at once,

---

[317] Daniélou. 2001. 59.
[318] Daniélou. 2001. 59.
[319] *The Life of Moses*. Daniélou. 2001. 111-116.
[320] Ibid.
[321] *Commentary on the Song of Songs*. Daniélou. 2001. 224-225

and equally, are the establishment of effect as a being. Essentially, any thing's way of being itself is reversion to its cause.[322] Perl goes so far as to say that God cannot make beings without their active cooperation: that there is something analogous to freedom and personhood at every level of being.[323] This reality both affirms the goodness and beauty present within each hierarchical level of being, while allowing space for the soul to soar to infinite heights of glory.

Re-Entry

The phenomenon of pilgrimage which ever seeks to abandon the familiar in order to encounter the sacred and partake of its holiness or wisdom has its roots, for Christians, in the classical Mediterranean world. The Nyssen scholar Anthony Meredith, confirms that St. Gregory was especially influenced by the classical world of late antiquity. He writes: 'Both in the formal character of his writings and in the assumed, if unexpressed, premises on which they rest, the influence of Greek philosophy, above all that of Plato, is everywhere evident.'[324] In Antiquity the act of pilgrimage was correlated with the term for seeing (*theoria*), where the pilgrim was called a '*theoros*' who 'travelled away from home to see some sort of spectacle or learn something about the outside world.'[325] It was a short step form this to make the term for seeing an intellectual symbol as well as an ocular one. It appears to have been Socrates who first defined the philosopher as a new kind of 'theoros,' writing that the philosopher's pilgrimage was to 'journey to and look upon Beauty itself.'[326] The philosopher then, was a new kind of 'Seer': 'A man who traveled to the metaphysical realm to see and experience the sacred in that region.'[327] But the journey never ended at the expected destination. Andrea Nightingale explains that the philosopher never traveled merely

---

[322] ED. Perl. *Theophany: The Neoplatonic Philosophy of Dionysius the Areopagite.* State University of New York Press. Albany. 2007. 38-39.
[323] Perl. 2007. 44.
[324] Meredith. 1999. 7
[325] AW. Nightingale. 'The Philosopher at the Festival: Plato's Transformation of Traditional Theoria.' in Elsner & Rutherford. 2005. 156-157
[326] Plato's *Republic.* (476b-c), cited in Nightingale. 2005. 169
[327] Nightingale. 2005.169

to see and partake. She writes: 'The vision of Beauty thus rendered the philosopher virtuous as well as wise: theoretical contemplation always led to the production and enactment of virtue in the practical sphere.'[328] And she continues: 'Theoria, in the classical period, followed the basic pattern of detachment from the city, the 'liminal' phase of the journey, in which the traveler opens himself to what is new and extramundane, and then his all-important re-entry into the polis.'[329]

St. Gregory would have known this ancient tradition well, and his exegetical commentaries on the *Life of Moses* and the *Song of Songs* also highlight the important stage of the 're-entry' of the spiritual pilgrim. He describes both Moses and the Bride, after having encounters *with* and participating *in* the Beauty and glory of the Divine, 're-entering the *polis*,' having similarly both, 'journeyed to see the Ideal Forms and, after having gained wisdom, returning to embody this (in words and in deeds) in the human world'.[330] Andrew Sterk, in his interesting study on monks as bishops in the early church also notices this pattern and rite of passage which St. Gregory brings out in the *Life of Moses*. He writes:

> Only Moses, who alone had climbed the mountain and penetrated to the interior of the cloud, was prepared to receive God's law and instruct multitudes. Moses was so intimate with God, St. Gregory writes, that he was transformed to such a degree of glory that the mortal eye could not behold him.[331]

Even so, far from this reality and experience being opposed to, or in place of the active life of pastoral care, he writes, the life of contemplation is presented in *The Life of Moses* as a fundamental requirement for effective priestly service. [332]

In the *Life of Moses* St. Gregory notices this progression from *Theoria* to active leadership, saying that:

---

[328] Nightingale. 2005.157
[329] Ibid. 157.
[330] Ibid. 173
[331] Exodus 34.29, *Life of Moses*. 2.217; Sterk. 2004. 124.
[332] Ibid. 124.

After Moses was instructed by the ineffable teaching of God while he was surrounded by that invisible darkness, and having surpassed himself by the aid of the mystical doctrines, he emerged again out of the darkness. He then went down to his people to share with them the marvels which had been shown him in the theophany, to deliver the laws, and to institute for them the sanctuary and priesthood according to the pattern shown him on the mountain.[333]

St. Gregory concludes: 'Practical philosophy is therefore joined to contemplative philosophy.'[334] At the end of the narrative, he also highlights the beauty of Moses' ascent and remarks on how this virtue was subsequently utilized for the life of his people. The mystical *theoria* made the patriarch into a holistic builder of civilization and culture.[335]

Again, even in the case of the Bride in the *Song of Songs*, the story, Gregory notes, does not culminate with the bride absorbed in her nuptial delight, but rather in the transforming effects that her pilgrimage has had on her which begin to impact her companions and the whole community around her. In the *13th Homily*, St. Gregory highlights the fact that the bride has now 'testified to her perfection because the covering of the head has been removed, by stripping off the old tunic, and casting away the veil from her face.'[336] For him this means that at this point the soul has come face to face with the truth. He points to her mystical transformation as a prophet: 'The bride says that she is thoroughly beautiful and cleansed from every stain and that she utters noting worthless but, following the example of Michaia [337], she speaks a word from God.'[338] Because of her mystical insight the bride has become a type of prophet, speaking truth to the on-looking maidens as a word straight from the Lord. She exhorts them saying they must now: 'faithfully look towards God and make

---

[333] *Life of Moses.* Daniélou. 2001. 46

[334] *Life of Moses.* Daniélou. 2001. 106

[335] *Life of Moses.* Daniélou. 2001. 133-136

[336] *Commentary on the Song of Songs.* Daniélou. 2001. 229.

[337] Zach. 9.17.

[338] *Commentary on the Song of Songs.* Daniélou. 2001. 230.

their lives free from passion as well.'[339] She also consequently becomes an apostle of divine magnitude. When the virgins and maidens who surround her now ask her: 'What is your Beloved, oh beautiful among women? What is your Beloved that you have so charged us?'[340] she now is able to instruct them in the true faith, as if she has become an apostle and a missionary telling the women exactly who this Lord is. By this point the virgins have observed her soul, going out and coming in, seeking Him who cannot be found by any signs, and crying out to him who is not summoned by any name. St. Gregory has the curious virgins respond eagerly to her mystical initiations, begging her to reveal to them the nature of the Lord so that they can see him themselves. [341] They are in a sense asking her: 'How then can we be saved?' The bride portrays her Beloved at this stage as, 'altogether desirable,' and closes by saying: 'This is my beloved, and this is my friend, Oh daughters of Jerusalem.'[342]

In both texts of *The Life of Moses* and *The Commentary on the Song of Songs*, both Moses and the Bride are depicted as sharing in the glory of God and as reflecting that beauty in their own being as well as manifesting it to the outside world. This beauty intrinsically contains an ethical element towards one's neighbor; because Truth and Beauty can never be separated from the Good. This fact encapsulates the ancient understanding concerning the transcendental God and Hans Urs Von Balthasar, commenting on the divorce between the Good, the True and the Beautiful in our contemporary context writes: 'In a world which is perhaps not wholly without beauty, but which can no longer see it or reckon with it; in such a world the good also loses its appeal, the self - evidence of why it must be carried out.'[343] But when the Beauty of the Divine retains its place among the essential attributes of God, then the true beauty and attractiveness of the good also preserves its potency and can be carried out organically, symphonically, and virtuously.

---

[339] *Commentary on the Song of Songs*. Daniélou. 2001. 256
[340] *Song of Songs*. 5. *Commentary on the Song of Songs*. Daniélou. 2001. 232
[341] Daniélou. 2001. 232.
[342] *Song of Songs*. 5.16. *Commentary on the Song of Songs*. Daniélou. 2001. 256
[343] H. Urs von Balthasar.1983. 19.

This non-linear pattern of perfection which has been explored in this paper, demonstrates that the life of salvation, according to St. Gregory of Nyssa, radiates from an intimate participation with Divine Beauty. The paths taken by Moses and the Bride should not be pressed to fit into any schematized progression of spiritual experience, but all of the important aspects of the pilgrimage to Beauty reoccur, mature, deepen, overlap and converge over time. St. Dionysios the Areopagite, who wrote a century or so after St. Gregory, encapsulates this fractal nature of salvation, where at every level of existence the whole is contained in its parts, by explaining how this is so is relation to the Divine Beauty. He offers the explanation: 'As well as being source and creating cause, Beauty is also the aim and ultimate limit of all things, their final cause.' [344] Being the starting point, it is equally the end-point. Longing (*eros*) for the Uncreated Beauty thus unites all created beings, drawing them together into a single coherent and harmonious whole. Dionysios continues: 'Beauty calls all things to itself and gathers everything into itself. Divine Beauty is in this way both fountainhead and fulfillment, both activating genesis and unifying objective.'

In the familiar triad used in Greek philosophy, and in the Church Fathers, Beauty was fundamentally still considered as one of the transcendental attributes of the Divine and was therefore ascribed, according to Von Balthasar: 'the same inwardly analogous form that we ascribe to the One, the True, and the Good?'[345] For the ancients, Beauty was an inseparable element of God's intrinsic attributes, vitally necessary for orienting all of one's mind and efforts towards the appropriate attitude and right approach towards the path of salvation. In line with this perspective, the life of perfection can be appropriately envisioned as a 'Pilgrimage of Beauty' because it is penetrated by the fullness of beauty at every stage of the journey. It involves an heroic, ecstatic, exodus towards the true beauty of God, a turning away from the slavery

---

[344] Cited in: Met. Kallistos of Diokleia. 2008. 11.
[345] Von Balthasar. 1983. 38.

of the ego and the senses, the constant kindling and fueling of holy desire as the sure guiding force, the ever extending participation and deepening of communion at the Holy Places of the Divine Glory, and finally the re-entering of the pilgrim into the *polis* as the witness and apostle of Divine Beauty. Without this spiritual context that Beauty and the pursuit of the Beloved provide, the spiritual life can easily be distorted as being arduous, lifeless, legalistic, utilitarian, or mechanistic.

St. Gregory concludes his discourse on the *Life of Moses*, stating that the purpose of his writing was: 'Briefly to trace in an outline, like a *pattern of beauty*, the life of the great Moses so that each one might copy the image of the beauty which has been shown to us by imitating his way of life.'[346] But what manner of Beauty is this? Is it a beauty that is self-aggrandizing, or fleeting; shifting with changing opinions of aesthetics, and tragically oblivious to the suffering and oppression that exist in the world? On this point Von Balthasar cites Karl Barth who attempted to reintroduce the Beautiful as a theological category in Protestant circles, explaining that the solution to this paradox must be found in the unity of Christ's humiliation and exaltation on the Cross. Von Balthasar writes: 'God brings His own form and proper beauty. Isaiah's phrase, 'He had neither form nor beauty', determines the precise locus from which God's unique beauty radiates. If we seek Christ's beauty in a glory which is not that of the Crucified, we are doomed to seek in vain. In this self-revelation, God's beauty embraces death as well as life, fear as well as joy, what we call ugly as well as what we call beautiful.[347]

The sacrifice of love initiated supremely by the Lord Jesus is thus appropriated and extended by the spiritual pilgrim in all stages of this pilgrimage: ekstasis, epektasis, re-entry. In the *Commentary on the Song of Songs*, Gregory alludes to this aspect of involvement in the real world of human suffering by poetically noting how the soul flies out towards the heart's desire with the wings of faith, but comes back within the self with fresh wounds of desire. St.

[346]*Life of Moses.* Daniélou. 2001.136
[347] Von Balthasar. 1983. 56

Gregory writes that this is the true meaning of St. Paul when he says that he is 'daily dying in Christ.'[348] We thus find the paradox of the cross at every stage of the mystical journey where the soul is simultaneously living within the joy and the sorrow of encountering and seeking the Beloved; conforming to Christ's cruciform pattern of self-emptying while enjoying the fullness of nuptial delight in his chamber; and dying to sensual pleasures and the familiarity of its created surroundings while the soul discovers a new birth in abandoning itself to the unknown.

Like Moses going out to meet God on the mountain, or the Bride going to encounter her Beloved, the person who is drawn on in the spiritual life is given an unfolding of ontology: the human awakens to his true identity as beautiful, while ever 'stretching forth' to encounter the Divine Beauty, progressively possessing this beauty in his own being as he is changed from 'glory to glory.'[349] It is only within this quest of love and desire that a person is truly 'born from above,' reacquiring a paradisiacal wholeness of personhood that enables the 'one who has seen' to act again liturgically as true priest of creation, sanctifying and uniting the creation in Christ as his role as mediator.[350] This pilgrimage, what Gregory calls the 'pattern of Beauty' proves to be an eternal process of becoming where (*Dostoevsky was right*) Beauty really does save the world, restoring man in its image and likeness, and empowering him to bring forth what St. Gregory calls the 'principle of resurrection'[351] which also lives poised in every living and nonliving element in the created world.

Awakening to the spiritual reality that it is truly divine beauty which activates, sustains, embodies, implies and inspires salvific action (because it manifests the glory of the Cross), is, I suggest, the very essence of St. Gregory's theological and pastoral cosmology. Within this fundamental theophany, Beauty and Salvation are simultaneously united at the foot of the Cross, and every

---

[348] 1 Cor. 15.31

[349] *Commentary on the Song of Songs.* Daniélou. 2001. 119.

[350] L. Thunberg. *Man and the Cosmos: The Vision of St Maximus the Confessor.* SVS Press. Crestwood. 1985.

[351] Daniélou. 2001. 17.

Christian is invited to internalize this reality so as to embrace the nature of the spiritual ascent and understand the context in which the life of perfection is appropriately pursued. In the end, the pattern and pilgrimage of beauty are not terms to be semantically unpacked and explained, but are rather meant to be embodied in the life of every Christian. Von Balthasar postulates that when this is achieved: 'Christian form is the most beautiful thing that may be found in the human realm. In any age, most especially our own, the Christian will realize his mission only if he truly *becomes* this form which has been willed and instituted by Christ.'[352] For St. Gregory, this is the cruciform pattern of Christ that one incarnates as he or she embarks on the Pilgrimage of Beauty.

Further Reading

Primary Texts
St. Athanasius. *Letter to Virgins Returned from Jerusalem. Nicene and Post-Nicene Fathers.* 2nd Series, vol. 4. 292-302.
St. Gregory of Nyssa. *On the Human Soul.* Belmont. MA. 2000.
Idem. *Ascetical Works. The Fathers of the Church.* vol. 58. CUA Press. Washington. 1967.
Idem. *Commentary on the Song of Songs.* tr. C. McCambley. Hellenic College Press. Brookline. 1987.
Idem. *Letter 2: On Pilgrimages. Nicene and Post-Nicene Fathers.* 2nd Series, vol. 5. New York. 1893. 382-383.
Idem. *Letter 3: To Eustachia, Ambrosia, and Basilissa. Nicene and Post-Nicene Fathers,* 2nd Series, vol. 5. New York. 1893. 542-545.
Idem. *The Life of Moses.* Paulist Press. New York. 1978.
Idem. *The Lord's Prayer, The Beatitudes. Ancient Christian Writers.* vol. 18. Paulist Press. Mahwah. NJ. 1954.

Studies
C. Cavarnos. *Spiritual Beauty.* Belmont. MA. 1996.
EJ Coleman. *Creativity & Spirituality.* University of New York Press. Albany.1998.
C. Foss. 'Pilgrimage in Medieval Asia Minor.' *Dumbarton Oaks Papers,* 56. ed. AM.Talbot. Washington . 2003. 129-151.
PJ. Griffiths. 'The Nature of Desire.' *First Things .* No. 198. 2009.
Met. Kallistos. 'Beauty will Save the World. *Sobornost.*30. 1. 2008. 7-20.
V. Kharlamov. *The Beauty of the Unity and the Harmony of the Whole.* Wipf & Stock. Eugene. Or. 2009.

---

[352] Von Balthasar. 1983. 28.

A. Louth. 'Beauty Will Save the World: The Formation of Byzantine Spirituality.' *Theology Today*. vol. 61. 2004. 67-77.

C. Mango. 'The Pilgrim's Motivation.' *Akten des XII Internationalen Kongresse fur Christliche Archaeologie*, vol. 1. Bonn. 1995. 1-9.

P. Maraval. 'The Earliest Phase of Christian Pilgrimage in the Near East' *Dumbarton Oaks Papers*, 56. ed. AM. Talbot. Washington. 2003. 63-74.

A. Meredith. *Gregory of Nyssa*. Routledge. New York. 1999.

Idem. *The Cappadocians*. St. Vladimir's Seminary Press. Crestwood. NY. 1995.

AW. Nightingale. 'The Philosopher at the Festival: Plato's Transformation of Traditional Theoria.' in: J. Elsner & I. Rutherford. *Pilgrimage in Greco-Roman and Early Christian Antiquity: Seeing the Gods*. OUP. New York. 2005. 151-180.

C. Olson. 'The Creative and Revolutionary Nature of Desire.' *Philosophy Today*. vol. 47. 2. Summer 2003. 205-217.

E. Scarry. *On Beauty and Being Just*. Princeton University Press. NJ. 1999.

N. Spyke. 'The Instrumental Value of Beauty in the Pursuit of Justice.' *University of San Francisco Law Review*. vol. 40.2. Winter. 2006. 451-477.

A. Sterk. *Renouncing the World Yet Leading the Church*. Harvard University Press. Cambridge. 2004.

AM. Talbot. 'Introduction.' in: eadem (ed). 'Pilgrimage in the Byzantine Empire: 7th-15th Centuries.' *Dumbarton Oaks Papers*. 56. 2003. 59-61.

Archim. Vasileios. 'Beauty and Hesychia in Athonite Life.' Alexander Press. Montreal. 1996.

H. Urs von Balthasar. *The Glory of the Lord*. Ignatius Press. San Francisco. 1983.

F. Vosmans. 'Ethics and Aesthetics: A Critical Evaluation of Their Relation.' in: W. van den Bercken & J. Sutton. *Aesthetics as a Religious Factor in Eastern and Western Christianity*. Leuven.2005. 385-393.

Beauty for the Rest of Us:
Re-considering St. Gregory of Nyssa's *On Virginity.*

VK McCarty

Among its many valuable lessons, *On Virginity* offers Gregory of Nyssa's inspiring teaching on the theology of beauty[353]. The heart of its wisdom is that the goodness of God is the very beauty of the soul. Gregory, the younger brother of saints Basil the Great and Macrina the Younger, explains that earthly beauty which is sensed and beheld is utterly insignificant compared to the glorious magnificence of the Archetypal Beauty of the Godhead. By being drawn to a glimpse of God's 'intolerable beauty'[354] and coming to participate in it, mankind itself begins to attain some measure of divine beauty. Examining Gregory's thinking on Beauty provides an invitation to engage with the Cappadocian bishop's earliest treatise, *On Virginity.* The mystical understanding of love enkindled by glimpsing the archetypal Beauty of God is startlingly illustrated by Gregory, whose work Rowan Williams considers: 'One of the more substantially original clusters of ideas in patristic theology.'[355]

Grounded in Platonic philosophy and called to defend the Nicene faith, Gregory's persuasive defense of the power of the Holy Spirit in the Orthodox theology of the Trinity has been praised by such distinguished writers as Jerome, Socrates, and Theodoret.[356] In modern times Denys Turner has spoken of: 'A fortunate convergence' of the Hebraic and Platonic mind-casts which is present in Gregory's thinking. While early in his life, Turner says, it may have been 'debatable which description is correct of Gregory of

---

[353] Although manuscripts of the work usually identify it as *A Treatise on Virginity,* Gregory's own title for the treatise is unknown. In the *Prologue* he refers to it as 'An Exhortation to a Life of Virtue.' *On Virginity.* 247.2.

[354] As he refers to it in his *Song of Songs Commentary.* See: Norris. 1998. This essay is dedicated to the memory of the late patrologist Canon Richard Norris.

[355] R Williams. 'Macrina's Deathbed Revisited: Gregory of Nyssa on Mind and Passion.' in Wickham & Bammel. 1993. 227.

[356] Introduction to the works of St. Gregory of Nyssa in: *A Select Library of Nicene and Post-Nicene Fathers of the Christian Church.* P Schaff & H Wace. (edd). Eerdmans. Grand Rapids. 1956. 1.

Nyssa's mind: whether he was a Greek Christian or a Christian Greek,' the theology developed in his mature writing clearly shows the priority of the Christian thinker.[357] For Gregory, as Richardson put it, 'philosophy becomes the handmaiden of faith.'[358]

Gregory of Nyssa was educated at home, by his sister the Great Macrina, and both at her feet, and at the desk of St. Gregory the Theologian who later became his tutor, he absorbed a special blend of late Platonic theology as mediated through the lens of the Christian theologian Origen.[359] His brother Basil, especially after the latter became Archbishop of Caesarea, drew him (reluctantly at first) deeply into church life, both political and theological; and had him ordained bishop of the very small town of Nyssa. After Basil's death he became a renowned defender of the Nicene cause. He was present at both the Council of Antioch in 379 and at the Council of Constantinople in 381, where he supported St. Gregory the Theologian, eloquently championing the Nicene theology. He was subsequently employed by the Emperor Theodosius to promote orthodoxy in the great imperial diocese of Pontus. He participated also in the Council of Constantinople in 394, shortly before his death. In his later years, he traveled considerably and was sought after in the highest circles as a preacher.

His treatise, *On Virginity*, shows Gregory's delight in demonstrating rhetorical flourishes, using especially strong metaphors. A soteriological analogy in ch. 4 describes how the soul 'like the sparrow, flying on the wings of virtue' escapes the teeth of the enemy of divine judgment.[360] Another striking example is

---

[357] Turner. 1995. 11-17.

[358] Richardson. 1954. 236. See also Laird. 2004. 76: who notes, 'Gregory is not simply placing the words of Diotima in the mouth of Abraham or attaching the wings of *Phaedrus* to the patriarch's back.'

[359] Origen had also been the tutor of St. Gregory the Thaumaturg, the Apostle of Cappadocia.

[360] See: *St. Gregory: Ascetical Works. Fathers of the Church Series*. ed. V W Callahan. CUA Press. Washington. 1967. 26. Citations from the *On Virginity* are taken from this edition.

his farmyard analogy in the service of illustrating an important teaching about the nature of Beauty:

> For just as the eyes of a pig are by nature trained on the ground and have no experience of the wonders of the sky, so the soul pulled down by the body can no longer look towards heaven and the beauties on high. Whereas if the soul looks up to the divine ... it will transfer its power to love from the body to the intelligible and immaterial contemplation of the beautiful.[361]

This early treatise was written before 371, perhaps in 368, four years before Gregory was consecrated as Bishop of Nyssa.[362] In chapters 11-12 of the work, Gregory assigns himself the apparently impossible task of describing the ineffable Beauty of God and of setting out the challenge facing mankind in recognizing it. Gregory sets out this intellectual path as a considerable feat: 'Let everyone have courage for this,' (*tharreito pas*) he says, arguing that acquiring a taste for the higher things of beauty can draw the soul away from even ingrained habits.[363] To seek God is to divest oneself of earthly desire and even of earthly beauty in order to sense the much vaster and infinite Beauty of its divine Archetype. Gregory writes that the experience of glimpsed transcendent ecstasy was of such 'boundless and incomprehensible beauty' for the Psalmist David that this is the reason why he cried out in the psalm: 'All men are liars.'[364] Indeed, the entire psalm can be interpreted as resonant with the comparison of the saving presence of God's beauty, contrasted with the deathly isolation of being away from him.

Gregory argues that an aesthetically sensed beauty (*to aistheton kallos*) is indeed within human ability to perceive and appreciate,

---

[361] *On Virginity.* Callahan. 1967. 28.
[362] From Gregory's reference to Basil as his 'bishop and father,' his brother was alive at the time of writing, which would indicate a *terminus post quem* for the treatise of 371; see Callahan. 1967. 3.
[363] W Jaeger. (ed). *Gregorii Nysseni Opera* VII. I. p. 288. line 10. Brill. Leiden. 1952: this edition/volume is hereafter referred to by editor, then page and line numbers. See also *On Virginity.* Callahan. 1967. 36.
[364] Ps. 115:2 (LXX) (RSV. Ps. 116.11). See *On Virginity.* Callahan. 1967. 37.

and he observes that it is this very beauty which we behold, for example, emanating from a holy icon. [365] On the other hand, a visible image of God's true Beauty cannot be brought into view because the celestial Archetype has no color, form, size or shape that can be comprehended by means of the material senses. Yet even in the face of this profoundly apophatic description of God's incomprehensible Beauty, he says: 'We must not despair of attaining what we desire because it appears to transcend our comprehension,'[366] for mankind is not excluded entirely from participating in that which is truly Good (*agathou*). [367] Goodness and beauty, while not interchangeable, are for Gregory essentially interrelated. The vision of God, which is impossible to us by nature, becomes possible by grace.

Gregory's *On Virginity* argues that when the human heart is inspired to transcend the earthly realm, it can begin to glimpse the truly beautiful, even if shrouded in mortal deficiencies. In an ascending progression toward this vision of the unseen Beauty, Gregory distinguishes different categories of people. The one who carelessly misses the mark and interprets superficially is contrasted with someone who educates his soul (*o dioratikos ten psychen*) to look beyond his eyes alone, so that he can perceive spiritual beauty without any illusion (*phantasia*) mixed into it [368]. The one who has 'purified the eye of his soul', on the other hand, will be able to use a beautiful visual image as a means to understand the actual exquisite form of God's Beauty (*te ton kalon idea*).[369] People in these two categories have the capability to discern and admire beauty, but the source of it eludes them, for Gregory stresses the inherent difficulty of such a comprehension. He blames an insufficient spiritual training, and the tendency for the weak-minded to limit their imagination of beauty (*to kalon horisanto*) to the elements he deems as lifeless: honor and glory and power.[370] If only they could turn aside from material obsess-

---

[365] *On Virginity*. Jaeger. 1952. 290. 20-21.
[366] Daniélou. *From Glory to Glory*. 1979. 106.
[367] *On Virginity*. Jaeger. 1952. 291.9.
[368] *On Virginity*. Jaeger. 1952. 292.7.
[369] *On Virginity*. Jaeger. 1952. 292.13.
[370] *On Virginity*. Jaeger. 1952. 293.2.

ions to seek the actual nature of supreme Beauty, which is perfectly simple and formless and immaterial, they would never be swept away by deception! As Gregory says: 'The more our reason shows us the magnitude of what we seek, the higher we must elevate our understanding and stimulate it with the grandeur of our objective.'[371]

And so, a further category of spiritual seekers is able to rise from earthly visible seeing to comprehend the invisible reality of God's Beauty, through the power of the Holy Spirit purifying the mind. They are able to use the earthly beauty of the skies to elevate their desire (*epithymian*) to the Supernal Beauty of which (as the psalmist says) the heavens tell the glory.[372] 'It is imperative,' Gregory writes, 'That we take hold of our understanding and, as it were, lead it by the hand towards the invisible with the help of that which we can perceive by the senses.'[373] In this way, whoever raises himself, as if on the wings of a dove, will find the only thing truly worth loving, and will become as beautiful as God's Beauty which he has come to know (*genesetai kai kalos to kalo prospelasas*).[374] 'The soul that is rising upwards,' Gregory notes, 'must leave all that it has already attained as falling far short of its desire; only then will it begin to grasp something of that magnificence which is beyond the stars.'[375]

Through this endless reaching out (*epektasis*) and this unlimited progression (*prokope*), the soul becomes attached to the imperishable God and by reflection (*mimesis*) is molded (*morphothenai*) in her own beauty to the Prototype of all Beauty. [376] Gregory warns the reader, however, that along this ascent toward the beautiful light of God, it is easy to be snared by sources of merely transitory beauty, all of which are ill-conceived and fade away. But, for those who leave all else behind and vigilantly seek that Beauty which has no source but itself, to them the essential beauty (*to mono te*

---

[371] Daniélou. *From Glory to Glory*. 1979.106.
[372] Ps. 18:1, LXX; Ps. 19:1, RSV.
[373] Daniélou. *From Glory to Glory*. 1979.106.
[374] *On Virginity*. Jaeger. 1952. 294.23-24.
[375] Daniélou. *From Glory to Glory*. 1979. 109.
[376] *On Virginity*. Jaeger. 1952. 296.8.

physei kalon) will become visible. [377] It is this stress on singleness (of mind, of vision and purpose) which gives him the entrance to the ascetic dimension of 'virginity', of course. This treatise is not simply a message to the ascetical community of virgins, who lived on his family's estates at Annesos (a community founded by his sister Macrina), but the trope of physical virginity is serving as a deeper analogy of that singleness of heart and mind (*monachismos*) which is at the root of the ascetic philosopher's quest for the vision of God. His argument is that as our senses are equipped to discern and behold physical beauty in nature and flesh, so too the purified heart seeks to discern and behold the Archetypal Beauty of God. Seeing God, the absolute and unrivalled source of all beauty and goodness, is thus the single goal of all spiritual progress.

This quest communicates beauty from God palpably. As Gregory puts it: 'Only someone who is transported by the wings of the Holy Spirit will become beautiful by being brought close to Beauty.'[378] Such an exhortation is set out for all, as the end and purpose (*telos*) of the spiritual life. But, we note of course that Gregory's thinking throughout this particular treatise is couched within a context which holds virginity as the exclusive means recommended to the attainment of beauty. The renunciation of bodily pleasure was widely thought to enable Christian ascetics to obtain access to the Beauty of God. In fact, for Gregory, virginity constitutes the first stage of man's return to paradise.[379] We need, therefore, to exegete the meaning of his term 'virginity' as being of critical importance; noting as we set out to do this, that he does not himself specify a precise definition of the term in his treatise, thus making it oscillate as a particular and as an abstract generalization, at one and the same time.

Virginity physically understood, of course, is an ideal which excludes the married Gregory himself, as he confesses: 'If only it were possible...but as it is now, for me the knowledge of the beauty of virginity is useless...We are only spectators of the beauty belonging to others and witnesses of the blessedness of

---

[377] *On Virginity.* Jaeger. 1952. 296.23.
[378] *On Virginity.* 11. See Mateo-Seco. 2010. 780.
[379] *On Virginity.* 14. See Mateo-Seco. 2010. 777.

others.' [380] Gregory sees himself partly excluded from the royal road to the glimpsing of true beauty. But he is not teaching that only physical virgins are able to attain to the vision. What is at play in his thought here is the *trope* of the virgin as the *monachos*, the single one who is single-mindedly dedicated to God. If it was his intent to teach that only the physically virginal ascetic was able to see the Beauty of God he would have excluded a large majority of the Church along with himself. This early treatise, however, does come closest of all to being an *encomium* of the monastic life as the best way to singleness of vision. Its dedicatees (female ascetical virgins) explain that emphasis. But what is being left unsaid, of course, is that the Christian philosopher-rhetor, while appearing to deprecate his own comparatively 'lowly' status, is actually setting out to teach these virgins the 'true meaning' of their virginal life: namely the ascent in mind and heart to the single-minded vision of Supreme Beauty. Thus, in spite of all he says about the supremacy of virginity, he does not fundamentally deprecate the overwhelming importance of the 'training of the mind' and the elevation of the soul's perceptive capacities. Physical virginity is, for Gregory, only one of the ways of ensuring a new epistemology: in which the one who ascends to true vision is constantly aware that material beauty, and human desire for it, are only the metaphors for the transcendent beauty which they depict as signs.

It is in chs. 3-4 of the *On Virginity* that St. Gregory offers the reader his famous 'diatribe' against married life. In a sustained critique he offers an overwhelming 'warts and all' picture; even describing the married state as a prime example of things that are 'dung' (*skubala*). He outlines a litany of abysmal facts about married life with its endless possibilities for 'smoldering grief.'[381] His literary intention appears to be the setting out of all possible 'tragedies on the contemporary stage of life whose sponsor is marriage.'[382] Does marriage, with 'its sexual and procreational

---

[380] *On Virginity.* Jaeger. 1952. 325.12-19.
[381] *On Virginity 3.* Callahan. 1967. 13.
[382] *On Virginity.*3. Callahan. 1967. 20. See also *On Virginity.* 20 as cited in: Barnes. 2001. 17.

core,'[383] run so radically counter to his vision for humanity's most grace-filled purpose? Or is Gregory here contrasting his definition of beauty with dire descriptions of worldly compulsions from his own discomfort with marriage as a life choice? (Some scholars have posited from this that he was very unhappily married!). Or do other factors contribute to Gregory's polemical outcry against marriage? Mateo-Seco is probably nearest the truth when he observes that Gregory here was following the prescribed literary genre of *encomium*, which calls for a section of diatribe against the 'opposite' factor one is praising. In writing to his audience of virgins, Gregory takes rhetorical license, therefore, and doubly damns marriage in terms he would not use for a general audience. Mateo-Seco says:

> One must take into consideration the literary *genus* of *De Virginitate* in order to place it in the proper perspective when it speaks of certain inconveniences of matrimony in chapters three and four. These are the most rhetorical pages of the entire book, in which Gregory is only seeking to make the beauties of virginity more visible, recalling the tribulations of matrimony according to the rules of the diatribe.[384]

As it stands, however, the diatribe rhetoric in *On Virginity* is founded on a somewhat immature image of monasticism, as well as married life. Gregory cites, against the advisability of married love, the prospect of inevitable grief from losing a spouse; yet within monastic communities all professed religious share intimately in the aging process of the community with whom they live, and grieve the deaths in their monastic family as one might grieve for a spouse. In fact, one element which Gregory characterizes as a troubling feature of married life (that in one's 'heart resounds the concern for his beloved ones'[385]) is actually also a

---

[383] See V A Karras. 'A Re-evaluation of Marriage, Celibacy, and Irony in Gregory of Nyssa's On Virginity.' *Journal of Early Christian Studies* 13.1. 2005. 118.
[384] Mateo-Seco. 2010. 774.
[385] *On Virginity*. 1. Callahan. 1967. 19.

guiding principle of Christian monastic community.[386] A melding of ascetical commitment and compassionate service to the poor actually characterizes Basil's monastic vision.[387] All in all, Gregory's rhetoric in this instance, concerning both the married state as well as the professed monastic state, displays elements of naïve artificiality.

MD Hart has attempted to set the anti-marriage diatribe in the wider intellectual context, arguing that here Gregory is speaking 'to the choir' but in the general cause of stressing the need to rise above material obsessions, pleasures, and symbols, to the spiritual archetypes. In short he uses virginity chiefly as a cipher for chaste single-mindedness, as part of a demonstration how the true seeker after divine beauty must always be aware that earthly loveliness is not synonymous with heavenly. Hart notes that Gregory's sense of virginity: 'Does not take part in the concessions to pleasure permitted to the common life but changes the direction of its erotic power from bodily things to the intellectual and immaterial contemplation of the beautiful.'[388] Thus, even if chastity is indeed a significantly ascetic element of focus in Gregory's use of the term, one must remember that it: 'Above all indicates a style of life which encompasses many more realities than those strictly indicated when one speaks of virginity.'[389] Since in his own spiritual economy, Gregory speaks of the significance of moving from 'marriage to virginity,'[390] he probably means the word to denote, above all, the virtue of single-minded ascetic focus, rather than simply the unrepeatable state of physical virginity.

Gregory 'conceives of virginity as a greatness of soul, so that at times he even expresses considering it compatible with matrimony.'[391] Thus, the treasure of virginity cannot be reduced to the

---

[386]The monastic principles discussed here are offered with grateful acknowledgement to the counsel of Rev. Clark Berge, Minister General S.S.F. and Rev. William Forrest O.S.B., St. Gregory's Abbey, Michigan.

[387] See W. Harmless. *Desert Christians: An Introduction to the Literature of Early Monasticism*. Oxford University Press. Oxford. 2004. 430.

[388] M.D. Hart. 1990. 465.

[389] Mateo-Seco. 2010. 775.

[390] *On Virginity*. 3. Callahan. 1967. 14.

[391] Mateo-Seco. 2010. 777.

repression of the flesh. It might be argued, for example, that one is virginal when in silent contemplation of the beautiful purity of being (*katharotes*) infinitely possessed by God, or of the Trinity, which Gregory Nazianzen himself explicitly calls: 'The first virgin.'[392] Ultimately, it is clear that for St. Gregory of Nyssa, 'the truly virginal life means not simply physical virginity, not even detachment from worldly concerns, but an active love for others as well for God.'[393]

The modern reader, therefore, 'needs to be advised' when reading this work. The keen regret Gregory appears to have experienced about his initial life choices, and the disparagement he heaps on the concept of married love, which is a pattern for the large majority of the Church: all of these things need to be set in the context of the times, and in the precise context of the demands of ancient rhetoric. They should not exclude readers from the saint's overall and very uplifting message about the source of all beauty. While Gregory contrasts virtue with the secular life in this treatise, it is perfectly conceivable that there are people for whom the progress toward partnership, with its routine of shared gifts and disciplines, may actually make possible and enhance the steps on the path to virtuous spiritual excellence that Gregory intends to laud. Whether single or married, the Christian's goal always remains the same: a single-minded focus on progress toward God's beauty through Christ. Indeed, for some it may be that the comfort and order of committed relationship may be the only possible escape from 'the world's anxieties;'[394] with the result that hand in hand in blessed partnership, 'the soul will reach out without ceasing towards the ultimate and incomparable beauty of God.'[395] Although an experience of divine beauty may certainly be easier to attain in a life directly focused on progress toward God to the exclusion of intimacy, perhaps a more helpful interpretation might be to re-frame Gregory's teaching on beauty by identifying virginity with determined progress in a continuum toward an ideal life of virtue. It is possible that Gregory's treatise may be

---

[392] *In laudem virginitatis.* 20. PG 37.523. See: Mateo-Seco. 2010. 778.
[393] See Karras. 2005. 120.
[394] *Introduction. On Virginity.* (edd. Schaff & Wace). vol. 5.1956. 343.
[395] Silvas. *The Letters of Gregory of Nyssa.* 2007. 23.

even more effective as an explication of Beauty than it is as recruiting material for a celibate lifestyle. Then, by the grace and power of the Holy Spirit, we can strive, as St. Gregory wants us, to live: 'for the soul alone and imitate, as far as possible, the regimen of the incorporeal powers, whose work and zeal and success consist in their contemplation of the incorruptible Father and in beautifying their own form through imitation of the Archetypal Beauty.'[396]

Further Reading

Primary Texts

St. Gregory: Ascetical Works. Fathers of the Church Series.
ed. VW. Callahan. CUA Press. Washington. 1967. (1990).
St. Gregory of Nyssa: Dogmatic Treatises. A Select Library of Nicene and Post-Nicene Fathers of the Christian Church. vol. 5.
P. Schaff & H. Wace. (edd). Eerdmans. Grand Rapids. (repr.) 1956.
Gregorii Nysseni Opera Ascetica. VII. I. W Jaeger. (ed). Brill. Leiden. 1952.
Plato. *The Symposium.* R. Waterfield. (tr.) OUP. Oxford. 1994.
The Rule of St. Benedict. T Fry. (ed). The Liturgical Press. Collegeville. 1982
Gregory of Nyssa: The Letters: Introduction, Translations and Commentary.
AM. Silvas. (ed). Brill. Leiden. 2007.
The Asketikon of St Basil the Great. A M Silvas. (ed). OUP. Oxford. 2005.
From Glory to Glory: Texts from Gregory of Nyssa's Mystical Writings.
J Daniélou. (ed). St Vladimir's Seminary Press. Crestwood. 1979.

Studies

MR. Barnes.	'The Burden of Marriage & Other Notes on Gregory of Nyssa's *On Virginity.' Studia Patristica* 37. Peeters. Leuven. 2001. 12-19.
D. Bentley Hart.	'The Mirror of the Infinite: Gregory of Nyssa on the *Vestigia Trinitatis.'* In S Coakley. (ed). *Re-thinking Gregory of Nyssa.* Blackwell. Malden. 2003. 112-131.
MD. Hart.	'Reconciliation of Body and Soul: Gregory of Nyssa's Deeper Theology of Marriage.' *Theological Studies.* 51. 1990. 450-478.
VA. Karras.	'A Re-evaluation of Marriage, Celibacy, and Irony in Gregory of Nyssa's *On Virginity.' Journal of Early Christian Studies.* 13.1. 2005. 111-121.
M. Laird.	*Gregory of Nyssa and the Grasp of Faith: Union, Knowledge, and Divine Presence.* OUP. Oxford. 2004.

---

[396] *On Virginity.* 5. Callahan. 1967. 27.

Idem.   'Gregory of Nyssa and the Mysticism of Darkness.' *The Journal of Religion*. 79 . Oct. 1999. 592-616.

JA. McGuckin.   *St. Gregory of Nazianzus: An Intellectual Biography*. SVS Press. NY. 2001.

A. Meredith.   *Gregory of Nyssa*. Routledge. London. 1999.

RA. Norris.   'The Soul Takes Flight: Gregory of Nyssa and the Songs of Songs.' *Anglican Theological Review*. 80. 4. 1998. 517-532.

CC. Richardson.   *Christology of the Later Fathers*. SCM Press. London. 1954.

CP. Roth.   'Platonic & Pauline Elements in the Ascent of the Soul in Gregory of Nyssa's Dialogue on the Soul &Resurrection.' *Vigiliae Christianae*. 46. 1992. 20-30.

L F Mateo-Seco (ed) *The Brill Dictionary of Gregory of Nyssa*.

& S Cherny (tr).   Brill. Leiden. 2010.

D. Turner.   *The Darkness of God: Negativity in Christian Mysticism*. CUP. Cambridge 1995.

R. Williams.   'Macrina's Deathbed Revisited: Gregory of Nyssa on Mind and Passion.' In L R Wickham & CP Bammel. (edd). *Christian Faith and Greek Philosophy in Late Antiquity*. Brill. Leiden. 1993. 227-246.

PART II

BYZANTINE

The Eros of Divine Beauty in
St. Maximus the Confessor (c. 580-662).

J A McGuckin.

St. Maximus: Life and Contexts

St. Maximus the Confessor is one of the most subtle of all the Byzantine theologians[397]. HG Beck once called him: 'The most universal spirit of the seventh century, and perhaps the last independent thinker of the Byzantine Church.'[398] His life has come down to us not only accreted with the usual hagiographic tales, but in two quite distinct, and sometimes incompatible, versions. There is a Greek tradition which had circulated from antiquity through Byzantine and into modern times (establishing the normative nucleus of his *Vita*) [399] and an ancient Syriac text only recently re-discovered by Sebastian Brock in the piles of *arcana syriaca* in the British Library [400]. This new divergence of foundational sources leaves the historian with several intractable problems as to which version to lean on for which period of

[397] For further reading see: G Berthold (tr). *St. Maximus the Confessor*. Classics of Western Spirituality. New York. 1985. *(Select texts;* L Thunberg. *Microcosm and Mediator*. Lund. 1965; A Louth. *Maximus the Confessor*. London. 1996; A Nichols. Byzantine Gospel: *Maximus the Confessor in Modern Scholarship*. T&T Clark, Edinburgh. 1993.

[398] HG. Beck. *Kirche und theologische Literatur im byzantinischen Reich*. Munich. 1959. p. 436.

[399] St. Theodore the Studite composed a *Vita* in the 8th C which was used by the later Studite Michael Exaboulites in the 10th C (PG 90. 68-109), along with several other sources. The tradition of the *Vita* is discussed by W Lackner: 'Zu quellen und datierung der Maximusvita (BHG.1234.' *Analecta Bollandiana*. 85. 1967. 285-316; and idem. 'Der Amtstitel Maximus des Bekenners.' *Jahrbuch der Osterreich-ischen Byzantinistik*. 20. 19171. 63-65.

[400] S Brock. 'An Early Syriac Life of Maximus the Confessor.' in: *Analecta Bollandiana*. 91. 1973. 299-346. The Syriac life was composed by the Monk George of Reshaina, and is contemporary with Maximus himself. It is a hostile account, the author being a leading Monothelite, who described Maximus as an illegitimate (thus poor) child, and a renegade 'Origenist' monk from the Great Lavra in Palestine.

Maximus' Life. It seems indisputable he once held high political office in the Byzantine court [401], and possibly headed the Imperial Chancery (*Protoasecretis*) in the shake-up that Emperor Heraclios gave to the administration in the aftermath of overthrowing the Phocas revolt in 610. It also seems highly likely that Maximus came from a Palestinian background (not a noble Constantinopolitan one as the Greek lives conspire to have it [402]). But how to combine the different data that the conflicting traditions of the *Vitae* offer is not clearly resolvable as yet. Louth rightly criticizes Kazhdan's whimsical solution in the *Oxford Dictionary of Byzantium*[403] (where he cuts the Gordian knot of the problem by simply using the Syriac evidence for the early years and the Greek evidence for the later life), as an implausible method [404]. The details of the saint's *Vita* only begin to clarify and harmonize after 630.

We know that by 618 Maximus was attended by a monastic disciple, Anastasios [405], who remained with him for the rest of his life. By this stage he was himself, therefore, clearly a scholar-monk, initiating his ascetical career at Chrysopolis, across the Bosphoros from Constantinople. His career in Heraclios' Chancery must predate this, but was probably not of long duration; and how he attained the rank and skills necessary for it, are not known, but surely derived from that amazing literary and philosophical education whose fruits are manifested from the beginning of his monastic writing career.

He then moved, circa 626 from Chrysopolis to the monastery of St. George at Cyzicus [406] where John was bishop, the addressee of his famous *Book of Difficulties*, or *Ambigua*. That was the year of the

---

[401] See Maximus' own reference to this in *Epistle* 12. 91. (Discussed in Lackner. 1971).

[402] Though his position in the Chancery would certainly have conveyed Constantinopolitan rank upon him.

[403] A. Kazhdan (ed). *The Oxford Dictionary of Byzantium*. Oxford. 1991. vol. 2. 1323f.

[404] A. Louth. *Maximus the Confessor*. Routledge. London. 1996. 199. fn. 11.

[405] At his trial in 655, Maximus says that Anastasios had been with him for 37 years. PG. 90. 128C.

[406] The southern littoral of the Sea of Marmara, now Erdek.

great Persian siege heading westwards towards Constantinople[407], with the Avar and the Slav tribes making concertedly for the city at the same time from the North. Maximus joined the refugee stream caused by these military disruptions and came via Cyprus and Crete, to North Africa by 630. In that year, and enjoying a buoyant reputation after his recovery of the True Cross from the Persians, the Emperor Heraclios celebrated a successful reunion of the Armenians with the Constantinopolitan Church on the basis of Mono-Energism; an ecclesiastical policy which the Egyptian Church also favoured[408]. But while this imperial theological policy was being advanced, an important Palestinian higumen named Sophronios[409] (later to become Patriarch of Jerusalem) then resident in North Africa, and a spiritual father to St. Maximus, raised strenuous objections to its orthodoxy, and took his case to Constantinople in 633, where his complaints were lodged and duly acknowledged in an Imperial *Psephos* [410].

Sophronios, who had arrived in the imperial city with a high standing as a leading ascetic, subsequently took on an extra-ordinary importance on account of his election as Patriarch of Jerusalem in 634, shortly after he had returned to Palestine. His Patriarchal accession statement of faith put the cat among the

---

[407] The occasion of the composition of the new opening stanzas for the famous Akathist Hymn, when Patriarch Sergius paraded the Icon of the Virgin around the Walls of the City.

[408] Bishop Cyrus of Phasis was translated in 631 to be the imperially sponsored (hence Chalcedonian or Melkite) Patriarch of Alexandria and commissioned to unite Egyptian Christianity around the Mono-Energistic formula. In 633 he celebrated a eucharist of reunion in the Alexandrian cathedral where many of the Monophysite clergy came over to his side. His formula of agreement (*The Nine Chapters*) was read at the 6th Oecumenical Council in 681.

[409] Further see C. von Schönborn. *Sophrone de Jérusalem: vie monastique et confession dogmatique.* Paris. 1972.

[410] The Imperial *Psephos*, or adjudication that was issued, forbade the use of language referring either to one or two activities in Christ, but advocated the single divine subject in the Lord which precluded the existence of two wills which were contrary to one another. It was effectively a *judicatum* that acknowledged Mono-Energism, as a policy of broad reconciliation of the parties conflicted over Chalcedon, was no longer able to work. The collapse of this arm of imperial reconciliation policy stimulated the next stage of the same, which was to move to be Monothelitism.

international pigeons, however, by denouncing Mono-Energism as tantamount to arguing Christ had merely one will (Mono-thelitism) a stance, he said, which would contradict a Chalcedonian Christology of union, in favor of a Monophysite-leaning solution. Rome which had been at first inclined towards the Mono-Energistic solution under Pope Honorius, backed away from it anxiously after Sophronios raised this red flag. The response of Emperor Heraclios and Patriarch Sergios of Constantinople to this turn of events (one which put their whole ecclesiastical policy of union in jeopardy) was to issue a decree known as the *Ekthesis* in 638.

The *Ekthesis* met Sophronios' challenge head on, and took Mono-Energism one stage further towards a position that the Incarnate Lord did in fact possess only one divine will and centre of his moral and spiritual energy among humanity. It answered Sophronios' charge of latent Monophysitism by claiming that this Oneness (*henosis*) of moral action in Christ was the result of the single unification (*henosis*) that occurred between the divine and human natures. It was this language of *henosis* that St. Cyril of Alexandria had advocated in his writings before and after the Council of Ephesus (431) [411]: and thus the imperial party continued to claim the mantle of Cyril, thereby following the capital's traditional ecclesial policy that a strongly Cyrilline Chalcedonianism would be the best way of positively nuancing Chalcedon for the disunited East. Monothelitism was thus really the last hope for the emperor's intention to reunite the Chalcedonians and Monophysites.

In the same year that the *Ekthesis* was published, Sergius of Constantinople died and was succeeded as Patriarch by Pyrrhus, who continued the imperial policy until 641 when the emperor Heraclios died, and he himself was deposed from office[412]. By at

---

[411] See JA. McGuckin. *St Cyril of Alexandria and the Christological Controversy.* Brill. Leiden 1994; & repr. SVS Press. New York. 2004.

[412] He had taken the part of Heraclios' widow Marina, in her bid for power, but her own ascent to the throne was widely regarded as illegitimate as she had been the niece of Heraclios. After his death she and her sons, and the patriarch, were

least 640, if not earlier, St. Maximus had decided that Sophronios' position was right and the imperial policy had clearly become excessively monist, and heretical. But by this stage Sophronios himself was largely ruled out of the debate, for in that very year he had to surrender Jerusalem to the Islamic Arab invaders. Alexandria, and almost all the East were lost to Byzantium in 642. All Byzantine affairs were thus reduced to massive turmoil and the prospects of any imperial policy for Church union looked very bleak. It was now that Pyrrhus came to Carthage in North Africa, hoping to get a hearing [413] from Gregorios, the Byzantine Exarch there. But it was also here that he encountered Maximus, whom he had known as a junior monk in the monastery of Chrysopolis when he himself had been Higumen, and with whom he had corresponded when Maximus had written to him to criticize his agreement to the *Ekthesis*.

Under Exarch Gregorios' authority, a formal debate on the merits of the Heraclian church policy was organized in 645 at the Greek monastery at Carthage with Maximus and Pyrrhus the chief debaters. The publicity given to this event signaled to Constantinople that Gregorios was acting as a kingmaker. For who adjudicates the settlement of religious policy in the empire other than the emperor? In 646 Gregorios came into the open by accepting acclamation as emperor by his troops in Africa. But he was killed the next year fighting against Arab armies. It is partly this unstable background which explains the later savagery attendant on St. Maximus and Pope Martin when they fall into the hands of the Byzantine emperor; who has already taken note of them as enemies. Maximus was credited with winning the debate on that occasion and Pyrrhus agreed to abandon the Monothelite cause and declared himself in agreement with Maximus. He would soon enough renege on his statements when it became clear, two years later, that the fallen usurper Gregorios was certainly no ticket back to grace and favor in the capital.

---

banished, and Constans II, Heraclios' grandson by his first marriage, assumed power.

[413] If Gregorios did (as was rumored) have aspirations for the throne of the capital himself, Pyrrhus might find his way to re-instatement by being a source of Gregorios' legitimation for a revolt.

In 646, however, the anti-Monothelite cause looked hopeful as Maximus and Pyrrhus came to Rome where they were received gladly by the Greek pope Theodore; and Pyrrhus was honored as an 'orthodox' hierarch. The pope, hearing from Maximus that several African synods had condemned the *Ekthesis,* then openly broke off communion with Paul, Constans' II's patriarch at Constantinople. But in 647, when Pyrrhus heard of Gregorios' death in battle, he immediately fled for refuge to the Byzantine Exarch Olympios at Ravenna, and declared he was reconciled once more to the imperial theology. Pope Theodore at Rome excommunicated him with a decree signed by a pen which he dipped into the altar's chalice, so deep was his disgust. The Emperor decided to try and bring an end to the whole set of arguments in 648 by issuing a decree known as the *Typos* which basically forbade any public debate or 'any discussion of one will, or one energy, two wills or two energies.' At Rome that same year Theodore died, and Martin succeeded to the papacy, refusing to seek the usual confirmation of his election from the Emperor at Constantinople or the Exarch at Ravenna: and thus declaring an outright break. The *Typos* arrived in due course and Martin's reaction was to call a council in the Lateran basilica in 649, where Maximus served as a theological expert to the attending bishops who numbered one hundred and five. While avoiding any personal excommunication of the Emperor, the *Ekthesis* and the *Typos* were declared heretical; and the Patriarchs of Constantinople: Sergius, Pyrrhus and the incumbent Paul[414] were explicitly anathematized.

The Emperor responded immediately by calling for the arrest of Pope Martin. It was the public violent opposition to his soldiers that probably decided Exarch Olympios to start looking for his own chances to the throne. Knowing he would need Martin's legitimation eventually, he allowed the Pope to carry on undisturbed. In 652 he himself died, in Sicily, while trying to make an alliance with the Arabs so as to march against Constans II in the capital. After that time Martin was unprotected. The new Exarch at Ravenna, Theodore Kalliopas, arrested the ailing pope in 653 and transported him to Constantinople where he was tried

[414] As well as the theologians Theodore of Pharan, and Cyrus of Alexandria.

for treason and deposed by the new patriarch Peter, ill treated, and sent into exile in the Crimea; where he died in 655. His successors as popes, Eugenius and Vitalian, quickly declared their state of being in communion with the Constantinopolitan patriarch, though neither of them formally endorsed either the *Typos* or the *Ekthesis*. Their silence was indication enough that the policy of the *Typos* was now being respected.

Only Maximus refused to keep quiet. But he too was soon arrested in Rome for refusing to sign agreement to the *Typos*, and transported with two of his disciples to Constantinople. His trial took place there in 655 on the grounds of treasonable association with Pope Martin and the usurper Gregorios. In his theological defence Maximus raised the argument, from St. Athanasius, that the Emperor has no right to determine the church's dogma. His sentence was exile to Thrace; but he refused to remain docile, and was recalled to Constantinople for a second trial where he was censured for speaking and writing against the emperor, and sentenced to the mutilation of his tongue and his hand, before being exiled to Lazica in Georgia; where he died on August 13th 662, aged over eighty. Only his two disciples stayed with him. His memory was passed over. Even when, twenty years later, the cause for which he had given his life was finally triumphant, and the Monothelite school was finally dismantled at the Council of Constantinople III in 680, no mention was made in the capital or at the synod of his name or his theology.

Even so, St. Maximus, in all this welter of complex theological *apologia* emerges as a theologian who clearly combined rigorous intellectual capacity, with a deep and close reading of the Origenian theological tradition: including in that line of intell-ectual heritage: Saints Gregory of Nazianzus, Gregory of Nyssa, and Dionysios the Areopagite. In this latter aspect of his own intellectual policy, Maximus takes his compass bearing from Gregory the Theologian, and that master's attempt of three cent-uries earlier [415] to rescue Origen from his own excesses, in order to

---

[415] Throughout his *Discourses,* but especially in his compilation, with St. Basil the Great, of the *Philocalia Origenis*. See G. Lewis (tr.) *The Philocalia of Origen.* T& T Clark. Edinburgh. 1911.

retain for the Church's wider tradition the latter's most brilliant insights on the nature of the Logos' redeeming activity in the soul, and the luminous character of the inspiration of the holy scriptures. This work of rescue was necessary in Gregory the Theologian's time, namely in the first period of the Origenian controversy, and rendered doubly acute for Maximus after Justinian's catastrophic attacks on Origen's reputation in the events attending the Fifth Oecumenical Council of 553.

If ever there was a quintet of sophisticated and subtle theologians in the history of the Orthodox Church it was these five: Origen, Gregory the Theologian, Gregory of Nyssa, Dionysios the Areopagite, and Maximus the Confessor. The four later readers of the Alexandrian ancient, all having this in common with their ancient patron that they welded together a profoundly philosophical anthropology with a mystical apprehension of the Logos' salvation of the human race by deifying redemption. It is at, and within, this juncture of anthropology and mysticism that St. Maximus works. At one and the same moment it explains for us why his aesthetic theory is an ascetical mysticism: how his role as a monk demanded his involvement in the sharp clash of the politics of the day: and why he saw the theologian's highest vocation as that of being a public intellectual. In him aesthetics, soteriology, culture, philosophy, sacramentology and ethics, all converge. He is the Byzantine *par excellence*; and his mind is as difficult to exegete as his Greek is to translate.

St. Maximus on Beauty

If we now turn to look specifically at his thoughts on Beauty, expounding them from Maximus' *1st Century on Charity*[416], and the *5th Century of Various Texts* [417], we will be in a position to ask not only what he meant by this boldly Christian reinterpretation of Plato's ideas of the ascent of the soul to Beauty, by the energy of divine *Eros*, but also to clarify how this perception of the innate

---

[416] *1st Century on Charity*. (Chapter 85). Text in E.T. in: G. Palmer, P. Sherrard, and K. Ware (edd). *The Philokalia*. vol.2. Faber. London. 1981. 133.
[417] *5th Century of Various Texts*. (Chapters 83-92). Text in E.T. in: Palmer, Sherrard, and Ware (edd). *The Philokalia*. vol. 2. Faber. London. 1981. 280-282.

Eros of the beautiful in the race, relates fundamentally, and by no means peripherally, to his Christological theory and his advocacy of the model of how the Christological union demonstrated the form (*eidos*) of the salvation of humanity by deifying trans-cendence. So let us make a beginning with his thought on Beauty. We begin in the Soul. Where else?

Plato's suggestion that the soul was comprised of several levels was very influential on later Christian ascetical thought. Two 'late Platonic' tendencies in Christian mystical writing, brought into focus first by Origen, but significantly developed by both Gregory the Theologian and Gregory of Nyssa before they are developed by Maximus, are (a) this aspect of the triadic levels of the soul [418] and (b) the concept of the soul's movement (its *energeia*) as ascentive.[419] In terms of its inner structure, the soul in its lower aspects is appetitive (*epithymic*). It is the psychic element in the human nature concerned with thoughts and awareness primarily as rooted in bodily consciousness. Such a psychic life turns around the primary axis of material self-interests such as protection, shelter, aggression and so on; and is rooted in material consciousness. It is a psychic awareness, not merely a material one, but its proximity to the body means that it's range of 'empathies' is profoundly psycho-somatic; its emotions and affects are close to those of the animal body. There is, however a second and higher aspect of psychic life: the soul's domain of emotions and aspirations which are more elevated from their material 'foundations' and impulses. We might take, as an example, the soul's functions as the organizer of human empathies, altruistic affection, and higher emotions (not so much anger and desire for revenge, but a passion for justice, let us say). These higher emotions correspond to the soul's mid-level affective energies, and while, at their lower range, they overlap closely with the

---

[418] It is more elaborately described in JA. McGuckin. 'The Shaping of the Soul's Perceptions in the Byzantine Ascetic Elias Ekdikos.' SVSThQ. 55.3 2011. 343-363. Elias was a later medieval commentator on Maximus.

[419] As described more completely in its philosophical context by Sergey Trostyanskiy earlier in this volume. See also RJ. O'Connell. 'Eros & Philia in Plato's Moral Cosmos.' in: *Neo-Platonism in Early Christian Thought*. H. Blumenthal & RA. Markus. (edd). London. 1981. 3-19

material inspirations for these energies (a more universalized desire for justice is akin to the base instinct for 'fight or flight', for example) they nevertheless ascend above these particularities towards a more refined set of deeper-horizon attitudes. The psychic energies of the two levels of soul differ, therefore. At the mid-level soul's lower end it is akin to the lower soul's material consciousness at its upper end. Between the lower soul (body consciousness) and its interests and desires, there is not so much kinship with the mid-level soul in its upper range. Someone 'working' psychically at the lower soul's bottom range (in their attitudes and aspirations and instincts is what I mean) might well describe the entire world as driven by a 'selfish gene'. Someone working at the mid-level soul's upper end will habitually describe the world as an ascent to universal values (compassion, love, justice, and so on). What the Christian mystical tradition does, after Origen, is to explicate this aspect of various soul levels as fundamentally triadic. The third level, clearly the highest level of psychic consciousness possible to humanity, is described by the Byzantine writers chiefly through the semantic of *Nous*. Unfortunately, the history of the base Greek terms in English language scholarship has been tortuous. There has been little attempt to recognize these things as a new and important technical vocabulary seeking to describe a new Christian theory of cognitive ascent. Be that as it may. English language scholarship is only now beginning to take the ascetical writings of the Byzantines seriously, and even to this day most theologians do not even see this literature as 'theological' (I pass over in silence to what extent the modern theologians have even read it).

The Soul, or we may say, the psychic cognitive capacity of the human is, therefore, triadic for Maximus. It is a triad that runs from the lower soul, through the middle soul, to the *Nous*. In each of the levels there is an upper and lower range, and on the borders between all three there is close kinship, such that each level can communicate with the other adjacent to it - can affect it. The mid-level capacity of the *Psyche* towards higher values, can be lowered by the strong passions of the lower soul, if they are allowed to dominate. The more universalized and altruistic affects (*agape*) of the mid-level soul can, equally, bring refinement and ordering to

179

the passions of the lower soul: again if they are allowed to dominate. This is why the moral life is above all else rooted in the
psyche and consists of an issue of how the *psyche* is ordered; given
order (*taxis*) an order that quintessentially means the subor-
dinating of the lower particular impulses to the higher more
universal values. This subordination was described by Plato in the
image of the soul as a chariot and its horses needing to be
controlled by a firm hand[420]. The Byzantines preferred to use the
simpler image of the *Nous* being the Director (*higumen, proedros*) of
the three parts of consciousness; and moral order being fulfilled
when the middle and lower soul concur with its *paideia*. Disorder,
and therefore moral catastrophe, occur when the lower soul takes
charge of a human life and acts as *higumen*. This leadership is not
a valid governance by a Director, rather a disordered tyranny; and
there was always a deep connection in patristic thought, accordingly, between the understanding of sin as moral defect, and
as disorganized ignorance ('ontological sickness'); making the
Eastern church's moral theology generally more therapeutic in
character than the forensic character its Latin theologians evinced.

The central importance of the moral life considered as the soul's
ascent through the passions to dispassion (*apatheia*), and the
mind's ascent from psychic cognition to logos cognition and on to
noetic cognition, is a driving idea in all the work of Origen of
Alexandria, and the many fathers who subsequently followed in
his school. When Maximus discourses on Beauty, therefore, he
shows himself to be a profound commentator on Origen, who is
himself a very important critic of Plato. Maximus knows, quite
consciously, all the nexus of texts which he is citing, either directly
or allusively; and is well aware of the previous patristic tradition
and the manner it had woven together a biblical soteriology and
this major question of contemporary aesthetical philosophy.

---

[420] *Phaedrus*. 246a-254e. The charioteer (reasoned consciousness or *to logistikon*)
drives a chariot led by two powerful horses; one dark one white. The dark horse
is *to epithymitikon* (the appetitive part of the soul – its desires and instinctive
drives). The white horse is *to thymitikon*, the irascible part (the soul's nobler
instincts, its courage, its 'spiritedness'). Plato uses this model of the soul (and
resumes it in the *Republic*) to speak of the philosopher's task of making the soul
ascend to higher truth.

His approach to the question of ascentive beauty is set out in two particular places which I wish to consider in this present essay; the *First Century on Theology*. cc. 85-86, and the *5th Century of Various Texts*. cc. 83-86. Both of these passages had a large circulation among Byzantine monastics and formed an important set of intellectual scaffolding for the monastic spirituality of the refinement of the soul. Both of them came to have a significant place in the later Orthodox tradition of the *Philokalia*.[421]

In the *First Century in Theology*, St Maximus states the question in this way:

85. The 'darkness' [422] is that formless, immaterial, and bodiless state which embraces the knowledge of the prototypes of all created things. Whoever enters it like a second Moses, even though he may be mortal by nature, understands things that are immortal. Through this knowledge such a person depicts in himself the beauty of divine excellence, as if painting a picture which is a faithful copy of Archetypal Beauty. Then, he comes down from the mountain and offers himself as an exemplar to those who wish to imitate that excellence. In this way he manifests the love and generosity of grace he has received.

86. Those who apply themselves with a pure heart to divine philosophy derive the greatest gain from the knowledge it contains. For their will and purpose no longer change with circumstances, but readily and with firm assurance they undertake all that conforms to the standard of holiness. [423]

The *Centuries*, as a genre of Byzantine writing, are sets of philosophical *aporia*, or puzzles, sometimes simpler maxims or

---

[421] *St. Maximus 1st Century on Theology*. cc. 85-86. *The Philokalia*. vol. 2. London. 1981. 133. (*presented here with some emendations to the translation); and 5th Century of Various Texts*. cc. 83-86. in: *The Philokalia*. vol. 2. London. 1981. 280-282. *(again with some emendations)*.

[422] The biblical 'type' of which Moses encounters in the Sinai Theophany, which Maximus is referring to here as a symbol of the divine nature. His *aporia*, or set puzzle, is how the Christian can approach the Unapproachable Godhead.

[423] *The Philokalia*. vol. 2. 1981. See f.n. 26.

aphorisms, meant to offer the individual monk, or reading circle of like-minded zealots, a 'text for the day'. It is, of course, the continuation of the ancient theme of *Lectio Divina*, but in the way it was functioning in Maximus' day, the books of *kephalaia* present dense and meaty short sections of text which are designed to be taken away to form the focus of the day's monastic meditation. In this section, in chapters 85 and 86 we find two closely related sets of reflections. The second in 86 is a simpler iteration of the more complex proposition in 85.

Let us begin, then with 86. Here it is, set in a form of parallelism with its precedent, arguing that the vocation to philosophy is itself the true path of the monk. Philosophy is now, and has been since the time of St. Gregory the Theologian who coined the term: 'Our Philosophy', by which he meant the Christian ascetical life. Maximus, who is also a very close reader of St. Gregory [424], takes that theme forwards. Divine philosophy is able to be exegeted only by the pure heart. This is because it is not perceptible merely by virtue of intelligence. It is a matter of divine vision. Echoing Jesus' own words: 'Blessed are the pure in heart for they shall see God' [425] Maximus stresses the ascetical life as involving not merely the purification (*katharsis*) of the body, through celibacy and poverty and fasting, but also the issue of the clarification of the mind; so that it can see, more fully and more truly, divine realities. The whole section in 86 is not merely a generic moral *encomium*, but rather functions as a quite precise definition of a concept that had a long pre-history in Christian ascetical writing: namely *apatheia*. In what did *apatheia* consist? The passionless state of the perfected monk (an ideal to which the ascetics strove to be conformed even in this life) is carefully rendered by the modern translators of the *Philokalia* as 'dis-passion', to distance it from the Hellenistic overtones of the notion, and to focus it as a moral factor connoting for Christians the way that fixity of moral

---

[424] His *Ambigua* are very precise *scholia* on the *Orations* of the Theologian.
[425] Mt. 5.8. Further on this theme see: JA. McGuckin. 'The Prayer of the Heart in Patristic and Early Byzantine Tradition.' in: P Allen, W Mayer, & L Cross. (edd). *Prayer & Spirituality in the Early Church.* vol. 2. Queensland. 1999. (Australian Catholic University. Centre for Early Christian Studies). 69-108.

purpose renders the power of the bodily and lower-soul's temptations less and less, as the ascetical philosopher becomes more
and more grounded in the life of wisdom. In short, the pure in
heart are able to enter into divine philosophy, become stabilized
within it, and thereby set fast within the ambit of holiness. He has
not exactly stated this explicitly, but the unitive ethos of the whole
text is much to the fore. It is the ascent to union with the divine
presence of the Logos within the soul of the ascetic (as its
archetype) that is the basis and energy of the ascent of the
creature to union with divine wisdom. The union is itself the
energeia of holiness. Holiness is the presence, and being within the
presence. Now this, as we may see, is substantively a re-iteration
at a slightly different tangent, of the previous passage about the
ascent to Divine Beauty: the connection being given by the fact
that Divine Beauty is hypostatically understood within Christian
tradition: that is, as none other than the Person of God, archetype
of all beauty.

Maximus' main point in relation to beauty, set out in c. 85, derives
from the biblical typology of the Sinai theophany (Exod.19.9f;
24.15f). His chief motif is that the type of divine presence (the
approach to divine being) is symbolized in the dark and impenetrable cloud that shrouds the face of God (the presupposition
always understood among the Fathers who use this symbolically
impenetrable 'darkness' being that the cloud shields human eyes
from the unbearable brightness of the lightning flash [426] of the
deity within). Maximus elevates the darkness as the type of the
immaterial transcendence of the deity which is the prototype of
all created things. There is therefore, in the very experience of
bewilderment of a limited creature approaching the threshold of
transcendence, nevertheless a true intimation of its own essential
nature. It is the paradox of authentic revelation: that the
unknowing is, at the same time, a deeper knowing of the self than
is possible using the normal channels of materially-based cognition. The soul, especially in its higher forms as the human *Nous*,

[426] Gk: *astrapé*: the biblical theology of God's presence uses the concept of the
kabod (the 'glory' in the form of the shadowing cloud) to connote the presence
(*shekinah*) of the Holy One, in the manner that this is mediated to limited human
sense.

183

has a kinship with the divine; since the Divine *Logos* made the *Nous* in his own image and likeness. The human creature has, therefore, a root-creational affinity with its God. When Maximus speaks of the initiate 'understanding things immortal' he means it in a double sense: the genuine perception of realities (divine transcendence) which are beyond its own cognitive capacity, and a realization of its own inner nature, which material senses deny to it; namely the growing awareness that this mortality we now bear is truly an immortal glory; the gift of the resurrectional life in the Logos incarnate. Maximus, having set out this dense paradox of revelation, in the form of an *aporia*, comes to its suggested resolution in the final section of c. 85 when he turns explicitly to the theology of beauty.

This *gnosis* of the paradox allows the human soul to mirror within itself, or faithfully iconize, the beauty of the divine archetype. So it is that the initiate becomes a second Moses, who now descends the mountain to stand as the icon of divine beauty to the larger church, the manifestation of God to others through love and grace[427], just as the *theophaneia* was a manifestation to Moses, and he demonstrated it to Israel on the plains below, by his enduring radiance of face. This is, of course, fundamentally an ethical meditation, but how deeply Maximus has set his ethical anthropology within the ontological glory of the Godhead. It is classical patristic thought, but evidently worked through the pen of a master.

St. Maximus comes at the same idea in another interesting set of passages in *5th Century of Various Texts*. cc. 83-86. Here he says:

> 83. The beautiful is identical with the good, for all things seek the beautiful and good at every opportunity, and there is no being which does not participate in them. They extend to all that is, being what is truly admirable, sought for, desired, pleasing, chosen and loved. Observe how the divine force of love – that erotic power pre-existing in the Good – has given birth to the same blessed force within us, through which we

---

[427] He means to suggest *agape* and *charis* (love and grace) as Christian renderings of the Sinaitic covenant virtues of *Hesed* and *Emet* (loving-mercy and faithfulness).

long for the beautiful and the good in accordance with the words: 'I became a lover of her beauty' [428]; and also: 'Love her and she will sustain you; fortify her and she will exalt you.' [429]

84. Theologians call the divine force sometimes an erotic force, sometimes that which is intensely longed for and loved [430]. Consequently, as an erotic force and as love, the divine itself is subject to movement; and as that which is intensely longed for and loved, it moves towards itself everything that is receptive of this force and love. To express this more clearly: the divine itself is subject to movement since it produces an inward state of intense longing and love in those receptive to them; and it moves others since by nature it attracts the desire of those who are drawn towards it. In other words, it moves others and itself moves since it thirsts to be thirsted for, longs to be longed for, and loves to be loved.

85. The divine erotic force also produces ecstasy, compelling those who love to belong not to themselves but to those whom they love. This is shown by superior beings through their care for inferiors; by those of equal dignity by their mutual union; and by lower beings through their divine conversion towards those that are highest in rank. It was in consequence of this that St. Paul, possessed as he was by this divine erotic force, and partaking of its ecstatic power, was inspired to say: 'I no longer live, but Christ lives in me'[431]. He uttered these words as a true lover and, as he himself says, as one who has gone out from himself to God [432], not living his own life but that of the Beloved, because of his fervent love for Him.

86. One must also, in the name of truth, be bold enough to affirm that the Cause of all things, through the beauty, goodness, and profusion of his intense love for everything, goes out of Himself in his providential care for the whole of

---

[428] Wisdom 8.2.
[429] Proverbs. 4. 6,8.
[430] cf. Dionysios the Areopagite. *Divine Names.* 4.14. PG. 3. 712c.
[431] Galatians 2.20.
[432] cf. 2 Cor. 5.13.

creation. By means of the hyper-essential power of ecstasy, and spell-bound as it were by goodness, love, and longing, he relinquishes his utter transcendence in order to dwell in all things while yet remaining within himself. This is why those skilled in divine matters call him a zealous and exemplary lover, because of the intensity of his blessed longing for all things, and because he rouses others to imitate his own intense desire, revealing himself as their exemplar; for in him what is desirable is worthy of emulation, and he deserves to be imitated by the beings under his care. [433]

Now this is a Niagara Falls in terms of the history of ancient theology. No one [434] among the Christian Fathers has been so bold as Maximus. He knows he is being shockingly radical: for he is ready to set aside the universal language of all ancient theology (common to Hellenes and Christians): that God as Absolute, is also impassible; and being impassible is not moved by external forces. What Maximus says here is that the force of love moves God, as it moves us, since love is part of the divine image within us. To be Un-Moved Mover is not, therefore, a perfection, rather a catastrophic limitation. To this end he describes the force of God's love as an *Eros*. This carries all the force of the concept of passionate love; and in describing God as passionate lover of the creation Maximus knows he is boldly marking off new territory. The speed with which the argument moves between cc. 83 and 86 is best slowed down for terms of commentary.

In the opening of c.83 Maximus begins with a simple statement of Platonic archetype theory in relation to the divine. The Good is the Beautiful, and accordingly is universally desired. No one in the ancient world would disagree with this. Because of the inherently desirable nature of the True Beauty, the human soul moves towards it and longs for it. Here he begins to specify his thought as Christian not Hellene. He locates his ethic in the midst of a theological *a priori*: in other words we have a strong attraction to

---

[433] E.T. in: *The Philokalia*. vol. 2. London. 1981. 280-282. *(here with some emendations to the translation).*

[434] Possible exceptions would be St. Gregory the Theologian in *Oration 31*, or Dionysios the Areopagite in *The Mystical Theology*.

Beauty because God has laid this innate longing in the bed of our being as type from the archetype. If this is so, he goes on (and this is where his thought becomes radical even for Christians of his era), then it demonstrates that in the archetypal beauty itself a passionate longing-for-union-in-love is demonstrable. Maximus has 'corrected' St. John the Divine [435]; for God is not *Agape*; God is *Eros*.

In c. 84, starting with an opening allusion to Dionysios the Areopagite in the *Divine Names* 4.14, Maximus explains that this is indeed Movement *(kinesis)* within the deity, but far from being a contradiction of the divine attributes (immovability, immutability) it is the shape of the actual *energeia* of the Godhead. God in Himself moves out to creation philanthropically: this is what is meant by God as erotic force: the true desire of all who live and know God. At the end of c. 84 he even suggests that God is as desirous to be loved, as we are to love God: an amazing theology, highly suggestive that love and beauty are the kinetic movement flowing from out of the very *ousia* of the Godhead, and lodged in the human soul as the *locus* of the Icon of deity God himself has placed there.

Section 85 reprises Plato's ethical teleology in his aesthetics; but once again Maximus refashions the actual *telos* of the ethic in a radically Christian fashion, rendering it into a double evocation of Christian themes. In the first place, the whole of section 85 is a clear allusion to the Dionysian hierarchies: how God's grace is transmitted in hierarchical series of mediation. For Maximus all the conjoined ranks and interrelated ministries, from angels and heavenly hierarchies, down to the hierarchies of service that comprise the Church, all conspire together to make God's *cosmos* (his 'beautiful' creation) a symphony of love. In the second place this joining together of love, caused by the ecstasy originating in God's own love for the world, creates that distinctive mark and characteristic *proprium* of love: which is to seek not to belong to the self, but to the beloved.

---

[435] 1Jn. 4.8.

It therefore, in Maximus' understanding, has an innately *kenotic nature*. The *Kenosis* of the Logos' own emptying out to be available to the creation in his incarnate ministry of love, is thus mirrored by the believer's love which similarly seeks the beloved's good not its own. In this way the lover's soul is conjoined with God, the heart and centre of it all, as well as with the community of heavenly and earthly church: which is indeed nothing other than a communion of love, held together by the Eros of God's ecstatic outreach. Maximus lifts up St. Paul at the end of this section as an exemplar of one who lives in the mystery of Christ's kenotic love for mankind.

Section. 86 presses this theology to its radical climacteric: for this mystery of *kenosis* is not simply allowed to be a model of the earthly economy of salvation, rendered as an historical or temporary thing; but is rather traced back into the eternal life of God. St. Maximus knows from the outset that this will shock both Hellene (readers of Plato) and Christian (readers of the earlier patristic tradition) and thus he prefaces his remarks in this section with a call to 'boldness'. He claims the audacity of truth, in a prophetic manner, to insist that God's infinitely loving Providence is not that of some distant deistic watchmaker, but the profound love of the God who leaves his royal splendor and: 'relinquishes his utter transcendence in order to dwell in all things.'

This immanence in lowly creatures, by the *energeia* of love is not incompatible with God 'remaining in Himself' (in other words remaining God-as-Himself). *Kenosis* thus becomes not a challenge to divine glory, but rather the proof of it; for it is the mark of an infinitely caring and self-sacrificial love, that forms the model for all who witness it to be moved and desire to emulate that kenotic *Eros* for God and the world. Beginning thus in divine pity (*synkatabasis*) Maximus moved to the motive for kenotic incarnation (*katabasis*) and demonstrated how the transfiguration of this dynamic of salvation results in a profound moral dimension (our *mimesis* of the merciful Lord, and our resultant deification, *theopoiesis*, in him).

We began this essay with a consideration of Maximus' Christological *foci*, and noted how his life's career was summed up, in a sense, by the Monothelite controversy. The latter has often been relegated in the theological text books to the marginalia of obscure theological controversies. For Maximus, of course, it was of one piece with his magnificent account of providential soteriology through this dynamic reworking of Plato's aesthetic theory. Long before Rahner, Maximus here insists that the immanent Trinity is the economic Trinity. And long before Barth, Maximus stresses that the core of the story of salvation is the 'Way of the Son of God into the far country.' For him, the key movement of divine love into sacrificial self-emptying is the Incarnation of the Logos into humanity, time and space.

For Maximus, the Monothelite position was a false piety that wished to spare the Son of God incarnate, the vicissitudes of the flesh. Embodiment, and thereby human consciousness, was seen in Hellenistic Antiquity as intrinsically unworthy of divine presence and thus incapable of being its true sacrament. Divinity, as a corollary, was seen as so purely a transcendental that any 'substantive' correlation of it with earthly existence had to be a primary category-mistake. In this matrix of thought, shared as a commonplace by Hellenistic religions and the Old Testament, God (or the gods) manifested themselves on earth solely in the form of epiphanies. For Maximus the Incarnation, understood as God's self emptying to assume a body and a fully human intellectual and moral consciousness to himself, makes for a radically new revelation of the Godhead.

The God and Father of Our Lord Jesus Christ, the Divine Lord who is himself crucified, and the indwelling Spirit of their holiness is, therefore, a divine reality of complex unity quite different from the gods of the Hellenes and from the understanding of God prevalent in the Old Testament. It is radically new, showing up both sets of theologies as opaquely antiquated. The Old Testament, as well as the Greek philosophers, were shadowlands for something new and bright that was to come. Maximus sees from the very beginning of his monastic career that one of the great flaws of Monothelitism is that it carries on, unreflectively, Hellenistic theological premises: intruding their paganisms unconsciously into the *kerygma* of the Church.

To present Christ as possessed of only one will, and that the divine one, was a step up from a simple pagan theology of epiphany that refused to consider the gods as 'truly' being at one with the form of mortals which they sometimes assumed; but for Maximus it is not a far step away from that. The acceptance of the human will in Christ, standing in perfect harmony with the divine will (but having to 'learn obedience' like all flesh: Heb. 5.8) was for Maximus the elevation of an incarnationalism that prioritised soteriology as its chief mechanism. It was also, in Maximus' hands, a major defence of the continuing validity of the freedom of the person. To attack the truncated anthropology of Monothelitism was for him a necessity in order to assert, as a contrast, a robust doctrine of the freedom of the human person, which is assured by the incarnation of the Logos. The incarnation, which Maximus sees as the high point of all human history, is for him the dynamic method and means of the deification of the human race; a spiritual re-creation of human nature that allows individuals the freedom needed to practise virtue, since all humans before the advent of the Logos into human flesh, and will, and mind, were wholly enslaved by the passions.

What is special to Maximus in fighting so vigorously for this high patristic doctrine of soteriological incarnationalism, is that he sees more clearly than many another before or after him, that this high doctrine of Christology is at root a doctrine of the perception of the beauty in God's ordering of the *Cosmos* (the place of beauty). He has seen the link between the doctrine of the ascent of human consciousness from material forms to immaterial perceptions (*aisthesis*): from the earthly creation to the divine realities: and understood most clearly that this ascent is also synonymous with a comprehension of the beauty of love as the explanation of all that God does in Christ. Maximus has kept faith with the ultimate reasons Chalcedonianism had insisted on the full Humanity of the Lord: he sees how necessary it is to protect the moral teleology at the heart of a true Christology. He keeps faith as a philosopher-theologian with the ever present call to ascend to truer and more beautiful perception (*aisthesis*), rising to Beauty from a beautiful life, and thus into the embodied experience of Beauty Hypostatized (the *Logos* made flesh). In a word, Maximus' theory of the Ascent to Beauty is not a separate treatise from his dyothelite Christology of deification. It is simply his teleologically moral expression of it. That this has not been generally witnessed in the commentators is a mark of how his acuity is still full of challenges to ours.

Beautiful Come-Uppance: A Theology of Platonic Order in Gregory of Nazianzus and Theodoret of Cyrrhus.

Todd E. French

The phrase, 'That is beautiful', is often used to describe a perfect harmonizing principle. It seems to emerge as the perfect description for a multitude of scenarios ranging from *schadenfreude* — that pertinent German term for joy in another's suffering — to a genuine appreciation for the perfect ordering of a series of life events. By what force these events unfold in such remarkable ways varies according to one's concept of how the universe functions: whether by serendipity, or divinely ordered retribution. Many early Christian communities witnessed the ordering of events as the imprint of the beauty of God on everyday life. The earliest Christians who faced martyrdom and myriad other earthly tortures were more likely to question whether God was interested in ordering the immediate world or the world to come. Later communities of Christians, those who had found favor with the Emperor were perhaps more intent to show that God's will extended into the everyday. Far from happenstance, the revealing of life's twists turned on the axis of God's providence. Everything was properly ordered in the universe according to the divine plan.

The term 'comeuppance' is rarely used today. Its antiquated sound connotes a tone of longsuffering in judgment. Although the examples utilized in this paper are often more expeditious, many maintain a comfort with the notion that judgment often occurs within God's rather than humanity's timeframe. In general, it is an excellent term for any situation in which one sees a person receive what is deemed appropriate to his or her actions. This sounds close to the notion of *schadenfreude*, but I want to make the case that, in the Byzantine religious literature it approximates something more reverent, and far more beautiful.

This paper will give a few brief examples of the roots of comeuppance in ancient texts and Christian scripture, then move ahead to two integral figures in the development of Eastern Christian thought during the late fourth and early fifth century: Gregory of Nazianzus and Theodoret of Cyrrhus. To any student of early Christianity this will seem like an odd pairing given Theodoret's relation as student to Diodore of Tarsus, and Gregory's public falling out with Diodore during his loss of the throne of Constantinople in 381.[436] Their uneasy connection through Diodore might bespeak disjunction if one was to focus only on the *minutiae* of the political landscape. Both of these thinkers, however, are champions of Nicene Christology and can be examined not only for a high level theology, but also more generally for their influence on contemporary Christian belief.[437] In terms of the investigation of the themes of providence and judgment, they make a very interesting pair. They are not at all the same, but they pair nicely, as something sweet often couples with something salty. It will be up to the reader to decide which one is the 'saltier' of the two. Their combination gives us a depth of flavor in the beauty of Christian comeuppance.

Comeuppance is an important and ubiquitous theme in ancient narrative. It has been given little attention in the study of early Christianity and is thus worth examining in its own right. In the context of Gregory and Theodoret, it gives the historian an indication of how the beauty of God's providence was understood by educated Christian bishops, and their less educated communities of followers. I will argue that the notion of Beauty in the ancient world is translatable in terms of order and symmetry to the Byzantine context—particularly in the works of Gregory of Nazianzus. Utilizing Gregory and Theodoret of Cyrrhus, I will show that there were two possible scenarios available to the late ancient mind: immediate comeuppance and otherworldly comeuppance. Both had their place and both contributed to the Byzantine notion of a beautifully ordered cosmos.

---

[436] For a comprehensive perspective on the intricacies of this political fallout, see JA. McGuckin, *St. Gregory of Nazianzus: An Intellectual Biography*. St. Vladimir's Seminary Press. Crestwood. NY. 2001. 229–370.

[437] Here I would point toward Gregory's Episcopal homilies as well as his influential *Theological Orations*. Theodoret is best known for his *History of the Monks of Syria* (tr. R.M. Price. Cistercian Publications. Kalamazoo. 1985) and also for his *Church History*. (P. Schaff & H. Wace. (edd). *Nicene and Post Nicene Fathers*. vol. 3. New York. 1892).

Comeuppance can be loosely structured by terms of revenge or vengeance; or, alternatively, disconnected from any particular actor. Revenge requires an actor, comeuppance can simply be rendered by someone 'getting their due.' If one adds in the element of divine judgment, the notion changes slightly. It may be that God acts through or alongside his favored person or people to right some situation. It may also be the case that God acts on his own to effect some desired outcome. I have chosen this term precisely because it works well with the notion of 'righting.' As will be seen in the coming examples, various situations merit divine correction in the religious thought-world of Late Antiquity.

There are numerous examples of comeuppance in the ancient world's literature. It seems, therefore, that this theme was dear also to the heart of the ancient hearer. Perhaps most famously, this theme is deeply embedded in the ancient epics of Homer.[438] If we consider Athene's revenge on Penelope's suitors who were Odysseus's antagonists, we see a clear picture of comeuppance. As you will recall, the suitors were eating up Odysseus's wealth while trying to win his wife's hand. In the end Athene steps in to help Odysseus orchestrate the murder of all 108 suitors, as well as 12 household maids who had betrayed Penelope. It is difficult to separate Athene's will from Odysseus's hand; they act in concert to serve comeuppance.

Moving forward to a genre equally influential on early Christian thinkers, one locates the theme of comeuppance in the Hebrew Scriptures. In the story of Elisha, one reads, 'He went up from there to Bethel; and while he was going up on the way, some small boys came out of the city and jeered at him, saying, 'Go away, baldhead! Go away, baldhead!' When he turned around and saw them, he cursed them in the name of the Lord. Then two she-bears came out of the woods and mauled forty-two of the boys.'[439] This remarkably violent story of Elisha is an excellent example of comeuppance. It is fascinating for the unequal

---

[438] On Gregory's profound knowledge of Homer, see McGuckin. 2001. 44.
[439] NRSV, 2 Kings 2.23-24.

retribution it portrays and has forced countless of generations of readers to try to make sense of its gratuitous violence.[440] There doesn't appear to be any reason for Elisha's revenge, other than a simple name-calling. With this in mind, we start to see a theme developing in this literature. One must not cross the holy man, for it is tantamount to crossing the almighty God in heaven. Examples in Hebrew Scripture are manifold, but it will help to show some New Testament examples that are closer to our context.

Perhaps the most closely related to our theme is the story of Ananias and Sapphira. This narrative of the prototypical Christian community gives us a clear indication of how judgment can be swift and irrevocable. The book of Acts relates:

> But a man named Ananias, with the consent of his wife Sapphira, sold a piece of property; with his wife's knowledge, he kept back some of the proceeds, and brought only a part and laid it at the apostles' feet. 'Ananias,' Peter asked, 'why has Satan filled your heart to lie to the Holy Spirit and to keep back part of the proceeds of the land? While it remained unsold, did it not remain your own? And after it was sold, were not the proceeds at your disposal? How is it that you have contrived this deed in your heart? You did not lie to us but to God!' Now when Ananias heard these words, he fell down and died. And great fear seized all who heard of it. The young men came and wrapped up his body, then carried him out and buried him. After an interval of about three hours his wife came in, not knowing what had happened. Peter said to her, 'Tell me whether you and your husband sold the land for such and such a price.' And she said, 'Yes, that was the price.' Then Peter said to her, 'How is it that you have agreed together to put the Spirit of the Lord to the test? Look, the feet of those who have buried your husband are at the door, and they will carry you out.' Immediately she fell down at his feet and died. When the young men came in they found her dead, so they carried her out and buried her beside her husband.

---

[440] On the subject of apology for overt violence, Theodoret takes the opportunity to try and explain the deaths of Ananias and Sapphira. See *History of the Monks of Syria* 1.9. Price. 1985. 16.

And great fear seized the whole church and all who heard of these things.[441]

The haunting line, 'you did not lie to us, but to God,' highlights the strangely liminal nature that the holy apostles and ascetics embodied in the late antique world. They were proxies or representatives of God and wielded a similarly charged power of God within the cosmos. With these examples of comeuppance in mind, one can begin to think about how a properly ordered world might look in antiquity as well as in our Byzantine context.

Beauty in the ancient world

One can find the term 'beauty' carefully considered in a large number of Platonic works. Several of the well-known dialogues, including *the Symposium, the Republic, Phaedrus* and even *Timaeus* deal with beauty as an important notion in understanding the highest aspects of wisdom.[442] Beauty is held up as an ultimate virtue next to love, knowledge and excellence. The Platonic form of beauty was something that was naturally imbued with order and symmetry. Any type of disorder or deformity was considered a disjunction between the entity and the excellence of god.[443]

Plato's *Timaeus* (*30b*)supports the idea that the world is beautiful because it was created by god. The text relates:

> What is perfectly good can accomplish only what is perfectly beautiful; this was and is a universal law. So the god took thought and concluded that, generally speaking, nothing he made that lacked intelligence could ever be more beautiful than an intelligent product, and that nothing can have intelligence unless it has soul. And the upshot of this thinking was that he constructed the universe by endowing soul with intelligence and body with soul, so that it was in the very nature of the universe to surpass all other products in beauty

---

[441] NRSV, Acts 5. 1-11

[442] There are many more, but these instances serve as a solid foundation for later Neo-Platonic influence.

[443] Divinity in Platonic thought is a somewhat fluid concept. When I refer to 'god' here I am referencing the *demiurge* or the highest creative being in Platonism.

and perfection. This is the likely account, and it follows that we're bound to think that this world of ours was made in truth by god as a living being, endowed thanks to his providence with soul and intelligence.[444]

Because the god is perfectly good, in Plato's scheme, he is only capable of creating beauty. This worldview that readily accepts creation and the natural structure of the cosmos as a beautiful and balanced entity was highly influential on later Eastern Christian thought.[445]

As Plato describes how the world was fashioned, he readily embraces geometry as a telling aspect of how the *Kosmos*[446] was ordered. Arguing that there is beauty in particular shapes, such as the particular scalene triangle, which in the combination with itself forms a perfect equilateral triangle. These arguments from geometry to positions about the nature of beauty and creation sound strange to the modern reader, but they begin to show the emphasis that Platonic thought laid on symmetry within creation.[447]

---

[444] R Waterfield (tr.) *Plato, Timaeus and Critias*. OUP. Oxford. 2008.

[445] Here I distinguish between the East and the eventual turn—in the West—toward a theology of sin as the predominant descriptor of an ugly and fallen creation. These, of course, are not straightforward categories.

[446] The very word means 'beautiful'.

[447] *Timaeus* states, 'We have to decide, then, which are the most beautiful bodies that can be created. There should be four of them, and they must be dissimilar to one another, but capable (in some cases) of arising out of one another's disintegration. If we succeed at this task, we'll know the truth about the generation of earth, fire, and the bodies that act as proportionate means between these two extremes. For we will never agree with anyone who claims that there are or could be more perfect visible bodies than these four, each after its own kind. So we should do our best to construct our four substances, each of outstanding beauty, and to reach a position where we can claim to have adequately understood what they are like. Of our two triangles, the isosceles one is essentially single, whereas there's an infinite number of right-angled scalene triangles. What we have to do, then, if we're to start properly, is select the most beautiful of this infinite plurality of scalene triangles. If anyone can demonstrate that his choice creates more beautiful structures, we'll welcome our defeat, not resent it. But until then our position is that there is one that is the most beautiful, and surpasses all other scalene triangles, and that is the one which is a const-

For the Platonists, creation was a chaotic mess that needed order imposed upon it. The initial elements were in need of structure and this structure naturally came from god. Timaeus explains to Socrates:

> To repeat, then, one of my original assertions, the god found the four bodies we've been talking about in a chaotic state and made each of them compatible with itself and with the others, in as many ways and respects as they could be proportionate and compatible. For at that time none of them had its characteristics, except by chance, and in fact none of them had the slightest right to be called by the names that are now used of it and the others—'fire', 'water', and so on. So he first imposed order on them all, and then he created this universe of ours out of them, as a single living being containing within itself all living beings, both mortal and immortal. He himself was the craftsman and creator of the divine beings, and he gave his own offspring the job of creating mortal beings. In imitation of their father, once they had received from him the immortal seed of soul, they proceeded to fashion a mortal body in which to enclose it, and to assign the whole body to be its vehicle.[448]

One can envision this Platonic notion of god as a craftsman (*demiourgos*) and harmonizer, a god that creates order from chaos. Whether or not god acts to organize everyday life in such a manner, the imposed basal structure god provides pokes through the fabric of creation, allowing one to glimpse the divine hand.

---

ituent of the equilateral triangle, with two triangles making the equilateral one as a third. It would take rather a long time to explain why, but if anyone challenges our claim and finds that we were wrong, we won't resent his victory. So these are our choices for the two triangles from which the bodies of fire and the rest were constructed—the isosceles, and the one whose essential property is that the square of the longer side is triple the square of the shorter side.' *Timaeus* 53e–54b.

[448] *Timaeus.* 69b–c.

Gregory of Nazianzus

Gregory of Nazianzus was a consummate theologian. He was classically trained—as many prominent Christian theologians were in that age—and was able to incorporate his knowledge of rhetoric and philosophy into his writings. While a prominent churchman, Gregory was also no stranger to the ascetic life—whether through direct participation or connection to the ascetics that surrounded the countryside of Nazianzus. He was known simply as 'The Theologian' to later generations, and was well regarded for his style in poetry and prose. Gregory can be seen to maintain rules of rhetorical style even in his *Funeral Oration for his Sister Gorgonia*. He explains, 'We have omitted most of the details in order to keep some due proportion in our discourse, and not to seem greedy for her praise.'[449] Brian Daley comments in a footnote to this translation of Gregory's orations that, 'As in the traditional conception of virtue, so in the ideals of rhetorical style, proportion and self-restraint were considered by the Greeks to be the key to excellence and beauty.'[450] Gregory embodied these considerations of rhetorical style in his nearly 17,000 lines of poetry.[451]

Gregory's connection to the Platonic worldview is well documented in his use of Plotinus as well as a range of other classical thinkers.[452] This crafting of his intellectual heritage took place when he studied in Athens, prior to his work as priest and bishop. While Gregory utilized the notion of order in his rhetorical style, he also incorporated it into his own theology. His

---

[449] Cited in B. Daley, *Gregory of Nazianzus*. Routledge. Abingdon. 2006. 8.19.
[450] Daley. 2006. 214, fn. 60.
[451] Daley. 2006. 1.
[452] John Whittaker, 'Proclus, Procopius, Psellus and the Scholia on Gregory Nazianzen,' *Vigiliae Christianae* 29. No. 4. December. 1975. 309–313. On his classical influence McGuckin states: 'The explicit references in Gregory's writings to the classical authors are wide ranging and impressive. Anaxilas, Apollonios of Rhodes, Aratos, and other poets of the Palatine anthology, Aristophanes, Aristotle, Callimachos, Demosthenes, Diogenes Laertios, Evagoras, Heraclitus, Herodotus, Hesiod, Homer, Isocrates, Lucian, Lysias, Philo, Phocylides, Pindar, Plato, Plutarch, Sappho, Simonides, Socrates, Theocritos, Theognis, and Thucydides.' McGuckin. 2001.57.

is a theology that is deeply connected to order and comeuppance. In *Oration Fourteen*, Gregory states:

> The events of this present life are of a different form and have a different moral purpose, although all lead in the same direction; surely what seems to be unfair to us has its fairness in the plan of God, just as in the physical world there are prominent and lowly features, large and small details, ridges and valleys, by which the beauty of the whole comes into visible existence in their relationship to each other.[453]

For Gregory, God would ultimately be the judge of what is fair and what is unfair. Like the prominent hills in comparison to the lowly valleys, so too, are humans raised to points of prominence while others struggle below. In a great example, Gregory's own political trajectory would be impeded for reasons that he could not or would not comprehend.

As with most great theologians of the early church, there was little outward recognition of any internal struggle over one's position on given issues. The rhetorician is always a wise master, rarely a doubtful seeker. Accordingly, truth claims are usually absolutes in ancient religious literature and responses to opponents were often accompanied by vitriol and violence.[454] If one did not succeed in persuading a broader group of bishops about one's claims, then the recourse naturally fell to God. One hears a familiar tone in this *Oration (14) on the Love of the Poor* to Gregory's future struggle in his deposition from the seat of Archbishop. His penchant for poetry allows a more introspective look at his feelings about what had transpired in Constantinople before and after the council of 381. Gregory shows 'a high degree of self-examination of all that had gone on in the turbulent time of his administration' and felt

---

453 Daley. 2006. 14.31.
454 One of the more violent examples came during the Easter Vigil services of 380. 'A concerted attack was made on the Anastasia [Church]....a crowd of monks and nuns from the city together with assorted troublemakers forced their way into the house Church. They let fly a hail of stones.' McGuckin. 2001. 257.

he had 'nothing to reproach himself for under the eyes of Christ.'[455]

Gregory could see the struggle in his own life (ascetic/political/familial/personal) as perfectly aligned with the disordered world of which God alone could make sense. He explains:

It is, after all, very much within the skill of the Craftsman (*demiourgos*) if he should adapt the occasional disorder and unevenness of the material realm to achieve the purpose of his creation; and this will be grasped and acknowledged by all of us, when we contemplate the final, perfect beauty of what he has created. But he is never lacking in the skill of his art, as we are, nor is this world ruled by disorder, even when the principle by which it is ordered is not apparent to us.[456]

For Gregory, human eyes were simply incapable of grasping the true beauty of what God was accomplishing in the world. If something looked out of alignment, it was only because it was not being seen for its true purpose. The 'final, perfect beauty' will be grasped by all, but only after the confused order of the world is translated by a grander perspective. He continues:

Recognize the source of your being, your breath, your power of thought, and (greatest of all), your power to know God and to hope for the Kingdom of Heaven, for equality with the angels, for the vision of glory — which now you have only 'in a mirror and in riddles,' but which someday will be more perfect and pure — for the chance to become a child of God, a fellow-heir with Christ, even (I make bold to say) to become yourself divine. From where do all these gifts come — and from whom? Just to mention the small and obvious things: who gives you the ability to look on the beauty of heaven, the course of the sun, the cycle of the moon, the multitude of stars, and the harmony and order that rules in all these things as in a lyre, always remaining the same? To witness the passing of the hours, the changes of season, the turning of years, the equal

---

[455] McGuckin. 2001. 372.
[456] Daley. 2006. 14.31.

measures of day and night; the products of the earth, the abundance of the atmosphere, the breadth of the sea as it constantly flows yet remains, the depths of the rivers, the blowing of the winds?[457]

Of particular interest is Gregory's acknowledgment that the beauty of heaven is associated with the 'course of the sun' and 'the cycle of the moon.' These correlate to the harmony and order that rules 'as in a lyre.' He connects the regular patterns of his early Platonic training to the natural world. The lyre, with its measured vibrations, accompanies the image relating the order of harmony with the order of the universe. For Gregory, the physical, social and spiritual worlds rest in a careful—though not always apparent—balance adjudicated by God.

In his *Evening Hymn*, Gregory touches on the beauty that God creates out of his ordering of matter. The passage is reminiscent of Timaeus's lines quoted above:[458]

> We bless you now, at twilight,
> My Christ, God's Word, God's brightness
> From light that knows no dawning,
> And steward of the Spirit—
> Your threefold radiance woven
> Into one strand of glory!
> You have abolished darkness,
> Forming, on light's foundation,
> A world that light embraces,
> Shaping unstable matter
> Into a stable order—
> This beauty that delights us.[459]

Beauty is a natural outcome of properly ordered nature. When God sets his hand to correcting the surging elements that make life unappealing, humans can witness the true beauty of order in

---

[457] Daley. 2006. 14.23.
[458] Plato. *Timaeus*. 69b–c.
[459] Daley. 2006. 167.

the cosmos. This concept of divinely ordered correction is also deeply influential on the hagiographers of the early Byzantine world.

Comeuppance in Hagiography

Theodoret of Cyrrhus, writer of the *History of the Monks of Syria* or the *Religious History (Ascetic Life)*, examines the ascetic life in terms of order and harmony. He explains, 'Although the (*demonic*) enemies have an invisible nature, they could not master a visible body subject to the necessities of nature; for its charioteer and musician and helmsman by holding the reins well induced the horses to run in proper order, by striking the strings of the senses in rhythm made them produce sound that was perfectly harmonious, and by moving the rudder skillfully put an end to the blows of the billows and the blast of the winds.'[460] Like the divine craftsman who orders the elements of the world, the ascetic orders his own internal elements, aligning them to avoid discord. The image of turning one's rudder in order to sail with the wind supports Theodoret's argument that the visible body only struggles when it goes against the natural harmonies created by God. This beauty of internal harmony in the ascetic life, he argues, is often besieged by worldly circumstances that require the ascetic to engage with disordered humanity. Using Theodoret's image one could envision the ascetic sailing with the wind in the midst of many misdirected and struggling ships fighting against the wind. And yet, the order so intrinsic to the ascetic life had the possibility of quickly becoming compromised.

Comeuppance is a prevalent theme in early Byzantine hagiography. In many instances, it is the very reason a text is called hagiographical. By claiming God's action through or in conjunction with the holy person, literature that would have otherwise been considered historical narrative is diverted into the hagiographical category. In every instance of comeuppance there is an interesting, and, at times uneasy, conflation of God's power with human concerns. Both work together to harmonize and order human existence.

---

[460] Theodoret. *A History of the Monks of Syria.* 6.

A primary example of comeuppance and its relation to cosmic order comes from Theodoret's treatment of James of Nisibis. James is perhaps best known as the saint who beseeched God to 'grant what would benefit the churches,' regarding the great heretic, Arius. James brings about Arius's death through prayer.[461] Theodoret explains in a very famous narrative:

> While in a disgusting and stinking place that wretch was evacuating the refuse from his gluttony, he evacuated its receptacle as well; so with his inwards dissolved and ejected along with his excrement, the miserable creature instantly breathed his last and underwent this most shameful death; called to answer for his stinking blasphemy in a stinking place and slain by the tongue of the great James.[462]

In this remarkable example of comeuppance, Arius receives a fitting punishment for his crimes against the church. Theodoret offers well-crafted wordplay with his retelling of the story, comparing Arius's teaching itself to excrement.

In his section on Sapor, Theodoret similarly explores the possibility of engaging in punishment of the outsider while leaving the door open to future conversion. The text tells of Sapor, the third century Sassanian king, and his interest in sacking the city of Nisibis. Theodoret proceeds to tell the story as if it were ultimately a showdown between the Christian holy man James and the pagan Sapor. Faced with the onslaught of elephants and eventually a river redirected against the city walls, James takes action. When 'they all begged the man of God to appear on the wall and rain down curses on the enemy; he agreed and went up, and seeing the innumerable host besought God to send on them a cloud of gnats and mosquitoes.'[463] This of course sent the animals running in all directions and caused enough confusion to inhibit the attack. Theodoret explains in the next section:

---

461 *History of the Monks of Syria.* 17.
462 *History of the Monks of Syria.* 17–18.
463 *History of the Monks of Syria.* 1.11.

I myself, in addition to this, am also filled with admiration at the way James, when applying a curse, did not ask for the introduction of thunderbolts and lightning, as the great Elijah did when each of the commanders of fifties came to him with his fifty....Therefore he did not ask for the earth to gape under them nor did he call for the army to be consumed with fire, but rather that it be wounded by those tiny creatures and, recognizing the power of God, at some later date learn piety.[464]

What does this passage tell us about beauty in the ancient world? I would begin by pointing out Theodoret's tone in the passage. His is not the concerned tone of one who feared the demise of his God. He acknowledges that ultimately God is capable of maintaining a symmetry of justice that surpasses his own immediate historical perspective. Did Sapor deserve death? Perhaps, but it was not something that Theodoret felt he could question. From his perspective, it was not necessary to kill Sapor because a greater plan was undoubtedly at work.

In another section of his work, Theodoret tells the story of James of Nisibis being duped by a group of fraudulent mourners. Asking for money to bury their friend, James helps them by praying for the man's soul and asking God to count him worthy of the choir of the righteous. At his prayer, the man's soul then left his body, effecting death. When his friends realized he was dead they quickly returned to James explaining the situation and begging for forgiveness. James responds by restoring the man to life. In his commentary, Theodoret relates this deception to the story of Ananias and Sapphira in Acts 5. He has no problem relating the power of the apostle to the power of James, but has to account for the implacable harshness of the apostle, since James graciously brought the man back to life. About this he explains, 'while the divine Apostle did not release the dead from their misfortune—for terror was needed in the first stage of proclaiming salvation— James, who was full of the grace of an Apostle, both applied chastisement as the occasion demanded and

---

[464] *History of the Monks of Syria.* 1.13.

then swiftly revoked it, since he knew this was what would benefit the wrongdoers.' [465] In this 'economic' manner Theodoret justifies the harshness of the Apostle vis-à-vis the mild actions of the saint.

On another occasion, we are told, James is traveling in Persia, the frontier empire which abutted the Roman empire near Nisibis, when he came upon some girls who were washing their clothes in a stream near a spring. Rather than reflect modesty, the girls stared at James 'with brazen looks and eyes dead to shame,' and refused to let down their tucked-up clothing as the holy man passed.[466] James, the consummate educator, sees this as an opportunity to correct. Rather than lecturing the young women about modesty, he decides to 'display God's power opportunely' through a miracle.[467] He curses the spring, which dries up the stream and then proceeds to curse the girls with premature grey hair. The girls, who now looked like 'young trees decked in spring with leaves of autumn,' ran into town to tell of the situation.[468] The townspeople beg James to reverse the sentence and he agrees, returning the spring to working order. When the girls do not return, however, 'he let the punishment stand, as a lesson in self-control, a reason for good behavior, and a perpetual and clear reminder of the power of God.'[469]

Theodoret takes the opportunity of James's encounter with the girls to examine the possibility that the holy man could have been harsher in his judgment. He reminds the reader of Elisha and the bears in 2 Kings 2:24, and states that by 'applying a harmless correction that involved only a slight disfigurement he gave them a lesson in both piety and good behavior....while possessing the same power [of Elisha], he performed what accorded with the gentleness of Christ and the new covenant.'[470] God's power to

---

[465] *History of the Monks of Syria*. 1.9.
[466] *History of the Monks of Syria*. 1.4.
[467] *History of the Monks of Syria*. 1.4.
[468] *History of the Monks of Syria*. 1.4.
[469] *History of the Monks of Syria*. 1.4.
[470] *History of the Monks of Syria*. 1.5.

correct and order social interactions is accessed and deployed easily from his holy man, James.

There are numerous stories in the Byzantine hagiographies — indeed far too numerous to list here—of holy men engaging in raw retributive actions against those who cross them or the God they serve. I have chosen these passages about James of Nisibis precisely because they are so nuanced.[471] Substituted for the harsh judgment the ancient reader expected to (wants to?) hear, is the tender pastoral care for a 'could be' Christian soul that God may indeed see fit to conquer one day. Although the stories of immediate retribution, seen in James of Nisibis's own action praying for the 'solution' to the problem of Arius, indicate the theme of symmetry and a return to order, so do the less harsh examples of James and Sapor or James and the deceiving mourners.

Neil McLynn has noted that Gregory's treatment of life's inequalities has a different feel than Theodoret's vignettes of holy men. McLynn explains, 'Gregory's first person perspective creates one obvious difference between *de vita sua* and Theodoret's biographies. The humiliating defeats which Gregory describes, where his persecutors 'caw in triumph' over him (*De vita sua*. 1926), seem very different from Theodoret's studies of 'power in action.' However, Gregory was not conceding real defeat: like any other 'athlete of Christ' he knew that his competition would not be won in this world.'[472] McLynn is right that Theodoret's examples deal

---

[471] Many hagiographical stories show a less forgiving power-wielding structure. Theodoret mentions several retributive acts in his *History of the Monks of Syria*. In the story of Aphrahat (*History of the Monks of Syria*. 8.10), his persecutor jumped into a pool of boiling water thinking that it was a bath of mixed water ready for his bathing. The moral comes through clearly in Theodoret, 'As a result fear fell on the emperor and on all those in arms against piety; the story echoed throughout the city of how that wretch had paid the penalty for his insolence against Aphrahat, and all continued to hymn the God of Aphrahat.' Aphrahat was a subject of Sapor II in Persia, and of Constantius II after 360 when he moved to Antioch. He had to contend first against Sapor's fear of pro-Roman Christians in his territory and, after 360, of anti-Nicene sentiment in Antioch.

[472] Neil B. McLynn, 'A Self-Made Holy Man: The Case of Gregory Nazianzen,' *Journal of Early Christian Studies* 6. no. 3. 1998. 464.

largely in immediacy while Gregory languishes.[473] I would nuance it slightly, however, given the example of James of Nisibis. He does not see the need to condemn the enemy in every circumstance. Theodoret allows that some things, including the possible conversion of a ruler like Sapor, could wait on God's final imprint on the situation. We should also acknowledge here that Theodoret had certain facts to deal with in his narrative. If James had been able to kill Sapor as a result of his prayers, Theodoret would surely have swung the commentary to match.

It is possible to draw a direct line from the Platonic notion of beauty as constituted by order straight through to Gregory. Whether the claim can be extrapolated to other early byzantine writers such as Theodoret is a moot question. One can be sure that the proper ordering of the natural world and, more importantly, the interactive personal world of the Christian, was something that was deeply connected to the concept of beauty. As the example of Gregory makes clear, comeuppance was something that was not always immediate but was always a sure eventual prospect. God's extra-temporal perspective could be counted on to correct for any earthly inequalities, rendering beauty from imbalance. Theodoret's examples of holy persons rectifying worldly situations that had fallen out of balance with God's plan show an attention to the details of how God could be counted on to restore beauty to his creation. This was certainly a theological update to a Christianity which had moved past the days of martyrdom and

---

[473] 'The enemies who 'nodded and whispered' (*Carm.* 2.1.1. 548) at Gregory will not have been his brother's creditors, but resentful sceptics at home who relished the humbling of the aspirant holy man's spiritual pride (*Carm.* 2.1.1 561). In reply, Gregory raised the stakes dramatically, outdoing any criticism that can conceivably have been voiced against him with a lurid picture of himself, wallowing miserably in slime 'or below the earth, in a yawning pit' (*Carm.* 2.1.1. 501-2); after which he swiftly forgets his avowed renunciation of self-righteousness and proceeds (in a development which recalls *Oration* 2) to confess the pain in his heart when he contemplated wicked men who were thought to be good, those lying sepulchres who 'reek inside of putrid corpses, while gleaming outside with whitewash and charming colors . . .' (*Carm.* 2.1.1. 513-17). Gregory cuts down both himself and his enemies to their proper size, trembling beneath the 'great eye' which saw into their minds, and before the prospect of the 'purifying fire' that would judge their deeds.' See McLynn. 1998. 471-2.

maltreatment but had yet to show how it could function as the religion of late antiquity *par excellence*. For that, it would need to show that it could explain and maintain cosmic order, in ways comparable to the avenging fates of the old gods of Rome, and could secure the victories that the old gods had repeatedly shown possible to pagan eyes.[474] Hagiography was the Christian vehicle of choice for such an endeavor.

Does this answer our question as to whether one can create a theology of beauty that is contingent on comeuppance. The literature of Hagiography would say so. Either every ancient monk and common person was greatly interested in vengeance, or the theme of comeuppance played a more influential role in the theology of the cosmos. If every wrong action was sure to meet its due, if every unfair situation was sure to be righted, then all was balanced in the world. God was truly in control and the *Kosmos* was beautiful by being in a perfectly symmetrical state. For the Byzantine Christians these stories were living proof that their world had meaning and that the random actions of the evil ones would only manifest themselves as disorder until such time as God was ready to order them according to his will. Disorder, chaos and injustice would only rattle out of tune for so long, until harmonizing providence would inevitably press them into beautiful symmetrical tones.

---

[474] The pagan religions of Rome and Christianity were long in uneasy competition. One is reminded of the struggle for divine authority on the battlefield of Diocletian when the *haruspices* are unable to find the proper markings on the livers of the sacrificed animals. PS. Davies, 'The Origin and Purpose of the Persecution of AD 303.' *Journal of Theological Studies*. 40. no. 1. 1989. 78–79.

The Beautiful Bishop: Physiognomy and Holiness in the *Life of St. Eutychius of Constantinople*

Nicholas Marinides

A well-known anecdote from *The Sayings of the Desert Fathers* recounts the importance of the sense of sight for appreciation of holiness: [475]

> Three Fathers used to go and visit blessed Anthony every year and two of them used to discuss their thoughts and the salvation of their souls with him, but the third always remained silent and did not ask him anything. After a long time, Abba Anthony said to him, 'You often come here to see me, but you never ask me anything,' and the other replied, 'It is enough for me to see you, Father.'[476]

This vignette from the *Sayings* captures a deep-seated intuition of the spiritual life.[477] We feel that it expresses our own experience of meeting living holy men or women, or even of the contemplation of an icon of a venerable ascetic painted by a great master such as Manuel Panselinos or Andrei Rublev.

---

[475] In relation to the growing field of historical studies treating the senses, a concise introduction is given by: M. Jay. 'In the Realm of the Senses: An Introduction.' *American Historical Review*. 116.2. April 2011. 307–15. The major study of the importance of sight for appreciation of Christian holiness in Late Antiquity, primarily in the Egyptian monastic dossier, is that of: G. Frank. *The Memory of the Eyes: Pilgrims to Living Saints in Christian Late Antiquity*. University of California Press. Berkeley. 2000. For a more focused study of certain key concepts in this area, see: T.M. Shaw. '*Askesis* and the Appearance of Holiness.' *Journal of Early Christian Studies* 6.3. Fall 1998. 485–99. A necessary background for any discussion to do with the body in Christian thought is, of course: P. Brown, *Body and Society: Men, Women, and Sexual Renunciation in Early Christianity*. Columbia University Press. New York. 1988.

[476] *Apophthegmata Patrum*. Alphabetical Collection. 'Anthony'. 27. (PG. 65.83). Tr. B. Ward. *The Sayings of the Desert Fathers: The Alphabetical Collection*. Cistercian Publications. Kalamazoo. 1984. 7.

[477] Cf. Palladius of Helenopolis. *Lausiac History*. Preface. 15–16. (excerpted in Paul of Evergetis. *Evergetinon*. 1.18.1).

As we might perhaps expect from literature of the *Sayings* genre, the exact nature and significance of the gaze of St. Anthony's visitor is not elaborated. But it is part of long-held beliefs regarding physical appearance as an indicator of moral or spiritual qualities, in both the Judeo-Christian and Greco-Roman traditions. One of the most succinct summaries of this view is found in the Wisdom of Sirach: 'From appearance a man will be recognized, and from a meeting in person a rational person will be recognized. A man's clothing and a laughter of teeth and a person's gait will announce things about him.'[478] Physical appearance here consists of both the appearance of a man's face and his comportment in normal daily activities. This Scriptural passage does not specify whether it refers to any natural features of the face or simply to habitual expressions and behaviors. But then again, Greco-Roman theorists of the supposed-science of physiognomy, such as the anonymous author of the pseudo-Aristotelian *Physiognomica*, who was writing around 300 B.C., and the second-century A.D. sophist Polemon, did not clearly distinguish between such cases of nature or nurture.[479]

Of course such theories had many detractors, both then and in more recent times. Apart from the scientific questionability of their hypotheses, there is a fundamental philosophical and spiritual objection to equating outward appearance with inner quality. The amusing description of Socrates by Alcibiades in Plato's *Sym-*

---

[478] Sir. 19:29–30 (19:26–27 in some versions). Here I quote the intentionally literal NETS rendition of the text.

[479] For the Greco-Roman physiognomic tradition, see especially E.C. Evans, *Physiognomics in the Ancient World*. American Philosophical Society. Philadelphia. 1969; M. Gleason, *Making Men: Sophists and Self-Presentation in Ancient Rome*. Princeton University Press. Princeton. 1995; and the first three chapters in S. Swain (ed). *Seeing the Face, Seeing the Soul: Polemon's Physiognomy from Classical Antiquity to Medieval Islam*. OUP. Oxford. 2007. The first chapter in this work, by G. Boys-Stones, 'Physiognomy and Ancient Psychological Theory,' 19–124, draws careful distinctions between full-fledged physiognomy in a philosophical key (defined primarily by the idea that physical traits reflect one's *innate* and relatively unchangeable nature) and other, looser, applications of the term. This latter looseness reflects the difficulty of pinning down physiognomy. As Gleason notes (1985.55-58), traits that were supposed to be innate in fact were made and maintained by obsessive self-discipline and self-cultivation.

posium, as a Silenus statue that is ugly on the outside but full of beautiful wise thoughts on the inside, is a classic instance of this objection, and has been expressed in stone and metal by countless Greek and Roman sculptors.[480] This is paralleled by the Christian emphasis on the prophet Isaiah's description of the Suffering Servant of the Lord as being having 'no form nor comeliness,' as well as by St. Paul's testimony that 'we do not look at the things which are seen, but at the things which are not seen.'[481] These seem to point to a definitive rejection of physical appearance as a marker of spiritual beauty. To these ancient testimonies we might add a certain contemporary reaction against the excesses of the cult of the idol of sexual beauty in our own times, a reaction that would seek to emphasize that true beauty is within.

But as the anecdote about St. Anthony mentioned at the beginning suggests, it is not all so simple.[482] Even in the *Symposium*, which ends by emphasizing philosophical comeliness, this only comes at the end of a long development of the idea that physical beauty can serve as a stepping-stone to contemplation of eternal ideal Beauty. And the Christian tradition of course must deal seriously with testimony of Scripture such as that quoted above from Sirach.[483]

---

[480] *Symposium* 215b, 221d-222a; for the statuary, see P. Zanker, *The Mask of Socrates: The Image of the Intellectual in Antiquity*. University of California Press: Berkeley. 1995.

[481] Is. 53.2 and 2 Cor. 4.18. For an early Christian tradition claiming that Jesus was ugly, based on the Isaiah passage and others, see G. Dagron. 'Holy Images and Likeness.' *Dumbarton Oaks Papers* 45. 1991. 23–33 (esp. 28).

[482] In addition to the *Apophthegmata*, the *Life of St. Anthony* mentions the effect of Anthony's appearance several times: c.f. Athanasius of Alexandria, *Vita Antonii* 67.4–8 (NPNF Series 2, Volume 4, 214): 'And besides, his countenance had a great and wonderful grace ...' The passage cites several scriptural examples of revelation through the countenance for support (Prov. 15.13, Gen. 31.5, 1 Sam. 16.12). See also *Vita Antonii* 72.3 (NPNF 2. 4. 215), where, according to the English translation, when two pagan philosophers visited Anthony he 'recognised who they were from their appearance (*ek tou prosōpou suneis tous anthrōpous*)'; presumably the standard philosophic garb and cut of the hair and beard would have assisted such an identification, but perhaps a more physiognomic recognition is implied.

[483] One could add 1 Sam. 16.12, cited in the *Life of St. Anthony*, which refers to David's youthful beauty. But the entire episode (1 Sam. 16:6-13) is ambiguous, turning as it does on God showing Samuel that he looks not at the appearance or

This is especially so because Christianity repudiates the soul-body dualism of Platonic philosophy by its affirmation of the goodness of matter as a creation of God, and its redemption and glorification in the Resurrection of Christ, eventually affecting all humanity.[484] Ascetical and psychological considerations have also played a part in patristic reflection. Thus Basil of Ancyra, glossing the passage from Sirach, states:

> For because the souls which are in bodies are unable to converse nakedly (*gymnōs*) with each other concerning virtue, they use their bodies that cover them like instruments, by means of voice and look. And one who is unable to see the beauty of the soul walled up inside the body, or hear it by means of reason, sees the movements of the body in which it exists, and listening to the voice through this (body), analogously assesses its beauty by these. And it is not only the voice or even the look that displays the image of the soul as if in a mirror; but even a man's dress and laugh and gait testify concerning it.[485]

This passage, from a treatise *On Virginity*, might serve as a more sophisticated exposition of the idea underlying the silent monk's encounter with Abba Anthony. It explains the deep-seated need to pin our hopes and longings for holiness on some tangible, or at least visible, person. But always lurking in the shadows is the possibility that looks may deceive. In fact the text we cited from Sirach is immediately preceded by a warning to be on guard against the false mourning of hypocrites.[486] This insight was also equally used by several ancient authors to attack philosophical or theological opponents who, they claimed, put on a show of piety

---

stature of a man, but at his heart. Nevertheless, David's beauty is noticeably remarked upon, perhaps as an outward manifestation of his guileless goodness.

[484] Although even the Platonic tradition included a world-affirming side, expressed most clearly in the *Timaeus*. See J.M. Dillon. 'Rejecting the Body, Refining the Body: Some Remarks on the Development of Platonist Asceticism,' in *Asceticism*, (edd). V.L. Wimbush and R. Valantasis. OUP. Oxford.1998. 80–87.

[485] Basil of Ancyra, *De virginitate* 36. PG. 30. 741A-B; quoted in Shaw 1998. 490–91.

[486] Sir. 19.26–28.

and visible holiness but were in reality wolves in sheep's clothing.[487]

This seems to leave us at an impasse. But I would like to attempt to go some of the way toward a nuanced solution by reflecting on a relatively little-known text, the *Life of Eutychius of Constantinople*, a sixth-century patriarch, by his disciple Eustratius the Presbyter.[488] The genre of hagiography allows us to glimpse the issue from another perspective, than that of the two sources we have already considered. The kind of treatise written by Basil of Ancyra might reflect at length on appearance, but usually in an abstract and prescriptive manner. On the other hand, the comments on the venerable appearance of an ascetic in the *Sayings* tend to be too laconic. Even when certain details are given — as they often are in similar stories found in the *Historia monachorum in Aegypto* or Palladius' *Lausiac History* — they tend to be reduced to shorthand

---

[487] Cf. Shaw. 1998. 494–99.

[488] *Clavis Patrum Graecorum* 7520 (BHG 657). The modern critical edition is *Vita Eutychii Patriarchae Constantinopolitani*, ed. C. Laga, CCSG 25. Brepols. Turnhout, 1992. Further on Eutychius, see: A. Kazhdan, 'Eutychios,' in *The Oxford Dictionary of Byzantium*, 2.759. In the primary sources, for a friendly but more neutral view of Eutychius than the *Life*, see Evagrius Scholasticus, *Ecclesiastical History* 4.38, 5.16, & 5.18; and for a very hostile view, partially driven by the author's own sufferings as a Monophysite under Eutychius's Patriarchal administration, see John of Ephesus, *Ecclesiastical History* 2.31–40, 2.51–52, & 3.15–22. On the author Eustratius himself, see H G. Beck, *Kirche und theologische Literatur im byzantinischen Reich*, Handbuch der Altertumwissenschaft 2.1. Munich. 1959. 410–11 and the brief notice in the introduction to Eustratius the Presbyter, *De statu animarum post mortem*, ed. P. van Deun, CCSG 60. Brepols. Turnhout. 2006), IX-XI. The latter text (CPG 7522) is a polemical work arguing for the self-consciousness of souls after death and the effective presence and intercession of the souls of saints even before the resurrection. For an analysis see N. Constas, 'An Apology for the Cult of Saints in Late Antiquity: Eustratius Presbyter of Constantinople, *On the State of Souls after Death* (CPG 7522),' *Journal of Early Christian Studies* 10.2 . Summer 2002. 267–85. Eustratius also composed a *Passion of Golinduch*, a contemporary female Persian ascetic-martyr (CPG 7521; BHG 700-1). Only a few fragments by St. Eutychius himself are preserved: see *Clavis Patrum Graecorum* 6937–40 and PG. 86b:2390–2406. A quotation from a lost work by Eutychius *On rational and intellectual beings that are said to come to be as substances in 'place' in a secondary sense* (*Peri tous* [sic] *en topōi kata deuteron logon ousiōdōs ginomenōn logikōn kai noerōn*), is included by Eustratius in his treatise *On the State of Souls after Death* (*De statu animarum*. 1050–65).

formulas, evoking some Biblical figure by reference to isolated features (such as a majestically Aaronic beard).[489] But the *Life of Eutychius* contains two rather extensive reflections on physiognomy and comportment that could provide further insights on the question. Some difficulties with the text might give us pause at first. As a hagiographical text, and of encomiastic type at that, it requires a very critical reading. In addition, large sections of it are a tissue of quotations from older sources, especially the eulogies of St. Athanasius of Alexandria and St. Basil of Caesarea by St. Gregory Nazianzen, and the depiction of St. Macrina in Gregory of Nyssa's *Dialogue on the Soul and on Resurrection*. This debt is openly acknowledged several times by Eustratius.[490] Because of the nature of the text, certain scholars might be tempted to relegate it to the much-maligned category of Byzantine hagiographical clichés. But to anyone who reads it sympathetically it becomes clear that Eustratius is a master of the hagiographical genre. In his hands the older sources are reworked in an assured and elegant manner, contributing organically to his goal of portraying Eutychius as a worthy successor and equal to the great sainted bishops of the past. All this is enlivened by the author's own fervent admiration and love for his spiritual master. The combination of skillful handling of tradition and actual acquaintance with the subject make the text a challenging but potentially rewarding one. Its importance for the present study lies in the way that Eustratius, as hagiographer and theologian, expresses a certain spiritual appreciation of physical beauty.

The first passage on appearance emphasizes comportment, that is, conduct and bearing. It describes how Eutychius, a kind of 'golden boy' from a well-connected but pious family,[491] was dedicated early on to the Church and raised by his grandfather, a miracle-working local priest:

---

[489] Frank. 2000. 172–73.

[490] Especially at *Vita Eutychii* 2296-2319, 2760–70, 2795–2808.

[491] His father was a *scholarios* in the retinue of the great general Belisarius (*Vita Eutychii* 176–82).

And when he had completed the first age of growth, he was instructed by him in the tradition of literacy, but even more than this in ethos, in the gait of his walk, in dress, the manner of the soul, cheerfulness of countenance, and to put it simply, he was filled with all things that contribute to perfection.[492]

The passage is essentially a reworking of Sirach 19. But the context offers several clues to the historical reality underlying this ancient exercise in Hellenistic education. Just before, the author has recorded a reminiscence of Eutychius himself concerning his grandfather and how he had recommended to the boy that he return frequently to the font where he was baptized so as to kneel and pray for a good mind, to pray to learn his letters to and to excel over his companions.[493] Immediately afterward, Eustratius records that, as a child, Eutychius was playing at 'rulers and bishops' with his friends, and chose for himself the role of patriarch, carving the title with his name in the wall of the house where they were playing, where it was still to be seen when Eustratius wrote the *Life*. Both of these incidents bracketing the paraphrase of Sirach indicate that such a curriculum in comportment was part and parcel of an education geared toward getting ahead in the highly competitive male élite society of the Greco-Roman world.[494] While it is true that Eutychius' mind was set on the more spiritual of the dignities available in the *cursus honorum*, and even if his graffito was only the result of childish mischief (Eustratius sees it as a divine inspiration), the climate was not one of monastic humility. In particular, his grandfather's instruction to pray for divine aid in scholarly competition against his comp-

---

[492] *Vita Eutychii* 219-27.

[493] *Vita Eutychii* 213-15: *Kyrie, agathon noun charisai moi, hina mathō ta grammata kai nikō tous hetairous mou.*

[494] For general background on Greco-Roman education, see H.I. Marrou, *A History of Education in Antiquity*, tr. G. Lamb. University of Wisconsin Press. Madison. 1956. [original French 1948], especially Parts 2-3, 'Classical Education in the Hellenistic Age' and 'Classical Education and Rome,' respectively. For the importance of rhetorical self-presentation in this competition, see Gleason. 1995, xvii–xxix; and also Swain, 'Polemon's Physiognomy' in idem. 2007. 125–202, especially 126–56.

anions might strike us as odd advice coming from a venerable and miracle-working priest. All this would suggest that the physiognomic game had rules that were less than perfectly Christian.

Even so, the later, longer, passage describing Eutychius' impressive physical appearance is of a wholly different tone. It depicts the endless crowds of the faithful who attend the first liturgy that Eutychius celebrates at Hagia Sophia upon his triumphant return from exile:

> Nor could those accustomed to thinking rightly be sated with gazing on him, but inasmuch as one looked at him attentively, so much the more was one attracted by him, suffering something akin to iron's attraction to the magnetic stone, which by some ineffable force of nature is seen to attract it. Likewise the wondrous man drew all those who wished to see him close to himself by love; for he was entirely gracious in dress, comely in beauty both of soul and body, exalted in works, humble in mind, and unapproachable in the greatness of his virtue, but very approachable in conversation. He was meek, without wrath, sympathetic, sweet in word and sweeter in manner, angelic in appearance and even more angelic in mind.[495]

Thus far, apart from the general mention of beauty in both body and soul, the praise still addresses elements of comportment in conventional terms. But then Eustratius begins to describe more properly physiognomic features and flesh them out with spiritual references:

> For I am not capable of worthily describing all of this man's characteristics of soul and body: the situation and structure of the members of the entire body, by which the inner man is often characterized; the cheer and grace of the face, concerning which Solomon also says, 'When the heart rejoices' (in a godly way, of course) 'the face blossoms';[496] the joy-producing eyes,[497]

---

[495] *Vita Eutychii.* 2196–2207. The passage 'exalted in works ... mind' is a direct quotation from Gregory Nazianzen, *Oration.* 21.9 (PG. 35.1092).
[496] Prov. 15.13.

their modestly guarded pupils[498] (for such are they who look rightly and gesture justly[499]); the white teeth (for pure and heavenly is the nourishment of the righteous); the fiery red lips, the fire and purity of his speech and the graces that dripped from it [500]; the modest and straight ears, which received every divine voice; 'the neck built like a tower of David',[501] strongly bearing the easy and spiritual yoke of divine grace,[502] which was 'the care of all the churches'[503]; the whitened hair of both the sacred head and likewise sacred beard of the chin of Aaron,[504] signifying the brightness of his life and its perfection. And in addition to these, there was the fragrance of his body, 'like the myrrh that runs down the fringe of the high-priestly garb'[505]; the moderate physical height, showing the 'perfect stature in accordance with Christ'[506]; the broad-palmed hands manifesting the breadth of his generous distribution, the proportionately-sized fingers, skilled at writing divine sayings and dogmas; the feet straight and solid in all things, inclining neither to right nor left,[507] but treading the tried and royal road,[508] which 'the ox and ass tread'[509] — that is, the faithful people composed from both the Jews and the Gentiles. Who could fittingly sketch his orderly gait, the ordered movement of

---

[497] *Charopoious*; this could be a mistake for *charopous*, from *charopos* = 'fierce, flashing, bright' or simply 'bluish-grey' (LSJ) , but the critical apparatus does not indicate such a variant. According to LSJ, *charopoioi* is a *falsa lectio* for *charopoi* at Gen. 49.12 (LXX); but by Eustratius' time the reading might have become standard, and he is much more likely to be drawing on the Genesis passage here than on the reflections on eyes of *charopos* color in the physiognomists, especially since his attribution of white teeth to Eutychius, a line later, seems to draw on the same scriptural verse.

[498] Cf. Ps. 16.8.

[499] Cf. Prov. 4.25.

[500] Cf. Prov. 10.32.

[501] Song of Songs. 4:4.

[502] Cf. Mt. 11.29–30.

[503] 2. Cor. 11:28.

[504] Cf. Ps. 132.2.

[505] Ps. 132.2.

[506] Cf. Eph. 4.13.

[507] Cf. Prov. 4.27.

[508] Cf. Num. 20.17.

[509] Is. 32.20.

his whole body? For such is the movement of the meek and 'beautiful feet of those who preach the good tidings of peace', [510] whence is demonstrated their soul's godlike ever-moving dynamism. How shall I extol the pallor which bloomed on his face, like the rind of the pomegranate or like the redness and fragrance of the apple? For such is hidden life of those who are in truth continent and austere, possessing in their spiritual granaries the sweetness of varied edible fruits: fiery red and breathing forth the fragrance, as it is written, to some of 'the scent of death unto death and to others the scent of life unto life'[511] according to their respective choice. Who would not wonder at his persistent and emphatic and uninterrupted instructive discourse, which he did not leave off from ministering sacredly night and day?[512]

We can see that some of the same elements of comportment as in the earlier passage are repeated, but this time the context is wholly Christian. Eustratius takes as his starting point the hypothesis of physiognomy that the outer manifests the inner, although with the caveat that this is 'often' the case, and he then proceeds to use many of the physical marks that a classical physiognomist would try to interpret, such as the size and shape of the ears and hands. However, Eustratius does not interpret in terms of the prescriptions of the ancient physiognomists, nor does he use them to evaluate critically the moral character of an élite competitor, but rather as an opportunity for anagogical contemplation, drawing each physical characteristic into the spiritual plane by means of scriptural citations. Thus he depicts Eutychius as a kind of living statue of the holy man. But unlike the statues of the Hellenic sages of Antiquity, he offers a wholly Christian ideal of inspired divine wisdom. Eustratius' *ekphrasis* of this beautiful masterpiece of a

---

[510] Rom. 10.15.
[511] 2 Cor. 2.16.
[512] *Vita Eutychii* 2207–53. The description then transitions from Eustratius' own original description into a succession of (non-physiognomic) quotations from St. Gregory Nazianzen.

man becomes a vehicle for model of virtue to all those who hear his *encomium*.[513]

Once the Christian nature of Eustratius' physiognomy of holiness is recognized, we must ask whence it comes. Georgia Frank's study has noted how late antique Christian pilgrims, gazing on holy people, reconfigured certain elements of ancient physiognomy along biblical lines.[514] But the long and detailed description by Eustratius is markedly different from the brief and stereotyped sketches provided by the desert literature. The difference cannot exactly be framed with reference to the Greek rhetorical tradition that Eustratius was working from. I have called the description given here of Eutychius an *ekphrasis*; one might more narrowly identify the passage as an *eikonismos* or *charaktērismos*.[515] Gilbert Dagron identifies a difference between them: 'Contrary to the *ekphrasis*, which plays with artistic effects and establishes the place of the artist, *eikonismos* simply aims at characterizing a person, never putting him or her 'in context,' but making the subject appear posed, fixed, with a vacant expression, as in an identity photograph.'[516] We might designate Eustratius' passage as an *ekphrasis*, given its length and complexity and its context within a lively description of the crowds straining to gaze on him, but we might also call it an *eikonismos*, given the posed and fixed character of the saint, as if like a statue or an icon (*eikon*); but then again, the eloquence of the description certainly does not leave its subject with a 'vacant expression.' It is clear that we are dealing here with post-classical rhetorical developments that cannot be exactly mapped onto the ancient categories.

Given the rhetorical sophistication of the passage and Eustratius' evident penchant for drawing on the Cappadocian fathers, we might then seek his sources there. Yet unlike much of the rest of

---

[513] *Ekphrasis* can simply mean 'description', but in its more specialized sense as used here, is the 'title of works descriptive of works of art' (LSJ).

[514] *Memory of the Eyes*, 134–70, esp. 163ff.

[515] See G. Misener. 'Iconistic Portraits,' *Classical Philology* 19. 2. April 1924. 97–123; E.C. Evans. 'Roman Descriptions of Personal Appearance in History and Biography.' *Harvard Studies in Classical Philology* 46. 1935. 43–8.

[516] Dagron. 1991. 26.

this section of the *Life*, the physiognomy is not a quotation or even an allusion to the Cappadocians. This group of fathers were certainly capable of *ekphrasis*-type language. St. Gregory of Nyssa even expresses a clear physiognomic sentiment when he states, while representing the youthful bloom of the Forty Martyrs of Sebaste: 'The discourse likes to linger on the beauty of the bloom of youth, for it knows how, as Wisdom says, from the greatness and beauty of creatures to reckon also the beauty that is hidden; since the beauty of soul shone through the outward appearance, and the outwardly-appearing man was a worthy abode of the unseen.'[517] But here, as in other passages in the Cappadocians, the physiognomic sentiment is treated only paraleiptically.[518] Thus, at most, the Cappadocians may be credited as authorizing Eustratius' use of physiognomy as a key to representing holiness, but not as providing the exact model of his description.[519]

Fortunately, we have such a model much closer to Eustratius' own time and place: the *Ekphrasis of Hagia Sophia* written by Paul the Silentiary, delivered at the re-dedication of the Great Church of Constantinople on December 24th 562, after repairs necessitated by the collapse of the original dome.[520] The final seventy lines, 959-1029, are in praise of Eutychius, the current patriarch of Constantinople; the parallels with Eustratius' account are many. Paul mentions Eutychius' temperance (*sophrosynē*) and modesty

---

[517] Gregory of Nyssa, *In Quadraginta Martyres* (PG 46. 761b), alluding to Wis. 13:5.
[518] As noted by Hippolyte Delehaye, *Les passions des martyrs et les genres littéraires* (Bureaux de la Société des Bollandistes). Brussels. 1921. 214–15 (with citation of further examples from St. Gregory of Nazianzus and St. Basil of Caesarea).
[519] One might also consider St. John Chrysostom as an inspiration, especially his famous 'portraits' of the Apostle Paul in *Homilies on Romans* 32.2-4 (PG. 60. 678-72) and *Homilies on I Corinthians* 13.3-4 (PG .61. 110–12), discussed in M. Mitchell, 'The Archetypal Image: John Chrysostom's Portraits of Paul,' *Journal of Religion* 75.1. Jan. 1995. 15–43. Chrysostom uses an enumeration of body parts in both of these passages, as does Eustratius (along with a similar emphasis on the desire to behold and embrace the saint in question), but develops it quite differently, notably through specific references to Paul's well-documented adventures, accomplishments, and sufferings (in contrast to Eustratius' depiction of Eutychius in quite generic terms).
[520] Paul the Silentiary. *Descriptio Sanctae Sophiae*. (ed). O. Veh. Munich. 1977. 306–58.

(*aidōs*) from birth, and then enumerates elements of his comportment, some of them harking back to Eutychius' childhood education as described by Eutychius himself: 'Your meals modest, your desire well-tuned/ Modest too the sparkle of your eyes, modest the traces/ of your heels, and modest the word that moves your lips.'[521] Paul then continues with a description of Eutychius' appearance that evokes some of the physiognomic notes of Eustratius: 'You do not adopt a superciliously dour, clouded, air but rather yield your cheerful heart to Christ, bearing a calm and gracious glow; and in your countenance a sweet smile inscribes your reverend cheeks. Such marks you bear of a gentle-tempered heart ...[522]'

Having identified a likely immediate model for Eustratius' own *ekphrasis*, we nevertheless remain with the fact that Eustratius developed it in his own manner. Inspired by a small portion of Paul's larger work, he in turn incorporates a rendition of it into his own longer encomiastic *Vita*, in the process exchanging epic hexameter for a literate *koine* and reducing a series of poetic sketches into a systematic prose catalogue. This transformation allows Eustratius to address more directly the biblical and theological content of his holy man (something which his predecessor, restricted by the conventions of his archaizing genre, could only hint at through ingenious use of classical language for Christian ends).

The need for such theological exposition was elicited by controversies that dogged Eutychius' career, and particularly the need to defend the late patriarch against charges that in his teachings he attenuated the reality of the resurrected flesh. He was attacked on this front by both the Monophysite bishop John of Ephesus, and by the staunchly Orthodox Gregory the Great, at that time papal *apocrisiarius* in Constantinople. John, who is bitterly hostile to Eutychius for several reasons, not least for his role in anti-Monophysite persecutions that resulted in John's own imprisonment, accuses him of sharing the views of John Philo-

---

[521] *Descriptio Sanctae Sophiae* ll. Veh. 1977. 995, 997–99.
[522] *Descriptio Sanctae Sophiae* ll. Veh. 1977. 1000–4.

ponus, the eminent philosopher and theologian of Alexandria. The latter, as far as we can tell, argued that the resurrected body would be completely discontinuous with the current mortal frame, a wholly new creation.[523] Gregory's reminiscence displays more respect for the late patriarch.[524] In commenting on Job 19:26, he remarks that 'our body will not, as Eutychius the Bishop of Constantinople wrote, in that glory of the resurrection be impalpable, and more subtle than the wind and air: for in that glory of the resurrection our body will be subtle indeed by the efficacy of a spiritual power, but palpable by the reality of its nature.'[525] He goes on to recount the dispute in some detail; for his part, he seems to have relied exclusively on exegesis of scriptural texts. The disagreement became heated, until the emperor Tiberius intervened and, after hearing both men out in a private audience, decided in favor of Gregory and ordered Eutychius to burn his book written on the subject. The two disputants fell ill shortly afterwards, in Eutychius' case mortally. Gregory concludes by observing that he chose not to pursue the dispute further, seeing as the patriarch did not leave behind many followers, and that on his deathbed whenever he was visited by any *apocrisiarius* who came to see him, 'he used to take hold of the skin of his hand before their eyes, saying, 'I confess that we shall all rise again in this flesh;' which as they themselves avowed he was before wont altogether to deny.'[526]

We may doubt whether Gregory, formed in his own Latin theological tradition, had understood all the subtleties of Eutychius' position, forged in the crucible of the highly technical disputes over Christology taking place primarily in Greek.[527] But

---

[523] See L. R. Wickham. 'John Philoponus and Gregory of Nyssa's Teaching on Resurrection: A Brief Note,' in: H.R. Drobner and C. Klock (edd). *Studien zu Gregor von Nyssa und der christlichen Spätantike*. Brill. Leiden. 1990. 205–210.

[524] The dispute is mentioned incidentally, but in some detail, at *Moralia in Job* 14.56.72–74 (PL 75.1077–79); translation in: *St. Gregory the Great. Morals on the Book of Job*. Vol. 2. Parker. Oxford. 1844. 56.

[525] *Moralia.* 14.72.

[526] *Moralia.* 14.74.

[527] A detailed analysis of Gregory's position and its possible sources is found in Y.-M. Duval, 'La discussion entre l'apocrisiaire Grégoire et le patriarche Eutychios au sujet de la résurrection de la chair. L'arrière-plan doctrinal oriental et

based on his retelling, we can probably discount the charges of John of Ephesus that the patriarch shared the views of Philoponus on the resurrection body. If Eutychius was, in fact, in any error, it was not in believing the resurrection body to be a different entity, but in possibly over-spiritualizing its nature, rendering it 'impalpable,' and thus contradicting the post-Resurrectional narratives in the Gospels, as Gregory points out.[528] Our hagiographer Eustratius, for his part, is exceedingly reticent in naming any particular charges or opponents of Eutychius and only asserts that his hero was in full harmony with the patristic authority of the Cappadocians and of Dionysius the Areopagite.[529] But this is not his only defense of the patriarch: for his *ekphrasis* and its emphasis on the way that holiness permeates the very physical body of Eutychius himself, implicitly assert the saint's belief in the enduring substance of the flesh in the age to come. The very concreteness of its description, enumerating every part of the body and its scriptural significance, refutes any possible charge of hyper-spiritualization. And as the passage transitions from the physiognomic portion translated above to an enumeration of Eutychius' pastoral qualities, and from original description to

occidental,' in J. Fontaine, R. Gillet, and S. Pellistrandi (edd). *Grégoire le Grand. (Chantilly, Centre culturel Les Fontaines, 15-19 septembre 1982: Actes).* Éditions du CNRS. Paris. 1986. 347–66. Unfortunately, despite the essay's title, it concerns Gregory's western background much more than Eutychius' eastern one, thus shedding little conjectural light on the patriarch's own ideas. It does contain, however, two useful observations with regard to Eutychius' possible views: that he was unlikely to hold an extreme Origenist position on the resurrection body, having presided over the condemnation of such doctrines at the Fifth Ecumenical Council in 553, and that the LXX rendering of Job 19:26-7 is quite different from the Vulgate on which Gregory was relying, making its exegesis less cut-and-dried than the latter would have liked to believe.

[528] We may indeed suspect that Eutychius' views, whatever they were, were problematic at the least, given that only a few fragments of his writings exist, which is strange considering that Eustratius alleges him to have written voluminously while in exile, refuting Monophysitism and other errors (*Vita Eutychii* . 2420-48). John of Ephesus, a hostile source, claims that these texts proved an embarrassment to the patriarch on his return from exile, since they were rejected by most of their recipients. He also mentions the emperor Tiberius' rebuke of Eutychius for another (liturgical) innovation he introduced (*Ecclesiastical History* II.40); perhaps lending some support to Gregory's claim about the emperor's order for the burning of Eutychius' book *On the Resurrection.*

[529] *Vita Eutychii.* 2449-2502.

reliance on patristic quotations, Eustratius seems to be setting up Eutychius as a worthy successor to Athanasius and the Cappadocian fathers, a new holy and patristic bishop who in his own person mediates the tension between soul and body and thus between contemplative and active, monastic and clerical, desert and empire.[530] Accordingly, the context of the sixth-century theological controversies reminds us that, even if Eustratius' language here is wholly Christian in inspiration and avoids casting aspersions on a specific opponent, he is still playing a game that would be familiar to Polemon and his Greco-Roman physiognomic tradition, namely, staking his subject's claim to fame in a high-stakes political struggle.[531]

---

[530] See A. Sterk, *Renouncing the World Yet Leading the Church: The Monk-Bishop in Late Antiquity*. Harvard University Press. Cambridge. 2004, 214–18; cf. C. Rapp, *Holy Bishops in Late Antiquity: The Nature of Christian Leadership in an Age of Transition*. University of California Press. Berkeley. 2005. 295–302, with less focus on the *Life of Eutychius*. For the tensions that required mediation, see N.H. Baynes, 'The Thought-World of East Rome,' in *Byzantine Studies and Other Essays*. Greenwood Press. Westport.1955 (repr. 1974). 25–45 and G.V. Florovsky. 'Empire and Desert: Antinomies of Christian History,' *GOTR*. 3.2. 1957. 133–59.

[531] As Gleason notes, 'In some ways, a preeminent sophist, in his combined role of prominent educator, public moralist, civic spokesman, and tourist attraction, he was a prototype of the Christian bishop, disposing of the fiscal, political, and social crises of his adopted city while feuding energetically with his rivals.' (1995. 24). For a detailed investigation of Eustratius' selective presentation of his hero's career, glossing over the most controversial aspects, see Averil Cameron. 'Eustratius' *Life* of the Patriarch Eutychius and the Fifth Ecumenical Council,' in *Kathēgētria: Essays presented to Joan Hussey for her 80th birthday.*(Porphyrogenitus. Camberley. 1988. 225–47; and eadem. 'Models of the past in the late sixth century: The life of Patriarch Eutychius,' in *Reading the Past in Late Antiquity*. (ed). G. Clarke . Australian National University Press. Canberra. 1990.205–223; both are reprinted in A. Cameron. *Changing Cultures in Early Byzantium*. Variorum. Aldershot. 1996. With regard to Eutychius' first deposition from the patriarchal throne and his replacement by John Scholasticus, see P. van den Ven. 'L'Accession de Jean le Scholastique au siège patriarcal de Constan-tinople en 565.' *Byzantion* 35. 1965. 320–52. The essays by Cameron and van den Ven deal primarily with Eutychius' earlier difficulties, namely his presiding over questionable proceedings at the Fifth Ecumenical Council and his replacement by John Scholasticus as patriarch during the aphthartodocetist controversy in 565. Even his position as patriarch was questioned by some, since he had returned from exile without any official reversal of the decision of the episcopal council that had condemned him in 565.

These sobering considerations should not lead us to miss the theological implications of Eustratius' contemplative depiction of the beautiful bishop St. Eutychius. Based on the tradition of Orthodox practice, there is certainly a place for beauty. It is expressed simply in the saying concerning St. Anthony, and translated into the idiom of shape and color in the icons of Panselinos or Rublev. Its theological justification is articulated most fully in the theology of St. Gregory Palamas, with his emphasis on the participation of the body in the uncreated divine energies. In between these, the *Life of Eutychius* provides a verbal key to contemplating physical beauty as a manifestation of holiness, in a Scriptural language of moral excellence. With its preliminary emphasis on correct training in comportment, it indicates the cultivation of outward beauty in movement and speech as a means of cultivating the spirit.[532] How different this is from an earthly obsession with good looks is indicated by the observation that Eutychius, as part of his regime of ascetic mortification, never washed, but nevertheless his body was fragrant.[533] This paradoxical phenomenon is also found in holy monks of other times and places.[534] It recalls another famous scene from St. Anthony's life, when he emerges from his inner desert retreat like a new man. He is neither worn down by asceticism nor slackened by idleness, but in perfect equilibrium of body and soul. 'But he was altogether even as being guided by reason, and abiding in a natural state.'[535] In this way his beauty is described as the natural beauty of man according to the image of God.[536]

---

[532] For striking parallels to Eustratius' physiognomic language in an earlier Latin source, see Ennodius of Pavia, *Vita Epiphanii*. 13–17 with the corresponding commentary in: G.M. Cook (tr). *The Life of Saint Epiphanius by Ennodius: A Translation with an Introduction and Commentary.* Catholic University of America Press. Washington. DC. 1942. 36–39, 131–32.

[533] The vow of *alousia* is recorded at *Vita Eutychii*. 386–93.

[534] Further references can be seen on the Dumbarton Oaks Hagiography Database under the subcategory 'Human Body: Lack of care.' see:
http://www.doaks.org/research/byzantine/projects/hagiography_database/

[535] *Vita Antonii* 14.4 (NPNF Series 2. Vol. 4, 200).

[536] Cf. Irenaeus of Lyons, *Against Heresies* 4.20.7: 'For the glory of God is a living man; and the life of man consists in beholding God.' (ANF. Vol. 1. 490).

Beauty and the Military Saint: The Case of Alexander Nevsky

Sergei A. Holodny [537]

Prelude

In the currently political climate, leaders are often thought of as working without moral principles, whose decisions stem from the latest polls and image-makers.[538] Aside from the potential compromising of ethical principles and the ubiquity of personal moral failings, the role of a high political leader now, as in ancient times, is inevitably fraught with difficult decisions, not least sending soldiers to their deaths during wartime. But if the principles that guide political leaders so often appear to be pragmatism and self-interest, rather than the good of those who are governed, it raises the question of how such a culture of leadership can be compatible with Christian ideals.

Specifically, the Christian ideal of Beauty, which according to Dostoyevsky's Prince Myshkin will 'save the world', seems almost axiomatically irresoluble with the standard, current view of a political or military leader. Images associated with shrewd political maneuvering or modern (or medieval) warfare appear diametrically opposed to the kind of internal and external grace, calm and beauty that are depicted in Orthodox icons and sung of in its hymnography. In contrast to the 'profession' of a monk or a physician, which seem more compatible with altruistic saintliness, the 'job' of being a political or military leader by its very nature seems to demand compromise.

Orthodox hagiography, however, is filled with examples of military and political leaders who, in the Orthodox understanding, successfully combined careers as statesmen and military leaders with saintly lives. This paper focuses on the thirteenth-

---

[537] My thanks to Prof. Vera Shevzov for her valuable assistance and guidance; to Archimandrite Cyril Hovorun and Eugenia Temidis for their advice on sources; to Maestro Peter Fekula, Professor Peter Bouteneff, and Elizabeth Ledkovsky for assistance with liturgical questions; and to Elena and Andrei Holodny for their encouragement and help.
[538] c.f. D. Balz & H. Johnson. *The Battle for America.* Viking. New York. 2008.

century saint, Alexander Nevsky, who was able to govern his country successfully in difficult historical circumstances and yet, according to Orthodox tradition, was able to remain true to the Christian ideal. In the Orthodox view, St. Alexander was able to resolve the inherent tension between the demands of his political and military responsibilities and the requirements of a saintly life, including a sense of both inner and outer beauty.

Perhaps Orthodox iconography and hymnography can offer us the resolution of this tension? An icon or hymn, on the one hand depicts actual historical events from the lives of the saint; yet, icons and hymns as works of art, are inherently and quintessentially objects of beauty. Moreover, icons or hymns ideally depict not only the outer or physical circumstances of an individual's existence but also the inner conflicts which pervaded the life of the saint and his (or her) victory in this spiritual struggle. [539] This paper will examine how the harmonious solution to the apparent tension between a successful political and military career on the one hand, and a saintly life on the other, is depicted iconographically and hymnographically in the figure of Alexander Nevsky. The essay considers in particular the harmonizing of the seemingly jarring notions of beauty and politico-military prowess.

Historical background

Alexander Yaroslavovich Nevsky lived in a time of great peril for Russia as well as for Orthodoxy in general. He was born in Pereslavl-Zalessky in 1220, sixteen years after the great sack of Constantinople by the Latin Crusaders in 1204. He died in 1263, two years after the recapture of the capital of the Byzantine Empire by Michael VIII Palaeologos. In 1236, at the age of 16, Alexander became the prince of Novgorod. During the first few years of his tenure, Russian land was devastated and subjugated by the Mongols under the leadership of Khan Batu, the grandson of Genghis Khan. In 1237 and 1238, Khan Batu captured and destroyed essentially all of the major centers of northern Rus', including Vladimir. By 1240, the Khan annihilated Kiev and the

---

[539] c.f. V. Lossky & L. Ouspensky. *The Meaning of Icons*. St. Vladimir's Seminary Press. Crestwood. NY. 1999.

southern part of Rus'. During this campaign, Novgorod was spared probably because its surrounding terrain was inhospitable to the Mongol cavalry. Sensing the weakness of the Russian land, Swedes and Germans attacked Novgorod and Pskov from the West. In 1240, Alexander Nevsky and his numerically inferior forces decisively defeated the Swedish army on the Neva River. For this victory, Alexander was given the title 'Nevsky'. In 1242 Prince Nevsky defeated the Livonian Knights on Lake Ladoga.

Alexander also resisted the efforts of the Catholic Church and other political forces in the West who were agitating to form an alliance against the Mongols; and instead chose to become a vassal of the Mongol overlords. His policy of appeasement of the eastern conquerors, which committed him to the collection of taxes from his own people and the suppression of anti-Mongol uprisings (for example the Novgorod revolt of 1259) both avoided internal wars and was successful in gaining a respite from the devastating Mongolian forays. [540] His success in this diplomatic endeavor, which earned him the enduring love of his people, was highlighted by the subsequent failure of ensuing rulers to achieve these aims. [541] His two sons, Dimitri and Andrei, for example, fought endless wars against each other on Russian territory. In this struggle, each of the combatants brought Mongol armies to devastate not only each other but also the Russian land itself. [542] The chroniclers depicted the stark contrast between the rule of Alexander Nevsky and that of his children. The words of Metropolitan Cyril pronounced at Alexander Nevsky's funeral, and recorded in the *Second Pskovian Chronicle* proved prophetic: 'My children, you should know that the sun of the Suzdalian land has set. There will never be another prince like him in the

---

[540] *First Novogorodian Chronicle.* Synodal document. 136-8. [Cited in: FB. Schenk. *Aleksandr Nevsky in Russian Cultural Reminiscence: Saint, Statesman and National Hero.* in: *Novoye Literaturnoye Obozreniye.* Moscow. 2007. (Russian version, translated from the original German). 58, 68, 82].

[541] Alexander Nevsky was declared the 'main hero' of Russia's history by a recent popular vote. (Kommersant. 24th September 2008).

[542] NM. Karamzin. *History of the Russian State (Istoria Gosudarstva Rossiakago).* Moscow 1842-44. (repr. Khiga Press. Moscow 1989). Bk.1. vol.4. chs. 5-6. 81-103. (I reference here the 1989 edition).

Suzdalian land.' And the priests and deacons and monks, and all the people present, both poor and the wealthy, all responded: 'It is our end.'[543] Alexander Nevsky was considered a local saint immediately after his untimely death,[544] and the Russian Orthodox Church officially canonized him in 1547.

The Hagiographical Vita of Alexander Nevsky

Much of what we know about St. Alexander comes from a manuscript entitled 'Tale of the Life and Courage of the Pious and Great Prince Alexander (Nevsky), which was written soon after his death (henceforth referred to as the *Life*). [545] When reading this chronicle, one is struck by the combination of detailed descriptions of the battle scenes and of extensive quotes and allusions to religious texts and ancient, secular history. Zenkovsky understood this to mean that the chronicle had at least two different authors – an experienced warrior and a learned churchman. [546] However, the dichotomy between the military and political world and the religious/ethical and aesthetic mindset assumed here by Zenkovsky is an artificial construct of the modern mind and did not exist in the medieval world. In contrast, perhaps, to contemporary expectations, military and political leaders at that time were expected to be pious and godly. In a reflected image of the role the Byzantine emperor had been understood to play in the church from early times, the medieval Christian prince, generally, was invested with sacral characteristics. Current scholarship rejects the opinions of Zenkovsky and Serebryanky and acknowledges the symbiotic relationship existing between politico-military and religious-aesthetic figures in medieval life.

Contemporary researchers have emphasized that the stylistic melding of the strictly factual historical narrative with the

---

[543] K.Begunov. (tr.) *Second Pskovian Chronicle*. Isbornik. Moscow. 1955.

[544] Karamzin. 1989. 58; Schenk. 2007. 58.

[545] SA. Zenkovsky. (ed). *Medieval Russian's Epics, Chronicles, and Tales*. Meridian. New York. 1963. 224-236. Zenkovsky uses the version from *the Second Pskovian Chronicle*, published in *Pskovskie Letopisi*, vol. 2. Moscow. 1955. 11-16.

[546] N.Serebryanky. 'The lives of old Russian princes.' In: *Proceedings of the Imperial Historical and Archeological Society*. St. Petersburg. 1915. Vol. 245. Bk.3. 151. (Cited in, Schenk. 2007. 79; and see also ibid. 60).

spiritual dimension is an essential characteristic of the hagiography of the period.[547] Indeed, the historian, Werner Philipp goes as far as to maintain that the author of the *Life* in depicting the deeds of Alexander Nevsky, actually created a new type of saint.[548] As opposed to the *Vitae* of prior Russian princely saints (such as Boris and Gleb and Igor or Michael of Chernigov), the *Life* of Alexander Nevsky does not describe martyrdom for the Christian faith or for averting a fratricidal war. Rather, it serves to 'Canonize the godlike rule of the prince, and, in this way, the successful resolution of everyday, earthly, concerns with pious responsibility.' [549] Prince Alexander, then, achieves sainthood through his deeds for the good of society (*obschedstvennoye sluzheniye*). Phillip thus sees the dimensions of the sacred and the political as indissolubly intertwined in the figure of Alexander Nevsky.

The linking of the spiritual and the temporal is emphasized in the *Life* through a miraculous vision of two Russian saints Boris and Gleb, who were witnessed to be hastening to the aid of 'our relative Alexander' prior to the battle against the Swedes. [550] Why, however, was it the saints Boris and Gleb who were depicted in the vision? Their military achievements were rather modest during their own lifetimes. The answer can be gleaned from a textual analysis of the original *Life*. Prior to his battle with the Swedes, Alexander was cautioned by advisors against immed-iately attacking the invaders, since the enemy was numerically superior to the forces of the Novgorodians. According to the *Life* Alexander replied, 'God is not in strength but in truth (*Ne v sile Bog a v pravde*).' Being on the side of truth was more important to him than a tactical military advantage. In this attitude he perhaps saw himself fulfilling the advice of the Psalmist to the ancient Kings of Israel.[551]   In contrast to this we might note that the

---

[547] Schenk. 2007. 60, 78-79; referencing the work of Okhotnoikova, Begunov, Von Lilienfeld and Phillip.

[548] W.Philipp. *Heiligkeit und Herrschaft*. 66. Cited in Schenk. 2007. 81.

[549] Phillip. *Heiligkeit und Herrschaft.* 67. Cited in Schenk. 2007. 81.

[550] Zenkovsky. 1963. 228. See also Karamzin. 1989. 18.

[551] Ps. 20. 7-9: 'Some boast in chariots and some in horses, but we in the name of the Lord our God. Give victory to the king, O Lord; answer us when we call'.

phrase famously attributed to Alexander Nevsky in the 1938 film of the same name by Sergei Eisenstein (at Stalin's commission)[552] is quite different. Eisenstein has the prince say this: 'Who comes to us with the sword, shall die by the sword (*kto k nam s mechom pridet, ot mecha i pogibnet*).' These words, of course, distort the following verses in the Gospel of Matthew: 'Then they came, and laid hands on Jesus and took him. And, behold, one of those who were with Jesus stretched out his hand, drew his sword, and struck a servant of the high priest's, cutting off his ear. Then Jesus said to him: Put away your sword back in its place: for all those who take up the sword shall perish with the sword'.[553] Eisenstein quite dramatically alters the original meaning of Christ's words, which quite clearly admonished the Apostle Peter after his violent and futile attempt to defend Jesus from the arresting Roman soldiers. In Eisenstein's (or rather Stalin's) version of an inspiring ruler, physical power predominates and all mention of truth (*pravda*) is eliminated. In stark contrast to this, in the original description, written soon after the actual battle, Nevsky clearly subordinates strength to truth. For Prince Alexander, faithfulness to his ideals is as valuable as strategic considerations, even though (not least because!) he was a military leader soon to engage a numerically superior enemy on the field of battle.

The Liturgical Celebration of Alexander Nevsky

The Russian Orthodox Church celebrates the feast day of St. Alexander Nevsky twice during the year: first, on the day of his repose (November 23rd, Old Style; December 6th, New Style), and secondly on the occasion of the transfer of his relics to St. Petersburg in 1724 (August 30th, Old Style, September 12th, New Style). Archimandrite Vikentii, the abbot of the Nativity Monastery, composed the first liturgical service soon after the initial opening

---

Ps.33.17-19: 'The war horse is a vain hope for victory, and by its great might it cannot save. Behold, the eye of the Lord is on those who fear him, on those who hope in his steadfast love, that he may deliver their soul from death, and keep them alive in famine.'

[552] D. Bordwell. *The Cinema of Eisenstein*. Harvard University Press. Cambridge. 1993. 28-9.

[553] Mt. 26. 51-53.

of the relics of Alexander Nevsky in 1380. This service was later edited around 1540 by nobleman (*boyarin*) Mikhail (according to other versions by Vasili Tuchkov), in preparation for the saint's canonization in 1547, in the time of Metropolitan Makarii of Moscow (1482- 1563). A second service was composed in 1724 during the reign of Peter the Great. [554]

There are interesting distinctions in both the Church services, which reflect differences in the ideals and objectives of Russian society during these two eras. The earlier version was written when religion (specifically Orthodoxy) played a dominant role in the lives of the Russian people. As such, it can be argued that this earlier version is most likely a more accurate reflection of the times of the saint himself. The second service was written during the waning of religious life and the rise of the Russian Empire. We note that the earlier version is more concerned with the inner, spiritual life. In the pre-Petrine service, for instance, the saint is referred to as 'venerable' (*prepodobnyi*) as well as 'most faithful' or 'pious' (*blagovernyi*), whereas in the later version, he is referred to exclusively as 'most faithful'. Interestingly, *blagovernyi* is a term essentially reserved for princes and other high rulers. The term *prepodobnyi* usually refers to saintly monks and priests. Therefore, the earlier church service, while praising Nevsky's statesmanship, also emphasized his saintly and hieratic qualities. The later Petrine version preferred subtly to highlight the Prince's political and military deeds instead.

The different emphases of the two services are evident in their very titles. The earlier version gives prominence to the fact that Alexander became a monk at the end of his life. The title of the service includes the information: '… whose monastic name was Aleksei (*narechennogo vo inotsekh Alkseia)*'. This detail is absent in the later version. There are number of possible reasons. It is hard to overestimate the domination of Peter the Great over the political and cultural milieu of Russia at that time, and the Tsar

[554] FG. Spassky. *Russian Literature (Russkoye literaturnoye tvorchestvo)*. Publishing Council of the Russian Orthodox Church. Moscow. 2008. (Originally published by the St. Sergius Institute. Paris. 1951). The text can be referenced at: http://www.klikovo.ru/db/book/msg/17693 (as at Dec 1st. 2011).

regarded monastics in a jaundiced way, as evidenced by his monastic reforms. [555] Therefore, the author of the Petrine service probably thought it wise to underemphasize the final decision of Peter's glorious ancestor to take monastic vows. [556]

In reading the first service to the saint, one is struck forcibly by frequent references to the interweaving of spiritual and physical beauty: a characteristic currently not often associated with either political or military leaders. For example, we see the direct use of the word 'beauty' in the following phrases: 'You [Alexander Nevsky] are beautified most brightly by piety and faith (*blagochestiem i veroiu presvetlo ukrashen*).'[557] 'You are brightly beautified by good deeds, charity and purity and became the vessel of the Holy Spirit.'[558] 'In joy and beauty (*v radoste i krasote*).'[559] 'You shine beautifully like a star (*Yako zvezda siyaya krasno*).'[560]

One extraordinary phrase [561] references Alexander's fine voice: 'You were the beauty of Christ's Church and decorated her with your singing, O glorious one. Even now we pray to you, Alexander: Rescue those who sing of you from physical and spiritual warfare.' This is an interesting metaphor connecting the defeat of one's demons through the aesthetic value of singing in

[555] RK Massie. *Peter the Great: His Life and World*. Knopf. New York. 1980. 788.
[556] Moreover Peter the Great's son, who rebelled against his father and met his untimely demise (probably at Peter's behest, c.f. Massie. 1980. 704-707) was named Aleksei. The composer of the service subtly avoided the mention the name of Peter's son, even though it was the monastic name of his famous predecessor. The Petrine service contains a seemingly out of place reference to Absalom, the son of King David, who rebelled against his father (2 Samuel 14:25: Sticheron at the Lity). The biblical reference to the rebellious (and assassinated) son becomes understandable when one visualizes the contemporary situation.
[557] Third Sticheron, at the Little Vespers. The quotations from the Church service here and further are taken from: http://orthlib.ru which represents the current standard of the Russian Orthodox Church. Publishing Council of the Russian Orthodox Church. Moscow. 2002. Translations are by the present author.
[558] Ibid. Third Sticheron at the Lity.(*blagimi deli svetlo ukrashen yesi, milostinyami I chistotoiu sosud Svyatogo Dukha bil yesi*).
[559] Ibid. Canon. Ode 4. Troparion 3.
[560] Ibid. Canon, Ode 7. Troparion 4.
[561] Ibid. Canon. Ode 1. Troparion 3. (*Tserkvi byl esi Khristovoi krasota, peniem bo siiu ukrasil esi preslavne. I nynye molim tia: svobodi ny ot vsiakiia brani boritelya, poiush-chim ti, Aleksandre*).

Church. The composer of the service here parallels Alexander Nevsky's triumphs in actual, physical, warfare (*bran'*) with the spiritual (or unseen) warfare and seeks spiritual assistance for all manner of struggle. Another passage in the early service shows the parallel between the princely duties and the prince's Christian caliber: 'O pious father Alexander...you were named by God to wear the crown, and were brightly beautified by piety and truth, charity and chastity.'[562]

These (among numerous examples) illustrate the organic linking of Christian virtues, not least ethics and aesthetics, which, in the earlier service, blend seamlessly with the military and political achievements of Alexander Nevsky. Such an ecclesiastical glorification of the harmonious coexistence possible between these ethical-aesthetic values and political success, doubtless intended to hold up such a goal and aspiration to his political successors.

The later Petrine liturgical service differs from the earlier by the unremitting presence of imperial and nationalistic military references. Constant allusions to the martial successes of Prince Alexander Nevsky are meant to turn the attention of the faithful listener to the accomplishments of the reigning Tsar, Peter the Great. For example, Alexander [563] is hailed as a military leader and a builder, akin to Peter the Great. Most references to miracles, beauty, healing, and monasticism are missing in this service. The few surviving mentions of beauty in the second service are direct quotations from the medieval service.

The 1724 Petrine Service is coupled with another feast: the commemoration of the establishment of peace between the Russian Empire and the Swedish Crown. This feast commemorates the victory of the Russian Empire over Sweden (in 1721), which definitively established Russian presence in the Baltic Sea and significantly solidified the hitherto precarious position of the

---

[562] Ibid. Fourth Sticheron. Little Vespers. (*Prepodobne otche Aleksande... bogimenit ventsenosets bil yesi, prepodobiyem i pravdoiu svetlo ykrashen: milostinyami zhe I chistotoiu*).

[563] In the liturgical Sticheron -Aposticha on: 'Both now and ever.'

fledgling capital of St. Petersburg. [564] The service, consequently, consists of two interwoven narratives: one for St. Alexander and the celebrating the victory over the Swedes and glorifying Peter the Great, often by name. Frequently, the references to the two princes dovetail, making it difficult for somebody standing in church and not having the text in front of them to differentiate between the glorification of the two leaders. Both had claimed victories over the Swedes, secured the Baltic Sea, and were great leaders. One, however, was a canonized saint and the other was a contemporary ruler. [565] The sycophantic metaphors and similes set up here for the advantage of Peter the Great are numerous in this service. The service, for example,[566] refers to the saint and the contemporary Tsar as 'flesh from flesh and power from power' (*plot' ot ploti, i vlast' ot vlasti*).

Shlyapkin expresses the opinion that the canonization of St. Alexander in 1547 and the hagiography published at that time were acts done to support the cruel, imperialistic, policies of Ivan IV and shore up the faltering dynasty after his death. [567] However, this seems to me doubtful. Alexander Nevsky was canonized during the All-Russian Council of 1547. Ivan IV was crowned in January of that year, aged 16. During the first few months of his reign, there were no signs of the notorious future troubles. It is much more likely that Metropolitan Makarii the editor of the *Great Menaion* who also supervised the canonization of thirty eight other Russian saints, himself initiated the canonization of Alexander Nevsky as a model for princes. The compilation of the *Great Menaion*, including the preparation of documents for the canonization of such a large number of saints, was a laborious, time-consuming task that had been started prior to the elevation of Ivan to the throne. Analyzing the service composed in 1380, which was edited in 1547 for the canonization of the prince, it is clear that the main emphasis of the 1547 service was on the Christian characteristics of the saint, not least his beauty, piety,

---

564 Massie. 1980. 735-743.
565 Massie. 1980. 373-382.
566 Sticheron at the Vesperal Lity.
567 I.A. Shlyapkin. *Ikonographia Svatogo Blagovernago Velikago Knyaza Aleskanda Nevskago.* Typographia Aleksandrova. Petrograd. 1915. 11-12.

and monastic. There is, unarguably, a clear glorification of the saint's martial and diplomatic achievements in the 1547 service, but a propagandist exaltation of the current dynasty and comparisons to a living Tsar only appear in the Petrine version of 1724.

Shlyapkin references the veneration of the relics of St. Alexander by Ivan IV prior to the taking of Kazan, as evidence of the support the Church gave to the rule of Ivan. [568] The taking of Kazan, the capital of the Tatar Khanate of Kazan, by Tsar Ivan in 1552 was seen as a great strategic and political victory, which solidified the growing regional influence of the Russian state and underscored the waning power of the Tatars, Russia's conquerors. The veneration of the relics of Alexander Nevsky by Ivan IV immediately preceding this victory, however, cannot be seen as a reason for the canonization of the saint as the military triumph occurred (1552) after the actual canonization (1547). [569] Nor can an ecclesial act of national prayer in time of war be taken as a wholesale endorsement by the Church of the character of Ivan's rule.

A much later liturgical composition: *Akathist to the Holy, Pious, Great Prince Alexander Nevsky,* written in 1852 expresses much of the same sentiment as the 1548 service (rather than that of 1724).[570] Originating in the fifth century, the *Akathist* (originally a processional hymn dedicated to a saint or an icon of the Mother of God) experienced a revival in late nineteenth century Russia as an expression of both public and private piety. [571] An *Akathist* is a short liturgical composition and can be sung at any time, whereas the standard Orthodox services are, apart from being very long, generally reserved for the actually feastday of the saint in

---

[568] Shlyapkin. 1915. 11-12.
[569] Also, the Church at that time was far from being the handmaiden of the State. Metropolitan Philip of Moscow, the primate of the Russian Orthodox Church was killed by Maliuta Skuratov in 1569 on the orders of Ivan IV, and the Tsar on February 20th, 1570, personally beheaded Kornili, the higumen of the important Pskov-Pechorski monastery near Lake Ladoga.
[570] A. Popov. *Orthodox Russian Akathists (Pravoslavniye russkiye akafisti).* Kazan State University Press. Kazan. 1903. 149-153.
[571] V. Shevzov. 'Poeticizing Piety: The Icon of Mary in Russian Akathesoi Hymns.' St. Vladimir's Theological Quarterly. vol. 44. 2000. 343-373.

question. From the outset the 19th century Nevsky *Akathist's* opening phrases present the resolution of the two seemingly irreconcilable characteristics: being a warrior (*voyevoda*) and possessing beautification or ornamentation (*ukrasheniye*): 'The chosen warrior of the Russian Land, the bright beautification of the Orthodox Church, the holy, pious, great prince Alexander Nevsky.'[572] The liturgy of the Church is replete with similar examples where apparently incompatible features are harmoniously combined to emphasize a certain characteristic of the saint's life. A famous example is the Troparion to St. Nicholas of Myra in Lycia (which also serves liturgically as a general Troparion for feasts of saintly hierarchs): 'You have attained great heights through humility and great prosperity through poverty.'[573] In an analogous manner, the 1852 *Akathist* for St. Alexander emphasizes the unity of his Christian virtue with his success as a ruler. Rather than being a hindrance, it is *because of* these Christian characteristics, including beauty, piety, truth, charity and chastity, that God grants Alexander Nevsky the ability to be an outstanding statesman.

St. Alexander Nevsky and his Icon

St. Isaac the Syrian once wrote: 'Speech is the organ of this present world. Silence is the mystery of the world to come.' [574] Speech represents the unique human ability to chronicle our temporal states, while 'silence' here represents that eternal moment of beholding the Divine. Given that understanding, one might view Art, specifically Orthodox iconography, as maintaining a mysterious ability, by means of beauty, to act as a bridge and simultaneously connect to both realms. On the one hand, icons depict stories of the lives of saints. The icon, therefore, fastens itself to a certain time period in which that figure lived. This binding gives the icon the quality of 'speech' because it actively tells a story of the past. Saints strove to see God and eternal truths,

---

[572] Kontakion. 1. (*Izbrannomu voyevode zemle Rossiiskiya, svetlomu ukrasheniu Tserkve pravoslavniya, svyatomu blagovernomu velikomu knyaziu Aleksandru Nevskomu*).

[573] *Smireniye visokoye, nishchetoiu bogatoye.*

[574] Cited in: K. Ware. *The Orthodox Way.* SVS Press. Crestwood. NY. 1995. 178.

and consequently created a certain 'movement' in the icons. Yet, iconographers saturate their icons with universal symbols of the 'world to come,' in order for others also to see what the saints themselves were able to see. In this way icons manage concurrently to 'speak' (silently) of the individual and to 'see' the (otherwise invisible) universal, giving an onlooker the ability also to see these truths through the icon's storytelling.

In Russian ecclesiastical culture, beauty had a central position ever since Prince Vladimir chose the 'Greek faith' in 988 as the new religion for his realm. The *Primary Chronicle* famously notes that this was done, on his part, largely because of spiritual-aesthetic considerations:

> Then we went to Greece, and the Greeks led us to the edifices where they worshipped their God, and we knew not whether we were in heaven or on earth. For on earth there is no such splendor or such beauty, and we are at a loss to describe it. We only know that God dwells there among men, and their service is fairer than the ceremonies of other nations. For we cannot forget this beauty. Every man, after tasting something sweet is afterwards unwilling to accept that which is bitter. [575]

The concept of beauty is again shown to possess the unique ability to unite seemingly opposite things. In this important text we see that the delegates of Vladimir: 'Knew not whether [they] were in heaven or on earth', indicating that two opposing realms were blended together when they experienced something so ineffably beautiful. Because beauty can disintegrate the boundary created between binary oppositions, it has remained central in Russian Orthodox iconography; which often deals with opposing ideas such as those binaries of the military versus the ethical we have been considering here.

The iconographic representation of saints who were also powerful politicians begs the initial question: 'Can a successful politician really be saint?' and 'What role does the concept of beauty play in

---

[575] SH. Cross & OP. Sherbowitz-Wetzor. (edd). *The Russian Primary Chronicle: Laurentian Text.* The Mediaeval Academy of America. Cambridge. 1953.

the life of a statesman?' In light of St. Isaac's theology, however, we might view a political saint *vis à vis* the dichotomy of 'speech and sight'. In terms of speech, a politician or military leader participates in conquests, reforms, and other miscellaneous endeavors, giving the iconographer an abundance of stories to chronicle. In terms of sight, the political figure traditionally stands for certain ideals and attempts to move his people towards those ideals. Undoubtedly, there exists a tension between the career of the saint who is also a statesman and his spiritual life; that tension is mirrored by the overlap of time and eternity. While a modern misconception may assert that the friction inevitably leads to negative effects, in actuality, the double-sided pressure can, in certain circumstances, mold leaders into men and women of deep and saintly character. The ideals for which they struggled are then crystallized in Orthodox iconographic art.

In pre-Petrine icons St. Alexander Nevsky was occasionally depicted as a monk in the great *schema* (the monastic garb of the strictest order. A mid 16th century example of this can be found in the Sophia Cathedral in Novgorod; and sometimes he was depicted as a ruling prince. Iconographic instruction manuals recommend portraying the saint: 'In a schema and monastic vestments, with a lock of curly hair protruding from underneath the headdress, himself broad shouldered.'[576] The directive to portray a protruding lock of curly hair is very telling. Such a depiction would be exceptionally unusual for a classical ascetic saint. In this case, however, the interplay of the unruly hair and the severe monastic garb might be read as an artistic testament to the resolution of the tension between his princely on the one hand and his deep Christianity on the other. The 'broad shoulders' and the lock of curly hair represent the boisterous life of the forceful ruler. Both are veiled under the monastic garb, symbolizing the individual's deep submission to the Gospel.

After the time of Peter the Great, iconographers were generally instructed to portray Alexander Nevsky in princely garb only. An *Ukaz*, or directive of the Holy Synod, dated June 15th 1724 went as

---

[576] As given in the instructions of the *Stroganoff* Iconographic School.

far as to forbid his portrayal in the habit of a monk: '.. henceforth, it is forbidden to depict this saint as a monastic.'[577] Even in post-Petrine icons, however, Alexander Nevsky is depicted as having his crown placed on the table behind him and with a halo around his head, showing the spiritual first and the political second, while maintaining the importance of both aspects. With his eyes gazing up and into the light, he appears immersed in the light of God. In such symbolic ways the icons themselves express what we have seen in the liturgical texts concerning the prince: the issue of the resolution of two binaries: power and humility.

Conclusion

Orthodox iconography and hymnography depict not only a physical reality, but are also deeply concerned with the delineation of the interior life, and the structures of spiritual beauty. The early manuscripts connected with Alexander Nevsky, and his iconographic depictions, tend to show someone who was simultaneously a forceful statesman and an authentic saint. The tension in this conjunction of binaries: beauty, chastity, charity and piety on the one hand, and military prowess and clever statesmanship on the other; is resolved in the case of Prince Alexander Nevsky through beautiful artistic media, which seek to hold up the resolution of the binaries as an ideal aspiration.

---

[577] *Complete collection of the orders and directives regarding the Orthodox religion of the Russian Empire. (Polnoye sobraniye postanovlenii i rasporyazhenii po vedomstvu pravoslavnogo ispovedaniya Rossiiskoi imperii).* St. Petersburg 1876. vol. 4. 148. Nos. 1318 and 1328. Cited in Schenk. 2007. 164.

The Aesthetic of Typology: The Prophet Jonah In the Church's Liturgical Hymns [578]

Bruce Beck

This paper focuses on the typological use of the story of the prophet Jonah in order to gain a greater appreciation for the role that form and aesthetics play in the interpretation and use of biblical narratives in the Orthodox Church. I will present some examples of how the biblical narrative of the prophet Jonah and the gospel accounts of the death, burial, and resurrection of Jesus mutually influence each other through the art of typological exegesis.

Some of the larger questions that have motivated this particular study include: What are the methods for reading scripture as evidenced by patristic writings, icons, and the liturgical hymns? What are the hermeneutical principles that legitimated these methods? To what degree is the 'meaning' of a biblical narrative shaped by an aesthetic or poetic perspective, rather than our contemporary tendencies to reduce a text to its 'bottom-line' meaning? and: In what ways do form and liturgical context determine the use and usefulness of a biblical narrative in the early church?

In this brief examination I will draw from one of the *catenae* of biblical odes that undergird the service of Orthros according to the byzantine rite; this beautiful hymn demonstrates well the typological 'mind of the Church' in its comparing Jesus' death, entombment, sojourn in Hades and resurrection, to the events in the life of Jonah. Likewise, through this typological kinship, the story of Jonah is itself expanded and enriched based on Jesus' life. So, our topic is the art of patristic typology, and our scope will be the comparative narratives of Jonah and Jesus.

---

[578] I would like to thank the organizers of the Fourth Annual Sophia Institute Conference on: *Beauty and the Beautiful in Eastern Orthodox Christianity*. I would also like to thank my co-presenter at the conference, Kristin Dwyer, who presented half our paper on the iconographical use of Jonah in the early Church. This published version includes only the work of the present author, and does not treat the iconographic material illustrated at the conference.

It continues to be necessary to 'Mind the Gap' between us and the ancient Christians, recognizing that they lived in a foreign culture and long before the Enlightenment. At the very least, this should give us pause when describing ancient Christian practice, and hope for discovering new ways of viewing scripture and worship through our encounter with the past.[579]

In the case of patristic exegesis, one is justified in quoting the prophet Isaiah, 'My thoughts are not your thoughts, nor are your ways my ways, says the Lord.'[580] The act and goal (*skopos*) of reading has changed dramatically from their culture to ours, so it is therefore difficult for us now to comprehend or appreciate the 'exegetical moves' that are made in so much of the patristic corpus. Many contemporary orthodox scholars have consciously avoided using the word 'exegesis' to describe what the Fathers do with the scripture, since they recognize the fundamental difference between the word's current meaning in the context of historical biblical criticism and what the Fathers are doing with scripture.[581]

With respect to some of the fundamental differences between ancient and contemporary reading and interpretation methods, I am indebted to the insightful work of John O'Keefe and Rusty

---

[579] From a theological perspective, this historical chasm is ameliorated for Orthodox who study the writings of the early Church with a very strong sense of the communion of the saints. See the lively discussion of the relationship between St. John Chrysostom and St. Paul by Margaret Mitchell in her monograph *The Heavenly Trumpet: John Chrysostom and the Art of Pauline Interpretation*. WJK Press. Louisville. 2002.

[580] Is. 55.8

[581] c.f. J. Breck. *Scripture in Tradition: The Bible and its Interpretation in the Orthodox Church*. SVS Press. Crestwood. N.Y. 2001. 16-21; TG. Stylianopoulos. *Sacred Text and Interpretation: Perspectives in Orthodox Biblical Studies*. Holy Cross Orthodox Press. Brookline. MA. 2006; esp. the essays in that collection by Stylianopoulos himself: 'Perspectives in Orthodox Biblical Interpretation.' ibid. 325-336; and by JA. McGuckin. 'Recent Biblical Hermeneutics in Patristic Perspective: The Tradition of Orthodoxy.' ibid. 293-324.

Reno in their recent monograph *Sanctified Vision*.[582] In the first chapter, 'Scriptural Meaning: Modern to Ancient,' they narrate the difficulty they encountered when trying to understand patristic exegesis. They make here the following confession:

> We saw the vast ocean of exegesis, and yet we did not see it. We recognized that most early Christian writing is saturated with biblical particularity, but as we continued to think in terms of doctrinal development, intellectual context, and social systems, the actual exegesis remained obscure and unanalyzed. Slowly we became unsettled and dissatisfied.... We increasingly worried that we did not adequately understand the vast ocean of biblical sensibility upon which all the particular forms of patristic thought and practice floats.[583]

O'Keefe and Reno distinguish (rightly in my opinion) between tracing the history of patristic exegesis and actually understanding it (that is, gaining competency in the rubrics and inner logic, which drive and justify the patristic textual peregrinations).[584] Their goal, for example, was to understand how Origen read scripture, and to focus much less on the questions about the historical influences on his methods. So, in writing their monograph, O'Keefe and Reno asked many of the questions that are paramount for this paper, including: 'How did the fathers engage the specific details of the text? How did the figural or typological exegesis ... function? What controlled and guided the seemingly arbitrary exegetical moves? .... How did the fathers read?'[585]

A related question which I want to raise here is whether and to what extent the biblical and patristic tendency to compare one narrative to another should be considered a *hermeneutical form* or poetic expression of a scriptural passage. In other words, what if the patristic reading of scripture would have considered foreign our modern tendency to limit the meaning of a biblical passage

---

[582] J. O'Keefe & R. Russell. *Sanctified Vision: An Introduction to Early Christian Interpretation of the Bible*. Johns Hopkins University Press. Baltimore. 2005
[583] O'Keefe & Russell. 2005. 5.
[584] O'Keefe & Russell. 2005. 5.
[585] O'Keefe & Russell. 2005. 5.

primarily to its historical context? What if a more wide-ranging, aesthetic and literary set of options should habitually be put to use in attempting to appreciate the patristic forms of exegesis?[586]

Jonah as Type

The lively narrative of Jonah landing on the shores of the Assyrian empire from the mouth of a sea monster has proved to be extremely significant in both Jewish and Christian applications. Here we focus only on that part of the story where Jonah is given over to the 'heart of the sea' by the pagan sailors and entombed in the belly of a large fish for three days and three nights, and finally, disgorged on God's command so that he can preach to the Ninevites. This rather vivid description of a prophet's entombment in the womb of the sea provokes two separate applications within early Christianity: first, Jonah's deliverance from the fish's belly is used prolifically in the prayers of early Christians (both through funereal art and liturgical prayers) as a paradigm of deliverance from all 'danger and distress,' including prayer for the soul leaving the body at death (as is most likely depicted in the catacomb reliefs in Rome); and the second application of the story is Christological: beginning with Jesus himself who makes use of Jonah as narrated in Matthew and Luke, when he compares himself to the prophet Jonah in the belly of the fish. He says:

> But he answered them, 'An evil and adulterous generation asks for a sign, but no sign will be given to it except the sign of the prophet Jonah. For just as Jonah was three days and three nights in the belly of the sea monster, so for three days and three nights the Son of Man will be in the heart of the earth.'[587]

Both of these applications of Jonah's story demonstrate how a biblical narrative can be retold to meet the liturgical needs of communities of faith through the art of typology. In this essay, I

---

[586] See further O'Keefe & Russell. 2005. 9, for astute observations about modern reading practices being reductionist in nature, viewing the text as always referring to something else, rather than itself containing value or holiness.
[587] Matt. 12.39-40.

will look only at this second use, namely how the narrative of Jonah's sojourn in the 'heart of the sea' attached itself to the life of Jesus.

Patristic Jonah Typology

How does the prophet Jonah become associated with Jesus' three-day sojourn in the tomb and Hades, and his third-day resurrection, and his appearances? The foundations for this typological exegesis is already found in the New Testament itself, when Jesus compared himself (and his destiny) to that of Jonah the prophet, using the specific phrase 'like Jonah....' This *logion* of Jesus created an inexorable, yet peculiar, typological link between himself and the prophet who fled to Tarshish, refusing God's assignment in Nineveh.[588]

This kind of comparison (or intertextuality) between one biblical story and an older one is now generally called typological exegesis. However, ascribing a name to this creative interpretive phenomenon does not explain *why* it takes place, nor its internal logic or rules, nor its theological presuppositions. In addition, this term typology is a modern one that describes the phenomenon when two biblical stories are connected to one another by analogy or some other hermeneutical attraction. The older story is known as the type (*typos*), while the new situation is somehow anticipated, foreshadowed, or antiphonally narrated in the context of the former type, which is its anti-type. While the word *typos* certainly occurs in the New Testament and early Christian writings, it is used interchangeably with a number of other terms such as allegory. The aim here is to look at this phenomenon of *comparative narrative*, or intertextuality, from an aesthetic and form-critical perspective. What made this rhetorical move so pleasing to our predecessors, both the speakers and their audiences? Furthermore, once the association is made between

---

[588] The comparisons in Matthew and Luke are different, for in Luke it is Jesus' preaching that is compared with Jonah's preaching which caused the entire city to repent, whereas in Matthew the comparison is made between their entombment in the heart of the sea/earth and their being delivered on the third day. c.f. Matt. 12.38-40 and Lk. 11.29-30.

246

the two stories or figures, how wide a range of influence can the type have on its anti-type, and *vice versa*? I will explore these questions below in the fruitful, tradition-historical intertwining of the story of Jonah in the great fish, and Jesus' sojourn in the 'heart of the earth.'[589]

Jonah and Jesus: A Comparative Narrative

One might think it odd to compare a fugitive prophet who tries to escape his mission from God, with the Son of Man who emptied himself, being obedient, even to the point of dying on the cross[590]. But there are several aspects of the two stories that inevitably attracted each to the other. The saying by Jesus tells us the primary attracting aspect of the two stories: they both were three days (and three nights) in the tomb or 'belly of Hades.' For example, compare: 'Jonah cried out of the belly of hell' (Jon. 2:2) and 'from the heart of the sea' (Jon. 2:3), with Jesus' saying: 'So too must the Son of Man be hidden in the *heart of the earth for three days and three nights.*'[591] Also, though not explicitly stated, like Jonah, Jesus too would be disgorged by Hades, and would not *be corrupted* or digested by death's putrefying powers. Later patristic authors such as Theodore of Mopsuestia and Cyril of Jerusalem note also the similarity that Jonah and Jesus both brought repentance and salvation to the Gentiles.[592] So even though the larger

---

[589] Mitchell (2002. 131. fn. 74) comments on the word typology as follows: 'There is considerable debate about whether there was such a thing as 'typology' (the term itself is modern) and if among Christian authors 'typology' is different from 'allegory'....The present volume...demonstrates the extent to which the terminology is variable, strategic and apologetic, capable of harmonization or differentiation, depending upon the context and needs. The modern critic should not be bound to particular ancient scruples in this regard.' See also F. Young. *Biblical Exegesis & the Formation of Christian Culture.* CUP. New York. 1997. 140-160.

[590] Phil 2.6-8.

[591] Matt. 12.40

[592] St. Cyril of Jerusalem discusses the relationship between Jesus and Jonah in his 14th *Catechetical Lecture* (trans. L .McCauley & A. Stephenson. *The Works of Cyril of Jerusalem.* Fathers of the Church Series. vols. 61 & 64. CUA Press. Washington. 1969-70. In the case of Theodore of Mopsuestia, Jonah was a *type* for Christ in two respects: a) like Christ he was kept incorrupt in the sea monster (the tomb) for three days and nights, and b) his preaching to the Ninevites who

stories of Jesus and Jonah may, when compared, display some dissonance, the iconic image of Jonah in the belly of Hades for three days and three nights was inexorably drawn towards the narratives depicting Jesus' death, his sojourn in Hades, and the resurrection appearances. In this process, nothing is taken away from the biblical narrative of Jonah, rather something is added to it as we read it now, since we now read Jonah as Jonah, and also Jonah as Jesus; thus the story now has two synchronous readings. Jonah as a 'type' of Jesus provides motifs through which to interpret the life of Christ and, remarkably, the life of Jesus has had a reverberating influence on the historical narrative expansions of the story of Jonah. We will demonstrate an example of this bi-directional, typological, influence below.

Jonah on Holy Saturday

In Ode six of the byzantine service of Orthros (Matins) on Holy Saturday, there is a beautiful hymn about Jonah cast in the light of Jesus' resurrection. It reads:

> Jonah was enclosed but not held fast in the belly of the whale; for, serving as a figure [*typos*] of you, who had suffered and were buried in the tomb, he leaped forth from the monster, as from a bridal chamber, and he called out to the watch: 'You who keep guard falsely and in vain, you have forsaken your own mercy.'[593]

Here the hymnographer uses the word *typos* to explain the relationship between Jesus and Jonah. He seems to imply that because Christ was the anti-type of Jonah, what was true in the case of Jesus' resurrection must also have held true for Jonah's disgorgement from the belly of the sea monster. Just as Jesus was given over to burial in 'the heart of the earth,' but sprang forth as from a bridal chamber, so Jonah in this hymn is depicted in the

---

came to believe in the one God and repent of their vile ways prefigured the Gentiles coming to faith in Christ (c.f. *Theodore Bishop of Mopsuestia: Commentary on the Twelve Prophets*. R C. Hill. (ed). The Fathers of the Church Series. vol. 108. CUA Press. Washington. 2004. 187.

[593] c.f. *The Pentecostarion*. Holy Transfiguration Monastery. Brookline. MA. 1990. tr. slightly emended.

same way. In the icons and images that we have of Jonah, he is doing exactly that: being propelled out from the mouth of the great fish with his arms extended forward. During the first four centuries C.E., scenes from the Jonah narrative are among the most frequently depicted from among both Hebrew Bible and New Testament iconographic themes. Almost always, Jonah is depicted in three sequential scenes: a) Jonah swallowed by the sea monster; b) Jonah spewed forth from it; and c) Jonah reclining blissfully as an Endymion-like figure under a grape arbor. One of the most well known of these programs is the fresco in the catacomb of Callixtus in the so-called 'Sacrament Chapels'. The noted art historian Charles Rufus Morey remarks, apropos of this fresco: 'The Jonah scenes themselves were an obvious symbol of resurrection.'[594]

Jonah Cries out to the Watch

In the last line of the hymn from Ode six of the Holy Saturday Orthros service, we read an example of what is often called a 'narrative expansion;' Jonah is depicted here as having cried out to those standing guard on the walls of Nineveh the following:

> You who keep guard falsely and in vain, you have forsaken your own mercy.[595]

This verse is certainly not found within the narrative of the biblical book of Jonah; rather it is derived from the psalm prayed by Jonah from within the belly of the whale (c.f. Jon. 2.8), which reads according to the Septuagint (LXX) version: 'They that observe vanities and lies have forsaken their own mercy.' The hymn, evidently, has adapted Jon. 2.8, changing only the grammar from third to second person plural to fit its new narrative setting.

---

[594] This note on Jonah catacomb iconography is taken from the author's dissertation: *You Lifted Me Up from the Pit Alive: Exegetical and Theological Trajectories from the Book of Jonah in Jewish and Christian Sources.* (Harvard University. 2000. section 3.3.1). See also: CR. Morey. *Early Christian Art. An Outline of the Evolution of Style and Iconography in Sculpture and Painting from Antiquity to the Eighth Century.* Princeton University Press. NJ. 1942. 63.

[595] c.f. *Pentecostarion.* Holy Transfiguration Monastery. Brookline. 1990. (tr. slightly emended).

At first glance, this quotation from the psalm in Jon. 2 seems out of place as a narrative expansion of Jonah's deliverance from the great fish. Who is he addressing? There is no reference to 'a guard' in the biblical story; neither at the city walls of Nineveh, nor when he comes ashore. In addition, the psalm is prayed by Jonah when he is all alone within the fish's belly. In contrast, in the case of the narrative of the burial of Jesus, this verse from the Jonah's psalm is quite fitting, since when placed in the mouth of Jesus, he would have been addressing the guards standing watch over his tomb, as described in Matt. 27.

Who are the guards or watchers that Jonah would have addressed? It appears that this cry from the psalm of Jonah (2.8) has been added by the hymnographers to the content of Jonah's preaching to the Ninevites, through an artful typological interpretation. As will be shown below, this proclamation fits better in the scene of Jesus' resurrection than that of Jonah coming out from the whale.

In the LXX narrative, Jonah says to the people of Nineveh only these words: 'In yet three days Nineveh will be destroyed.'[596] The paschal hymn, however, may be reflecting a traditional patristic interpretation that found the paucity of Jonah's words to be an exegetical stumbling block, and developed the tradition that more words were offered to the Ninevites to effect their radical turn-about; in the case of this hymn, the additional content to Jonah's 'proclamation' (*kerygma*) is based on the prophetic psalm that Jonah offers from the belly of the fish, which would have outlined some of the particular evils of the Ninevites: 'observing vanities and lies.'

A number of other patristic writings take notice of the paucity of Jonah's prophecy regarding the city, and the fact that he does not call for repentance, but rather only proclaims the judgment by God that the city would be destroyed. The 'trouble' that these Fathers had with the plain reading of the biblical account is this question: 'How could the Ninevites have repented if this was indeed all that Jonah spoke to them?' It is an important question,

---

[596] Hebrew texts read here: 'in 40 days.'

one to which even Jesus refers when comparing his preaching to that of Jonah's, saying: 'The people of Nineveh will rise up at the judgment with this generation and condemn it, because they repented at the proclamation (*kerygma*) of Jonah, and see, something greater than Jonah is here!'[597]

Theodore of Mopsuestia (ca.350-428) represents an early patristic attestation to the exegetical tradition that Jonah preached to the Ninevites, instructing them not only on the pending punishment, but also about the God of Israel, his mercy, and about fasting. He writes in his commentary on Jonah:

> The verse, 'the men of Nineveh believed in God' (Jon 3:5), also brings out that he did not carelessly say only 'three days more, and Nineveh will be destroyed:' they could never have believed in God on the basis of this remark alone, from a completely unknown foreigner threatening them with destruction and adding nothing further, not even letting the listeners know by whom he was sent. Rather, it is obvious he also mentioned, the Lord of all, and said he had been sent by him.[598]

Returning now briefly to the line from the paschal hymn about 'forsaking your own mercy,' on closer examination it seems almost certain that this quotation was first put to use to illuminate the narrative in Matt. 27 about the guard at Jesus' tomb, and then only after it had served in this context was it read back into the narrative of the prophet Jonah. This being the case it would serve to demonstrate the bi-directional influence (dynamic reflexivity) of typological units such as Jonah and Jesus. What evidence can be offered in support of the proposed trajectory that Jon. 2:8 has first been used to interpret or expand the scene of the guard at Jesus'

---

[597] Matt. 12.41

[598] Theodore of Mopsuestia. *Commentary on the Twelve Prophets*. R Hill. (ed). 2004. 202. We may note the contrasting approach by St. John Chrysostom who emphasizes that the Ninevites had nothing on which to base their repentance other than the threat of destruction, and yet they demonstrated faith based on much less than what Christians typically receive. (St. John Chrysostom. *Homilies Concerning the Statues* 20.21. A. Ferreiro. (ed). *Ancient Christian Commentary on Scripture: The Twelve Prophets*. vol. 14. IVP. Downers Grove. Illinois. 2003. 145.

tomb? The word translated 'to keep or observe' in the phrase 'They that observe vanities and lies' can mean both 'to observe' as well as 'to guard' in Hebrew. The same semantic field applies to the Greek word that translates it in the Septuagint (*phylasso*), which means both 'to guard' and, in the middle voice, 'to keep or observe' as, for example the observing of the Mosaic law.[599]

In its context, within Jonah's psalm, the word should be translated as 'to observe or practice,' so the verse would read, 'those who practice vanities and malice....' The verb would not be understood as referring to 'those who guard,' as it is here in the hymn. But since both the Greek and Hebrew words *can* theoretically mean either 'to guard' or 'to observe,' the hymn renders it to mean the former due to being influenced by the image of the guard at Jesus' tomb. The translation of the verb in the hymn is unambiguous due to the phrase that precedes it: -and he called out *to the watch*: You who keep guard ....' The word here translated 'the watch' is *koustodía* in Greek. This same rare word is used to describe the military guard set at the tomb of Jesus in Matthew 27.65.[600] So, the phrase: 'he called out to the watch,' is an intentional typological connection with that watch set by the Temple guards opposite the tomb where Jesus was laid. It fits perfectly within this context; but when put back into the narrative of Jonah, it significantly stretches the story-line of narrative.

Here then, is a marvelous example of a *typos* (Jonah) influencing its *anti-typos* (Jesus), which then, in turn, reflexively enriches the *typos*. In other words, the stories of Jonah and Jesus in their descent into the depths of the sea and the earth are so interwoven that each narrative is made fuller by its association with the other. Here in Ode six of the service celebrating the resurrection of Jesus from the tomb, Jonah's exodus from the sea monster is described in terms of Jesus' coming forth from the jaws of Hades, 'as from a

---

[599] e.g. Matt. 19.20; see W.Bauer & F. Danker. *A Greek English Lexicon of the New Testament and Other Early Christian Literature*. 3rd edition. University of Chicago Press. 2000. 1068.

[600] This noun is very rare in the scriptures, used only three times in the Greek Bible, all three of which are in this context of the guard at Jesus' tomb. It is a Latin loan word, and its first literary appearance is here in Matthew.

bridal chamber.' 'This is the Lord's doing; it is marvelous in our eyes.'[601]

Conclusion

We have set out in this study to gain more insight into patristic typological exegesis by casting it as an artistic, or poetic, mode of expressing the *meanings* of holy scripture. It's creative energy is comparative, unpredictable, and subjective by nature; as it fuses biblical stories with one another. When the Jonah and Jesus narratives are read antiphonally, as they are during Holy Saturday, a productive cross-fertilization takes place. This creative act of comparing one story with another is dynamic and iterative. It is only comparatively recently that the reading and interpretation methods that are exhibited in the hymns and other patristic readings of the scripture have begun to be uncovered and articulated. This paper has been an exercise in trying to frame this phenomenon within the rubric of form and poetry, so that we might be able to receive a more aesthetic and fuller experience of scripture with the help of the Mothers and Fathers of the Church.

Finally, it is our hope that one of the suggestive findings of this study is that we should hold with some suspicion the modern tendency to extract only one key or 'single essential meaning' from a biblical narrative. Instead, let us try to enter into the more spacious patristic framework of reading scripture, allowing ourselves to experience the whole narrative in its various forms and typological associations; knowing, as St. Ephrem the Syrian says, that it is richer than us. Below are his beautiful words regarding scripture:

> Therefore, whoever encounters one of its riches must not think that that alone which he has found is all that is in it, but [rather] that it is this alone that he is capable of finding from the many things in it. Enriched by it, let him not think that he has impoverished it. But rather let him give thanks for its greatness, he that is unequal to it. Rejoice that you have been satiated, and do not be upset that it is richer than

---

[601] Ps 117. (118). 23.

you.... Give thanks for what you have taken away, and do not murmur over what remains and is in excess. That which you have taken and gone away with is your portion and that which is left over is also your heritage.[602]

[602] *Saint Ephrem's Commentary on Tatian's Diatessaron: An English Translation of Chester Beatty Syriac Ms. 709* . OUP. Oxford. 1993. 49-50; cited in S.H. Griffin. *Faith Adoring the Mystery: Reading the Bible with St. Ephraem the Syrian.* Marquette University Press. 1997. 16-17.

Christ-Jesus as the Terminal Paradox in the Poetry Of St.Romanos the Melodist.

Stamenka E. Antonova

Historico-Theological Setting.

Romanos the Melodist is among the most famous Christian poets of the eastern Christian empire, whose personal history is nonetheless shrouded in many unknowns. The exact dates of his birth and death are uncertain, but it is usually surmised by scholars that he was born at the latest between 466 and 493,[603] while his death occurred in the vicinity of 555 to 565.[604] He is said to have been born in Emesa and to be of Syrian origin. Some also think that Romanos was of Semitic background, most probably of Jewish stock, although this hypothesis has been disputed based on the anti-Jewish motifs in his works.[605] If, in fact, Romanos was a convert from this background, it would explain the way his writings demonstrate a solid knowledge of Jewish religious traditions and texts. What is known with certainty is that Romanos was a foreigner in the imperial capital of Constantinople, where he went toward the end the rein of the emperor Anastasios (d. 518).[606]

---

[603] JG. De Matons. *Romanos le Mélode et les Origines de la Poésie Religieuse à Byzance.* Beauchesne. Paris. 1977. 178.

[604] M.Arranz. 'Romanos le Mélode,' in *Dictionnaire de Spiritualité.* 13. Paris. 1988. 898.

[605] One proponent of his Jewishness is A. Korakidis, whereas others have contested this hypothesis, such as de Matons, *Romanos le Mélode.* 1997. 197-198; however, the latter concedes that there is no way of resolving the question with any degree of certainty.

[606] The information concerning Romanos' life is quite scanty; it has been gleaned from different sources and organized by de Matons, as follows: 'Romanos *hosios* où *hagios* était un Syrien originaire d'Emèse, qui devint diacre a Béryte , où il était attaché a l'église de la Résurrection. De là il passa à Constantinople au temp de l'empereur Anastase, et il y exerça son ministère à l'église de la Mère de Dieu située dans le quartier de Kyros. Il y vécut avec beaucoup de piete , et avait en particulière dévotion la Vierge des Blanchernes, dans le sanctuaire de laquelle il allait volontiers prier, notamment quand il y avait un office de nuit, une *pannychis.* Cependant, c'est à l'église du quartier de Kyros qu'il reçut le don poét-

Although none of the sources mentions which one of the two Byzantine emperors bearing that name (one ruling 491-518, and the other 713-716) it has been more or less unanimously accepted that the former is more likely to have been meant.[607] It is in Constantinople that Romanos' prolific career of a song-writer developed and brought him fame. The circumstances under which he started composing liturgical poetry are unknown, apart from a legendary account of his swallowing a scroll given to him by the Mother of God: a story which modern critical scholarship tends not to take seriously, noting that there is no internal literary evidence to indicate any personal evolution and change. The story of his swallowing of a scroll (*tomos hartou*) has a deep biblical resonance as, for instance, in Ezekiel 2.8 – 3.3, and can be best understood as the tradition's way of attributing his gift to divine benevolence. Most likely, Romanos possessed his remarkable literary talent before moving to Constantinople, where he came to employ it with more extensive patronage.[608]

---

ique. Une nuit, la Vierge lui apparut en songe et lui donna un livre en lui ordonnant de l'avaler; il lui sembla, en effet, qu'il ouvrait la bouche et qu'il avalait le volume ; cela se passait pendant la nuit de Noël. Aussitôt il se réveilla et, après avoir rendu grâces à Dieu , il monta à l'ambon et commença à chanter son hymne de la Nativité: 'Aujourd'hui la Vierge met au monde le Supra-substantiel'. Ce talent miraculeusement acquis ne le quitta plus, et Romanos écrivit encore bien d'autres kontakia pour d'autres fêtes, voire pour toutes les autres fêtes de l'année, notamment pour celles du Christ, ainsi que pour différents saints, les plus importants. Au total, il en composa un millier ou même plus de mille; on peut en voir la plus grande partie écrite de sa propre main à l'église où il fut diacre . Il mourut et fut enterré dans cette même église du quartier de Kyros, où l'on célèbre sa synaxe.' See De Matons. 1977. 163.

[607] For elaboration on this controversy and the scholarly consensus, see De Matons. 1977. 175-176. Opposed to this universal scholarly sentiment, however, are sources of different provenance, such as this: *Romanou tou poiētou kai melōdou tōn kontakiōn.Hōrmēto de ek Surias tēs Emesēnōn poleōs, diakonos genomenos tēs en Bērutō ekklēsias· katalabōn de tēn Kōnstantinoupolin en tois chronois Anastasiou tou basileōs, katemeinen en tois Kurou, en hō kai to charisma para tēs Theotokou elaben, tomon chartou epidousēs autō · hothen kai hupēgoreuse kontakia ton aprithmon peri ta chilia, kai teleiōtheis en eirēnē thaptetai en tē autē ekklēsia.* This is one among many synaxes dated around 1063; quoted from De Matons. 1977. 161.

[608] For instance, De Matons. 1977. 185, surmises that Romanos must have gained fame for his poetical works and thus have been transferred from Berytos to Constantinople on account of his talent.

One striking feature of his works is the self-identification that he leaves for posterity - the enigmatic signature on so many pieces: 'the humble' Romanos (*tou tapeinou Romanou*) which at once suggests his humility as a writer and highlights his insistence on his authorial rights (or perhaps responsibilities), implied by his composition. Despite this consistently recurring identification, Romanos remains largely an enigmatic figure whose personal history and motivations lie in darkness, and whose individual piety and understanding of the Christian religion must emerge from the pages of his writings.

Romanos lived in a time characterized by lively controversies in the (divided) empire and church concerned with the issue of Christ's personhood, his constitution of divine and human natures and the relation between these. These Christological controversies were longstanding in the church, but at this period they had developed to a pitch that endangered the stability and order of the wider Byzantine imperial society. The crucial question of Christ-Jesus was of vital importance not only for the sustenance of society and its *status quo,* but also for the rationality of individual faith and religiosity dependent upon it. Romanos does not differ in this respect from his contemporaries for he is deeply intrigued with the double condition of Christ as God-made-Man. His works profess a certain type of Christology which joins the ongoing conversation at his time as to who and what Jesus is. His poetry, at first appearing simply as beautiful verses, also contains very emphatic and polemical pieces with a clear theological thrust. Almost in every verse Romanos invokes the mystery and the depth of his God by a triple token: poetic language, musical rhythm, and paradoxical formulations; the latter being of primary interest for the scope of this paper. For Romanos, the language of theology is indeed that of poetry, music and paradox (that which transcends common conventional ways of expounding the divine to assume alternative avenues of expressing it in especially mysterious and incomprehensible modalities).

For Romanos, the only way to capture the quintessence of the Christ-event in human terms and to convey its meaning to the devotee is through language which transcends itself and points to something which is beyond it. This beyond-ness is presented in a powerful and impressionable manner in his poetry by a constant resort to one literary device: juxtaposed paradoxes. He habitually heaps paradox upon paradox in the text, because for him the truth and the mystery of Christ-Jesus is nothing else but the 'terminal paradox': two opposite and mutually-exclusive realities are brought into one single reality and, despite the inherent unity, both remain intact and whole. What else can convey this primary folly, overturning conventional wisdom for the human mind, other than that which (contrary to common opinion and expectation) is 'incredible' and paradoxical (*to paradoxon*)?

Furthermore, the language of Romanos comes very close to that of the Cappadocian fathers and to Cyril of Alexandria,[609] when they expound on the divine economy. In a parallel manner, Romanos resorts to the use of paradoxical language in order to render into words the Christ-event as above all else a question of the limitless becoming limited; the uncircumscribed becoming circumscribed; the timeless entering time; the creator and sustainer of all things becoming a creature. This device is especially emphatic whenever Romanos explores the overstepping of limits and the points of contact between the divine (in this case represented and embodied by Jesus) and the human, which is strictly located in the earthly sphere. The power of his verses and the force of his language rest in the probing of these border-lines, typically delineated between the two incompatible realms that come frighteningly close to each other, and yet remain distinctly separate. Contrary to de Matons, one of Romanos' earlier editors, who claims that : '[Il] n'a aucune des prédispositions naturelles qui font le théologien: le goût de la spéculation et de l'abstraction, le sens des nuances, la rigueur dans l'exposé, l'art de se servir des textes sacrés de manière à leur faire bien plus qu'ils ne disent, et à l'occasion le contraire,'[610] I would argue that the Melodist is not merely a penman who transfers the biblical passages into mellifluous verse, but in, addition to

---

[609] JA. McGuckin. *St. Cyril of Alexandria: The Christological Controversy. Its History, Theology and Texts.* Brill. Leiden. 1994. 175-222.
[610] De Matons. 1977. 264.

that, he propounds an apologetic for a certain type of theology, while denouncing others.

Although Romanos does not stick to a particular rigid terminology, such as that of the Niceno-Constantinopolitan creed, he does remain loyal to the gist of its theology by expressing it in alternative ways which are nonetheless semantically related to it. Indeed, for him the true *theologos* and genuine theologizing are intricately connected to the liminality of language, to the trans-cendence of (normal) human experience and the encounter with the beyond on every level of human perception and under-standing. Such is his personal *religio* which he does not reduce to a string of illogically combined concepts and words, but expresses through profoundly dynamic and pulsating terminology which invokes rather than describes, and approximates rather than verbally fixes.

Romanos' resort to paradox, which is otherwise in compliance with the ecumenical creed, testifies not only to his personal understanding and rendering of the mystery of God-Enfleshed, but also serves as polemical and propagandistic tool in his writings. The use of paradox is a scintillating literary and concep-tual device poised between the two major threats to the integrity of the personhood of Christ-Jesus at the beginning of the sixth century: namely Arianism and Monophysitism. Arianism, which sprang up much earlier than Romanos' lifetime, was then enjoying a heyday in the western part of the empire, where it had re-emerged as the ancestral Christianity of the invading Germanic tribes.[611] Arianism contested the divinity of Jesus and placed him on a lower level to that of the Father for want of 'sameness of nature' (*homoousion*) between the two, due to the fact that the Son was not seen as eternal or uncreated. Against the main body of Arians, who claimed only a 'likeness' (*homoion*) between the Father and the Son, Athanasius in the fourth century defended the position of the sameness in nature (*homoousion, tautotes tes ousias*) of the Son with the Father, and also used the term 'Godbearer' or

---

[611] E. Lash, *Kontakia: On the Life of Christ. St. Romanos Melodos.* Harper Collins. San Francisco. 1995. xxiv.

Mother of God (*Theotokos*) a concept which was ecumenically affirmed at the Council of Ephesus in 431, and which pervades Romanos' poetry.

Monophysitism, on the other hand, was another significant factor in Romanos' time, because during Justinian's rein, the personal favors of his wife, empress Theodora, leaned toward the proponents of one nature or *mia physis* of Christ-Jesus, whereas Justinian himself was a staunch supporter of Chalcedon's 'two natures' ineffably united. One of the main protagonists of the single-nature movement, Apollinaris, in the 4th century had proposed a compromise position by collapsing the divine and the human natures into one compacted-nature of Christ-Jesus. This nature was seen as best described as a mixure' (*mixis*) of the divine and the human proper; for Christ-Jesus had a human body (*sōma*), a human soul (*psychē*) but, for Apollinaris, no human spirit (*pneuma, nous*) for in place of the latter there was the divine *Logos*. As a result of this ad-mixture of human and divine ingredients, the oneness of Christ-Jesus was firmly secured, but at the expense of the integrity of his humanity.[612]

On the other end of the spectrum, at the opposite extreme to that of the Arians who vehemently denied the divinity of Jesus, was the teaching of Nestorius, who was on the verge of creating two separate persons constituting Christ-Jesus and clearly distin-guishable from each other at every single moment and act. Thus, Nestorius refused to call Mary Godbearer or Mother of God (*Theotokos*) and instead argued that the faithful should call her Christbearer or the Mother of Christ (*Christotokos*) since as mother of Jesus, she gave birth to what was human but not to what was divine: mothered the man, not God. By the mid 5th century this was widely seen as an unnecessary division of the two aspects of the person Christ-Jesus, the divine and the human, to the point of implying a fundamental dichotomy. Instead of one Christ-Jesus, Nestorius ended up with two: the Divine Logos and Jesus, as distinguished and distinguishable in their respective natures, as

---

[612] *Nicene and Post-Nicene Fathers.* Vol. 14. (edd). P. Schaff & H. Wace. Scribner. New York. 1900. 173-4.

well as in the characteristics and acts pertaining to each. For Nestorius, one act, such as the birth, could be attributed only to one nature; in that case the human; whereas another act, such as the miraculous deeds of Jesus, could be attributed to the divine nature alone. Steering his way between the Apollinarian and Nestorian poles Romanos shows himself to be a careful and conscious *poet-theologos* who selectively chooses his images and terms so as not to occasion any controversy and yet to nuance a Chalcedonian two-nature understanding of faith in Christ-Jesus, which is very sensitive to the predominating aspect of the unifying *henosis* of the two natures having a 'consilience to oneness' as the Council of 451 phrased it. His ability for accuracy and precision, as well as his refined sense of beauty, is best seen when his verses are examined more closely.

Christ's Conception and Birth as Paradoxes.

Christ-Jesus in the schemata drawn by Romanos has a personal history on earth which starts with his conception, continues with his birth, hisconsecration in the temple, then proceeds with his deeds, and ends with his crucifixion and burial, followed by his resurrection. Albeit seemingly portraying a normal course of an historical life, Romanos focuses on the points of Jesus' history that transcend the possibilities and the experience of the common run of men. Thus, for instance, Romanos stresses the seedless (and thus 'unheard-of' and 'unthinkable') conception of Jesus. When he relates the annunciation of Mary by Gabriel, Romanos emphasizes the incredibility of the situation before her: 'When Mary heard these paradoxical words...' (*Paradoxōn rētōn ē Mariam ōs ēkouse*).[613] The angelic being has arrived to announce the supra-natural conception of the Christ child, namely that a virgin will conceive without a natural course, 'seedless conception' (*asporou kuēsei*), and will furthermore become a 'Mother of God' (*Theotokos*)[614]. The normal human reaction to this startling news, surely one of consternation and fear, rather than joy and gladness, is attributed

---

[613] *Hymns of Nativity* (henceforward *Hymn*). 1.6. All quotations from the Greek are taken from the edition of J. Grosdidier de Matons. *Romanos le Mélode: Hymnes.* Paris. 1965.
[614] *Hymn* 3. Prelude.

by Romanos even to Joseph and Mary. Joseph is stupefied for having witnessed an awesome happening beyond human experience: 'Joseph was struck with wonder as he contemplated what was beyond nature' (*kateplagē Iōsēph to upper phusin theōrōn*)[615] and Mary, as she accepts the news that she is going to bear a fatherless child (since she has 'become a mother and a nurse of a fatherless son' (*apatoros uiou egenou mētēr kai trophos*) declares that Gabriel's words are 'unbelievable'[616]. Romanos tells the reader that not only is Mary to conceive in a miraculous and incredible manner, but her offspring is also demonstrated to be elevated above human nature: 'Today the Virgin gives birth to him who is above all being' (*hē parthenos sēmeron ton huperousion tiktei*).[617] It is rather curious that Romanos not only employs oxymoron-ridden language, such as 'seedless conception' and 'fatherless child,' but he also toys with such controversial and foundational Christological semantics such as nature (*ousia*) and instead of calling Christ-Jesus the co-substantial (*homoousion*) with God the Father, or of the same nature as humanity, he prefers to define the 'little child' (*paidion neon*)[618] as a 'supra-substantial' one (*hyperousion*).[619] However, this compound noun does not in any way indicate the willingness on the part of Romanos to attribute lesser humanity and greater divinity to the new-born God-Man, for in other parts of the very same hymn the author explicitly proves otherwise. Indeed, the force of this usage of 'supra-substantial' (*hyperousion*) resides in the stark contrast between the frail human nature of Mary, on the one hand, and the sublime and fully-fledged divine nature of her offspring. This occurrence can only be phrased in terms approaching contradiction through paradox, such as are witnessed in these very verses.

Romanos strives to express the wonder of the possibility of encounter and indwelling between the human and the divine in one that can be only perceived and accepted by earthly agents as

---

[615] *Hymn* 3. Prelude.
[616] *Hymn* 1.4.
[617] *Hymn* 1. Prelude.
[618] *Hymn* 1. Refrain.
[619] For instance, De Matons 1965. 51, also opts to translate *hyperousion* as 'supra-substantiel'.

being 'beyond reason' (*huper noun*) [620]. This confluence of human and divine (both in the person of Christ-Jesus and, by extension, in his mother who encloses him in her womb) are rendered through a number of images, all of which possess a counter-intuitive and counter-logical relationship. One image for the virginity of Mary is for instance either the 'bush unburned by fire' (*baton en puri*) [621] evoking the theophany to Moses in Exodus 3.2. as a symbol now of the presence of the divine and yet the survival of the human in its midst. As the bramble bush was being enveloped with fire and yet was not being consumed by it, so did the Virgin bear the presence of her God inside her. Romanos puts it: 'As once there was fire in the bush shining brightly and not burning the thorn, so now the Lord is in the Virgin' (*houtō pote kai pur en batō ēn phōtaugoun kai mē kaion tēn akantha, hōs nun en tē parthenō ho Kurios*). [622] Another important figure for the virginal mother of Christ is the 'rod of Aaron which blossomed' (*rabdon Aarōn tēn blastēsasan*)[623], a figure drawn from Numbers 17.23 connoting now the manifestation of divine power that surpasses all human expectation and capacity. The rod of Aaron is a pertinent image for it signifies, and in Romanos' view pre-figures, the blameless conception: as the Virgin conceived without the aid of a male, so did the rod blossom in the desert without being dewed with water: 'Now see Aaron's rod that blossomed without watering' (*tēn rabdon Aarōn tēn anthēsasan dicha ardeuontos*)[624]; and compare with the repeated refrain: 'without a seed a Virgin gives birth, and after childbirth remains still a virgin' (*dicha sporas parthenos tiktei kai meta tokon palin menei parthenos*)[625]. Indeed, nothing else but paradoxical expressions can capture the marvel of the conception for Romanos:

How is it that the grass carries fire and is not burned? A lamb carries a lion, a swallow an eagle and the servant, her Master.

---

[620] *Hymn*. 3.1.
[621] *Hymn*. 3. Prologue.
[622] *Hymn*. 3. 5.
[623] *Hymn*. 3. Prologue.
[624] *Hymn*. 3. 4.
[625] *Hymn*. 3. 2ff.

(*Pur pherōn ho chortos ou phlegetai, hamnas bastazei leonta, aeton de chelidōn, kai despotēn hē doulē*). [626]

Alongside the images of the burning bush and the blossoming rod, Romanos employs another more unusual one in order to render comprehensible the incomprehensible, namely the Ark of the Covenant. In trying to rationalize the dispensation of the divine economy or, as he phrases it how: 'God ... became incarnate from a virgin' (*Theos ... ek parthenou sarkountai*) and also how: 'He who is before the ages [is] taking our form' (*morphēn hēmeteran labōn ho pro aiōnōn*) [627], Romanos develops a scheme of transposing the tripartite Ark described in the Old Testament to be a model of the constitution of the God-Man in the following manner: the jar signifies 'the body of Christ' (*Christou to sōma*), the manna the 'Divine Word' (*Theios Logos*), and the Ark itself represents the Virgin (*parthenos*)[628]. As becomes evident from considering the aforementioned examples, Romanos is not so much concerned with using a unified language to depict the ineffable inter-mingling of the human and the divine that took place in the body of the Virgin; but rather he is content to pile up paradoxical expressions, even though they may lack a systematic consistency, as long as they can powerfully invoke a range of symbols to suggest the saving truth, namely that: 'in a mortal womb in a manner uncircumscribed, Mary carries my Savior as he wills.' (*gastri thnētē theon aperigraptos Maria emon sōtēra ekonta pherei*)[629].

The intimacy of this is designated by another notion which parallels Johannine evangelical language – for not only did God assume Adam in the womb (*tēs sēs koilias touton anelabe*) Romanos says[630] but he also is 'in her bosom' (*tēn se pherousan kolpois*)[631]. While the Gospel of John emphasizes the intimacy between the divine Father and the Son who is 'in the bosom of the Father' (*eis*

---

[626] *Hymn.* 3. 1.
[627] *Hymn.* 3. 1-2.
[628] *Hymn.* 3. 3.
[629] *Hymn.* 3.1.
[630] *Hymn.* 3. 8.
[631] *Hymn.* 3.6.

ton kolpon tou patros, John 1.18), Romanos highlights the proximity of the divine and the human, the intimacy effected between the divine Son and his human mother, as the key *energeia* of salvation by means in the Incarnation. This truth can, in Romanos' view, be presented in self-contradictory terms that transcend the apparent meaning of language and invite the believer to go beyond ordinary signs. Such is the purpose of the phrases he uses such as: 'rich poverty, precious beggary' (*penian plousian, ptōcheian timian*)[632] that disrupt ideas of value that are commonly expressed in logical ways; a manner of speaking that rends apart ordinary received notions.

Through a large arsenal of strikingly oppositional words and images, therefore, Romanos conveys the idea of a paradoxical divine incarnation, whereby God is at once 'with' Mary, and yet is 'before' although he is 'from' her, as well as her 'father' and her 'Son': 'See, the Lord is with you, and he who is before you is from you: your Father and your Son.' (*meta sou Kurios, kai ek sou ho kai pro sou, ho patēr sou huious sou*). [633] His piling up of images of contradiction aids the poet's purpose, which is not the elaboration of a single 'correct' way to describe the Christ-event; but rather to indicate the incredibility (and yet the credibility) of this supra-event through its re-enactment in language that itself reflects the actual historical occurrence of this terminal paradox. In his poems, therefore, language mirrors reality in so far this is allowed by the limits of a semantic pushed to the very edge and then shown wanting. Its utility consists precisely in its incapacity to enshrine that which the poet has set out to capture in words. The failure of language *per se* in this case works exactly for the sake of describing the 'Ineffable' Christ-event'; for where logic (and, consequently, the working of language) ceases to cohere, there the correct rendition of the sublime happening can take place. In Romanos' poetry, language imitates reality; the reality of the historical occurrence of a certain period and place that has been projected onto a supra-reality governed by the notion of sacred time; and it enacts it in front of the reader (listener) by transferring

---

[632] *Hymn*. 1.7.
[633] *Hymn*. 3. 7.

it to sacred time and transposing the reader (listener) to a different level of understanding and a different dimension of experience.

For Romanos, everything pertaining to the human race is characterized by its essential insufficiency, and a lack that can be undone and completed only by the divine beneficence. Earthly beings are typified by their poverty and misery, and are referred to as 'beggars' (*tois ptōcheusasi*)[634] steeped in ignorance and corruptibility. The human condition, as understood by Romanos, is deeply entrenched and entrapped in vain undertakings and enslaved to inevitably futile ends [635]. For this reason the Magi, who come to worship the Child-God, are presented as travelers who have made their way across the entirety of the earth in stark darkness:

> From the land of the Chaldeans, where they do not say, 'The Lord is God of Gods.' From Babylon where they do not know who is the maker of the things they reverence. (*Ek gēs Chaldaiōn, othen ou legousi · theos theōn kurios, ek Babulōnos, hopou ouk oidasin tis ho poiētēs toutōn ōn sebousin.*) [636]

For the same reason, when Mary converses with Gabriel on her manless gestation, she exclaims: 'My nature is dismal at night, and how will the sun shine out of it?' (*Nux ameidēs hē phusis emē · kai pōs eks autēs lampsei ho hēlios;*) [637]. A common reference to the human condition in Romanos' verses is the word 'thorny' (*akanthōdē*), that comes to designate the passing and impermanent nature of human beings, especially in the sight of the divine. To underline the vulnerability and fleetingness of humanity, as well as to suggest the decisive effect of the incarnation, the poet often describes Christ-Jesus as the 'light' that shines in. In the first hymn on the Nativity, Romanos makes several shifts in the reference to 'star' and other illuminating objects, such as 'lamp,' and 'sun.' Although at first the star (*astēr*) signifies the astronomical object showing the way to the wandering Magi, it soon comes to indicate

---

[634] *Hymn.* 1.3.
[635] *Hymn.* 1.13.
[636] *Hymn.* 1.13.
[637] *Hymn.* 3.11.

Christ- Jesus as himself the Star that gushes forth from his virginal mother (*astēr anatellein*)[638] and superseding all other stars being: 'A Star far more brilliant than the star which has appeared' (*astēr asteros tou phainomenou uperphaidroteros polu*), a star which is in fact: 'the maker of all the stars' (*astrōn poiētēs*)[639].

There is a progression of the Word of God's gifted illumination that starts from his mother, then dawns on the Magi and afterwards that on the whole of creation [640]. However, although human agents are described as realizing their insufficiencies and seeking the 'light of his face' (*to phōs tou prosōpou sou*) [641], they are tacitly transformed from seekers of light to possessors of it. Thus, the virgin-mother is called 'the shining one' (*hē pheinē*), while the magi are called the 'lamps of the East,' (*hoi tēs anatolēs lychnoi*) [642]. It is worthy of note here that not merely humans become partakers in the (divine) light springing forth from the source and epitome of all light; but also the reverse move is true. While expounding on the opening of the door of the cave and alluding to the unopened-and-yet-opened Virgin Mary, Romanos makes a series of transformations that come to converge into one image, that of the door (comparable to the way he collapsed the image of star/light/lamps from the most literal level to that symbolizing Christ-Jesus, and his seekers. In this instance the Greek word *thura*, first of all plainly means the door of the grotto where the Christ child is placed; then it comes to designate the Virgin-mother (*thura, pulē*) that is both unopened (*aparanoiktos*) and opened (*anoichtheisa*) [643]. Lastly, the term refers to Christ-Jesus, a borrowed image from the Gospel of John.[644] This inter-mingling of metaphors and images amounts to another of Romanos' paradoxical sayings: 'She opens the door; she, the unopened gate through which Christ alone has passed... She opened the door, she from whom was born the door itself, a little child, who is God

---

638 *Hymn.* 1.5.
639 *Hymn.* 1.5.
640 *Hymn.* 1.24.
641 *Hymn.* 1.24.
642 *Hymn.* 1.13.
643 *Hymn.* 1.9.
644 Jn. 10. 7, 9.

before the ages.' (*pulē... ēnoikse thuran, aph' hēs egenēthē thura, paidion neon, ho pro aiōnōn theos*) [645].

The Paradoxical Touch.

As in the case with the supra-natural conception and counter-logical virginity preserved before and after birth, the human touch with the God-Man encapsulates the supreme mystery and profundity of the Christ-event, albeit to a smaller degree. Whereas before it was Mary, along with Joseph, who was stupefied by the happening willed and executed by God himself, it is now the angelic choir that declares the incomprehensibility of the fact that the one who created Adam is now carried in the hands of an elderly man as a child:

> From heaven the bodiless ones are amazed as they look on him and say: 'Wondrous and paradoxical, incomprehensible, ineffable are the things we now see, For the One who created Adam is being carried as a babe. The uncontainable is contained in the arms of the elder. He, who is in the uncircumscribed bosom of his Father, is willingly circumscribed in the flesh, but not in the Godhead...' (*Ouranothen hoi asōmatoi blepontes ekseplēttonto legontes · 'Thaumasta theōroumen nuni kai paradoxa, akatalēpta, aphrasta · ho ton Adam gar dēmiourgēs ōs brephos · ho achōrētos chōrreitai en agkalais tou presbutou · ho epi kolōn tōn aperigraptōn huparchōn tou patros autou ekōn perigrapsetai sarki, ou theotēti...*) [646]

The exact location of the Child-God becomes the sole focus of the cosmic drama for the attention of the heavenly and earthly beings is directed toward that which is enfolding below. Romanos makes an extensive use of vocabulary employed by the Cappadocian fathers to describe the divine economy. Apart from epithets such as 'uncontainable' and 'containable' (*achōrētos, chōrreitai*), uncircumscribed' and 'circumscribed' (*aperigraptōn ... perigraphetai*) [647], 'of the same essence' (*homoousios*), 'co-beginningless' (*sunan-*

---

[645] *Hymn.* 1.9.
[646] *Hymn.* 14.1.
[647] *Hymn.* 14.1.

archos)[648] and others in support of the accepted terminology of his day, the poet plays with words and concepts that might not have been palatable to many of the earlier fathers, who were so much more invested in fixing, with utmost precision, of language the divine economy.

For Romanos, however, language is here to be pushed to its own limits in order to illustrate the liminal nature of human understanding. This, it seems, is his way of saying that such a theological semantic is the only possible way of describing the awesomeness of God-and-Man-in-One; that is the union between two (apparently) mutually exclusive realities and entities that have been brought together in Christ. Romanos sometimes uses, but refuses fully to subscribe to, the language of any fixed *formulae* in order to render this union.. In addition to referring to Christ's birth as 'supernatural' (*hyper physin*)[649] and describing Christ-Jesus as a son of God 'by nature' (*kata physin*) and being a son of the virgin 'contrary to nature' and 'beyond nature' (*hyper physin*)[650] Romanos declares him to be the 'perfect imprint of the incomprehensible being of the Father' (*character ho panteleios tēs akalēptou patrikēs hypostaseōs*)[651]: a phrase (being referred to the Incarnated Lord, not simply the Eternal Word) that strains against the formulae laid out by the church fathers. The poet announces through the mouth of Mary the insufficiency of any title attributed to Christ-Jesus. She wonders to herself that the child she carries in her hands rules over all humanity and thus cannot simply be called 'human being' (*anthrōpon*) [652], not even 'a perfect human being' (*teleion anthrōpon*) [653].

Furthermore, Romanos suggests, he cannot simply (*haplos*) be called 'God' (*theon*) either [654] for he is in any other respect 'like a human being', as Mary exclaims: 'And if I call you God, I marvel

---

648 *Hymn*. 14.1.
649 *Hymn*. 14.3.
650 *Hymn*. 14.8.
651 *Hymn*. 14.6.
652 *Hymn*. 14.3.
653 *Hymn*. 14.4.
654 *Hymn*. 16.4.

as I see you like me in all things' (*kata panta moi homoion*)[655]. Thus, not any *single* title or word is sufficient to capture the true nature(s) of this being in human form, who is nonetheless beyond any being. This monologue of the Theotokos is seminal since it demonstrates the real power and, at the same time, the real failure of Romanos' use of language - it guides us to the edge and leaves us there in order to realize that which is otherwise impossible to realize, to bring us in touch with the transcendent through the crossing of boundaries, this time of semantics and logic rather than of the human and divine domains. The overturning of the logic and sequence of language signifies the overturning of the harsh boundaries hitherto prevailing between the divine and the human natures and spheres. The collapse of language and logic into themselves is therefore not a meaningless device suggesting helplessness on the part of the poet to communicate the Christ-event in truthful ways, but rather its masterful and colorful portrayal through enactment and reflection of the mystery in multiple words and images.

Any close encounter between the child (or the adult) Christ-Jesus with any other human being is an extremely pregnant moment that, for Romanos, highlights the immense and almost threatening co-habitation on earth of the divine and the human; in this case not because of their mutual in-dwelling within the same person but rather because of their co-existence on the same earthly plane and time-bound sphere as he 'lives with them' (*syn autois politeuetai*)[656] in the same human form. Interestingly enough, Romanos sets humanity at the center of Christ's works and privileges human actors over and above the bodiless angels of the celestial realm. The drama is all the more intense because the One who is otherwise inaccessible to the creatures of aether becomes available and readily accessible to the mortal human race: 'He whom angels cannot approach has appeared easily approachable to those born of earth' (*tois gēgenesin ephanē euprositos ho aggelois*

---

[655] *Hymn.* 14.4. Simple (non substantial) 'Likeness'; not, we may note, the 'consubstantiality' (*homoousion*) in Godhead (with the Father) and Manhood (with Humanity) assigned to him dogmatically by the council of Chalcedon.
[656] *Hymn.* 14.2.

aprositos) [657]. Not only does God assume the lowly human nature and position, but he also becomes dependent upon the actions of his own creatures. Thus, Christ-Jesus, 'the unapproachable light,' (*to phōs aprositon*)[658] approaches John the Baptist in order to seek his agency: 'The Master of the angels had come to a slave wishing to be baptized' (*pros doulon ho destpotēs tōn aggelōn elēluthe, thelōn baptisthēnai*) [659]. Furthermore, the poet indicates that, in fact, God is need of human cooperation for he supplicates John the Baptist for the lending of his hand. To John's request, 'What do you seek from a human, O Lover of Mankind?' (*Ti zēteis gar anthrōpou, Philanthrōpe*), Jesus responds plainly, 'I need to be baptized by you' (*egō gar chreian echo tou baptisthēnai hopo sou*)[660]. Indeed, the palm of the hand is likened to the mediation of the angel sent by God to those in need, for Jesus continues his pleading with Baptist, 'You too then, send me your palm as an angel [661], that you may baptize the unapproachable light' (*pempson oun kais u hōs aggelon tēn palamēn hina baptistēs to phōs aprositon*)[662]. What is more, the poet asserts that this stooping and the grasping of the 'head of my God' (*kephalēn kratounta tēn tou theou mou*)[663] by John's hand elevates him above the angelic world because of this fact of the very touch and the act of baptism, as Jesus indicates to him: 'In this way you will gain a dignity which does not belong to angels' (*ekseis gar dia touto axiōma hoper ouch hypērxen tois aggelois*).[664]

The encounter itself between Christ-Jesus and John the Baptist is triply paradoxical, as it is illustrated by the accumulation of three paradoxes in one verse alone: 'When he heard these ineffable and dread words, the son of the barren one said to the Son of the Virgin...' (*hrētōn arrētōn kai phriktōn ho ek steiras, phasi tō ek parthenou*).[665] The incredibility and yet even so the obvious

---

[657] *Hymn.* 14.2.

[658] *Hymn.* 16. refrain.

[659] *Hymn.* 16.4.

[660] *Hymn.* 16.6.

[661] He plays on the inherent pun (already used in the New Testament), in the term *angelos*: viz. angel or messenger.

[662] *Hymn.* 16.8.

[663] *Hymn.* 16.12.

[664] *Hymn.* 16.10.

[665] *Hymn.* 16.12.

factuality of the 'touch' between the God-Man and the human being is highly dramatized here, as one occurrence that both transcends the humanly possible yet is nonetheless made easily accessible. Romanos artfully reminds us that the hand or the palm of the hand comes in contact with its own Maker; a paradox in the same order as how the 'father' or the 'maker' of his own mother becomes her very son. He expresses this especially in Jesus' own words of supplication to the Baptist: 'Baptize me, do not hesitate. Just lend me your hand. I dwell in your spirit and I possess you wholly... I am within you and outside you.' (*baptison me, tēn dexian monon daneison moi ·to pneuma sou oikō kai holon se echō... endon sou eimi kai exōthen*) [666]. John the Baptist, like Mary and Symeon, grasps the importance and the unspeakability of the moment of touch and intimate contact with the God-Man. Just as in the third *Hymn on the Nativity*, Romanos indicates that it should not be considered an outrage, (*hubris*)[667] that God is enfleshed through a virgin (*theos... ek parthenou sarkountai*), so too does the poet teach that it is fitting for Symeon and John the Baptist to exceed the limits normally set to them as pertaining to humanity. Thus, Christ-Jesus cajoles John to be emboldened and baptize him by overstepping the boundary of the perceived separation between divinity and humanity in this way: 'I am not asking, Baptist, that you overstep the bounds... simply baptize me in silence and in the expectation of what is to follow the baptism' (*ouk apaitō se, baptista, tous horous hyperbēnai...*)[668].

Not only has God-Enfleshed crossed the boundary between the strictly divine and human realms, but he also enjoins human beings to do likewise in their own fashion. He, who has 'become flesh' and has been made like to humankind (*soi gar hōmoiōthēn*)[669] disregards the human discretion and fear of contact and invites a direct and immediate touch with different members of mankind. Christ-Jesus himself occasions and provokes the respective overstepping of human limits. Against the entreaty of John the Baptist to desist: 'Know yourself. Just how far can you go?' (*gnōthi sauton ·*

---

[666] *Hymn.* 16.9.
[667] *Hymn.* 3.2.
[668] *Hymn.* 16.10.
[669] *Hymn.* 16.10.

mechri pou parerchē) [670] Jesus responds with a command to act without fear. The human agent is pushed to respond to the divine condescension with elation.

The Terminal Paradox: Divinity Humiliated. Humanity Deified.

The physical contact with the Child-God or the God-Man is not a mere accident in the view of Romanos, for it has a real trans-forming power and an ineffaceable after-effect. This precisely is the juncture of the narration where Romanos' own invention and ingenuity intervene, for he somewhat alters the gospel accounts with his own interpretations. In so doing, he propounds a certain kind of theology, which in the Eastern Orthodox Church is mostly known as deification or *theōsis*. Romanos applies here the notion of sacred time, completely disregarding the flow of natural events to relate the anticipated human metamorphosis as immediate. In his poems, chronological time collapses into a timeless schema. Thus, after the Mother of God has born her child, she is fully transformed into something greater than the rest of the human race. Mary declares triumphantly: 'I am not simply your mother, compassionate Savior' (*ouk haplōs gar eimi mētēr sou*)[671] for she is turned into a shelter (*skepēn*), a buttress (*stērigma*) and a wall (*teichos*) for the sake of protecting humanity and, in this way, she becomes a mediating figure on behalf of all mankind.

In the story of the presentation of the Child-God to Symeon, Romanos alters the ending with an imaginary dialogue between the two. Symeon is granted his wish to precede God to heaven and is dispatched to be the first messenger to the angels of the news of the Incarnation.[672] The transformation of the human agent is most apparent with John the Baptist, however, only after the dramatic 'touch' between his hand and the head of his God. Whereas before this event John is timid, afterwards he is filled with boldness:

---

[670] *Hymn.* 16.7.
[671] *Hymn.* 1.23.
[672] *Hymn.* 14.17.

I no longer say as before, 'I may not loose the strap of his sandals, for see, I advance from the feet to the head. I tread no longer the earth but heaven itself, for what I accomplish is of heaven. Rather I have surpassed the things on high, for they carry, but do not see whom they carry, while I now both see and carry. (*Ouketi legō ōs to prin· Ou luō ton himanta tōn sōn hupodēmatōn. Idou gar ek bēmatōn epi tēn karan prochōrō· gyn patō ouketi, all' houton ton ouranon· ha gar telō ourania· mallon de kai ta anō paredramon· tauta gar bastazei all' ou blepei on bastazei· egō de nun blepō kai bastazō.*)[673]

Paradoxically, as it is God who is characterized as 'the only Lover of Humankind' (*ho monos philanthrōpos*) and who stoops to the level of his creation, so too it is the command and the destiny of the human race to surpass the limits of its own nature. Just as God took the shape of one of his creatures, so too all of humanity will be re-made in his divine likeness and will be glorified. Romanos expresses vividly this extraordinary potential for humanity to respond to the divine humiliation with its own ascent and participation in eternal life. The shattering of boundaries between God's realm and ours creates the possibility to re-gain what the human race had tragically lost, as a result of God's transformative 'touch' on every human being and, with it, humanity's complete metamorphosis.

---

[673] *Hymn.* 16.17. Lash (1995.46) here mis-renders *bastazō* as baptize, instead of carry.

St. Symeon The New Theologian & Nicetas Stethatos
On the Contemplation of the Beautiful [674]

Matthew J Pereira

The Beautiful in the Eastern Monastic Tradition

Ascetical practices associated with the eastern monastic tradition have often been sensationalized in the commentary literature and regularly caricatured for the severe and bizarre acts associated with the 'wild-eyed' holy fools of the desert. The performances of ancient Christian *askesis* can be certainly startling to modern sensibilities, but these acts of idiosyncratic holiness in themselves do not stand as the underlying foundation of the monastic tradition. The motivations behind some of these acts of radical self-abnegation are manifold, but certainly one of the concerns that motivated ascetics to strive to be free from the preoccupations of the material self, was their persistent striving toward the contemplation of the Beautiful. The monastic vocation, in part, was a call to free oneself from the entrapments of the flesh. This denial of the self, however, did not entail hatred toward materiality altogether as the Byzantine monks often spoke of appropriating the beauties embedded within this material world, and using them as ladders ascending up to the divine and ultimate beauty of God. In the ascetical tradition, however, there was clearly a privileging of the spiritual world over the material. Above all else, the searching out of the Beautiful represented the ultimate goal (*telos*), which orientated the spiritual journey of the Byzantine monk.[675]

A number of exemplary *Higumenoi* within the Byzantine tradition have written theological reflections on the contemplation of the Beautiful. The mystical theologians of the Christian East often reframed the Platonic notion of ascent toward the Beautiful by

---

[674] Sections of this study have appeared previously in: MJ. Pereira. 'Beholding Beauty in Nicetas Stethatos' *Contemplation of Paradise.*' Union Seminary Quarterly Review. 63:3-4. 2012. 51-61.

[675] See: JA. McGuckin. *Standing in God's Holy Fire: The Byzantine Tradition.* Orbis. New York 2001. 23.

interpreting the spiritual journey within the trinitarian life of the Father, Son and Holy Spirit. The tradition of Symeon the New Theologian and his ardent disciple Nicetas Stethatos [676] reveal one way in which Byzantine monastic theologians theologically framed a discourse concerning the beholding of the Beautiful. The widely diverse forms of early Christian monasticism had, by the medieval Byzantine era, given way to a more standardized tradition; so that by the time of Symeon of New Theologian, it is appropriate to speak of: 'An Orthodox ascetical and mystical tradition rather than merely an outline of different traditions, or streams of thought.'[677] Symeon's monastic theology, controversial perhaps in some of its details [678] , but generically a re-statement of Studite forms, itself became sanctioned as sacred tradition by his followers, most notably by Nicetas Stethatos. Nicetas contributed to the legacy of Symeon, in the generation following, by arranging the return of the relics to the capital (from their imperially imposed exile) and by writing his *Vita* as well as advancing his master's highly experiential vision of the mystical life. Symeon's *Ethical Discourses* and Nicetas' *Contemplation of Paradise* provide theological reflections on the contemplation of the Beautiful that stand as paradigmatic of the Byzantine monastic tradition of the eleventh century; and which also had much influence on successive ages of Orthodox monastic life.

The Triune Experience in Symeon's Ethical Discourses.

Both Symeon and his biographer Nicetas articulated a common vision of the monastic life, which was grounded in the Scriptures and the Greek Fathers. The biblical sub-text is a deep narrative woven throughout Symeon's *Ethical Discourses* and similarly provides a sub-text to Nicetas' *Contemplation of Paradise*. Nicetas' indebtedness to Symeon's theology is evident throughout the *Par-*

---

[676] St. Symeon Neos (c.949-1022) was higumen of St. Mamas in Constantinople; Niketas Stethatos (c. 1005-1085) was higumen of the Studium monastery.
[677] For further discussion, see G. Collins. 'Simeon the New Theologian: An Ascetical Theology for Middle-Byzantine Monks.' in *Asceticism*, (edd). VL. Wimbush, & R. Valantasis. OUP. New York 1995. 343 - 356.
[678] Such as the very heavy stress on the role of the spiritual father; and the necessity of tears and highly personalized *aisthesis*, or experience, of the divine grace (tears and visions given high priority).

adise. Nicetas had gained his close familiarity with the master's works in so far as he himself was surely the editor of a considerable section of the literary corpus, including the *Ethical Discourses*, and the *Hymns of Divine Love*.[679] It is here, in the *Ethical Discourses* that one receives what has been described as: 'St. Symeon's single most sustained attempt to set out for a wide readership his thought on... the direct experience of God.'[680]

For the Byzantine ascetic, the monastic emphasis on purifying oneself from the entrapments of the flesh was inexorably bound up with the vocation to worship the Triune God in truth. At the conclusion of the *Fifth Discourse*, St. Symeon, for example, ad-monishes the reader to: 'Hold in contempt everything visible' in order that 'we may attain to the good things of this present life and of the one to come, in Christ Jesus our Lord, to Whom is due all glory, honor, and worship, together with the Father Who is without beginning, and the all-Holy, good, and life-creating Spirit, the one unique and thrice-holy light, now and ever, and unto ages of ages.'[681] In the above excerpt and throughout much of his writings, the freeing of oneself from all things visible was a doxological movement, which allowed for the enlightened ascetic rightly to worship and experience the Father, Son and Holy Spirit. It is the attaining of the 'good things' within the life of the Triune God that provides the impetus for holding in contempt the visible things of this world.

The Triune God not only provides the ground and grammar of worship, but also this three fold divine outreach shapes the soteriological realities for the Christian. Symeon posits a corollary between the Triune God and the deification of humanity when he declares: 'Father, Son, and Holy Spirit are the one God Whom we worship. Body, soul, and God are the man who is created according to the image of God and made worthy of becoming

[679] Further, see A. Golitzin. *St. Symeon the New Theologian. On the Mystical Life, Volume 1: The Church and Last Things*. SVS Press. Crestwood. 1995. 19.
[680] Golitzin. 1995. 11.
[681] A Golitzin. *St. Symeon the New Theologian, On the Mystical Life, Volume 2: On Virtue and Christian Life*. SVS Press. Crestwood. 1996. 62.

god.'[682] The relationship between worship and salvation (deification- *theosis*) is inextricable within Symeon's theological outlook. The Trinitarian life is not one that is explicated by means of complex theological propositions (indeed the saint's contro-versial clash with Bishop Stephen, the Synkellos at the Imperial court of Basil II, was posited exactly on his rejection of theology as a purely intellectual argument) nor is the divine life one to be realized through reading and philosophical erudition. Symeon challenged a sterile and worn-out theology that is bound in books rather than founded on experience, thus he contended against those who believe the Christian receives: 'The full knowledge of God's truth by the means of worldly wisdom, and fancy that this mere reading of the God-inspired writings of the saints is to comprehend Orthodoxy, and that this is an exact and certain knowledge of the Holy Trinity.'[683] Symeon, at some cost to himself, challenged the hierarchal formalism of medieval Byzantine intellectualism through emphasizing the role of the Holy Spirit and energizing grace in the Christian's realization of the divine life. The divine mysteries, he argues, are revealed through, 'an intelligible contemplation enacted by the operation of the Holy Spirit in those to whom it has been given.'

These themes of intelligible contemplation, the role of the Holy Spirit, and the energy of God's free grace are all taken up by Nicetas in his treatise *Contemplation of Paradise*. The *Paradise* shares many obvious similarities with Symeon's *Ethical Discourses*. Both, for instance, appropriate the biblical narrative of the Adamic Fall in order to situate the starting point for the human predicament, the need for divine grace, and the call to strive towards the Beautiful. The following assessment will primarily focus on Nicetas' theological reflections of the contemplation of the Beau-tiful within the biblical and the trinitarian *oikonomia*.

Following in the charismatic tradition of his spiritual mentor, Nicetas was an enthusiastic 'theologian of the Holy Spirit'. Their collective zeal for the efficacious power of the Holy Spirit, and the

---

[682] Golitzin. 1996. 70.
[683] Golitzin. 1996. 113.

right to speak out as authoritative *pneumatophoros* which he gave to the theologian, was subversive in the church of their day, inasmuch as both Nicetas and Symeon opposed and heavily criticized the rise of Byzantine 'court-clericalism'. They castigated the apparent loss of authentic spirituality, which by the eleventh century had often been replaced with a stale ecclesial formalism.[684] For all its subversive potentiality, Nicetas' experiential spirituality was less than novel, inasmuch as he attempted to access the charismatic potentiality of the individual imbued with the Holy Spirit.[685] This emphasis on the vivifying energy of the Holy Spirit was already strongly championed within the writings and lives of the earlier church Fathers; and so, for all criticisms raised against them of 'novelty' (not least the disparaging nickname first given to Symeon as a 'New' theologian), they themselves claimed to stand as repristinators of the deep tradition.[686] In agreement with much of the eastern Christian tradition, from Origen of Alexandria to the desert fathers of the fourth and fifth centuries, Nicetas believed that the Holy Spirit allowed the saints to apprehend the divine realities (*logikoi*), which provided the possibility

---

[684] Nicetas's emphasis on lay spirituality reflects the thought of his famed mentor. In one memorable quote, Symeon asserted that the Holy Spirit: 'Was sent by the Son to the people: not to the perfidious and the ambitious, not to rhetoricians and philosophers, not to those who are curious about pagan writing, not to readers of profane books, not to the comedians of life, not to wits, artists of the word, not to those who carry famous names, not to the favorites of the powerful...but to those who are in spirit.' Cited in: T. Spidlik. *Prayer: The Spirituality of the Christian East*. vol. 2. (tr.) AP. Gythiel. Cistercian Publications. Kalamazoo. 2005. 162.

[685] J. van Rossum. 'Reflections on Byzantine Ecclesiology: Nicetas Stethatos' On the Hierarchy.' *St. Vladimir's Theological Quarterly*. 25, no. 2. 1981. 75-83, esp. 79.

[686] See. J A. McGuckin. 'St. Symeon the New Theologian (d. 1022) : Byzantine Theological Renewal in Search of a Precedent.' *Studies in Church History*. vol. 33. (*The Church Retrospective*). Boydell Press. NY. 1997. 75-90; Idem. 'The Notion of Luminous Vision in 11th Century Byzantium : Interpreting the Biblical and Theological Paradigms of St. Symeon the New Theologian.' In: *Work & Worship at the Theotokos Evergetis*. [Acts of the Belfast Byzantine Colloquium. Portaferry. 1995]. (ed). M Mullett. Queens University Press. Belfast. 1997. 90-123.

for orientating their spiritual quest for beauty and participating in it.[687]

In his treatise *Contemplation of Paradise*, Nicetas argues that the saints are utterly dependent on the Holy Spirit, who provides divine illumination, which in turn, makes it possible for them to ascend towards the comprehension of beauty.[688] Human beings, in their natural state, are unable to behold either the intelligible (*logika*) or spiritual (*noetika*) realities. If seekers of beauty dismiss the intellectual (*noeros*) work of the Holy Spirit, then they remain only capable of considering the visible world. The faithful saints, however, are able to discern good from evil while tasting even here and now of the tree of knowledge, so long as they remain entirely reliant on the operations (*energeia*) of the Holy Spirit.[689] Nicetas grounds his argument in the scriptures by returning to the words of the Apostle Paul, who asserted: 'The natural man (*psychikos*) rejects the things of the Spirit as foolishness.'[690] Contrary to the wayward (natural) ones, who reject the grace of the divine energy, the faithful (spiritual) ones participate in the Holy Spirit (*kata metousian*) and ultimately find rest in the pastures

---

[687] It should be noted that Nicetas' spirituality was not completely subjective, but rather it appears to fall outside of the rigid categories of the objective and the subjective. Spidlik, for example, rightly notes that the term *logikos* has both a 'subjective' and an 'objective' meaning in the Byzantine tradition. The saints participate in the Logos as they are simultaneously directed toward Christ the Logos. Spidlik. 2005. 474.

[688] On this point, Nicetas adheres to the Byzantine anthropological tradition, which emphasizes full dependence on God. As John Meyendorff expresses it: 'Thus, the most important aspect of Greek patristic anthropology, which will be taken for granted by the Byzantine theologians throughout the Middle Ages, is the concept that man is not an autonomous being, that his true humanity is realized only when he lives 'in God' and possesses divine qualities.' J. Meyendorff. *Byzantine Theology: Historical Trends & Doctrinal Themes*. Fordham University Press. New York. 1979. 139.

[689] *Contemplation of Paradise. Sources Chrétiennes.*(henceforth SC). 81. 224.

[690] 1 Cor. 2.14. Nicetas contends, 'As for others who have no regard for the things of God, who made no effort and had no zeal for intellectual work of the Spirit, because they can not imagine anything more than the visible, it would be notorious folly for naturalists like them, according to these declarations of the divine apostle: 'The natural man receives not the things of the Spirit, because they will be foolishness to him.'' *Contemplation of Paradise*. SC. 81. 174. 18.

of God.[691] Nicetas insists that the faithful are totally dependent upon the Holy Spirit within the framework of the trinitarian economy of salvation; which entails the ongoing transformation of creation into an ever more perfect communion with the Holy Trinity.[692]

In the final chapters of the *Paradise*, Nicetas examines the relationship between the theologian and the Holy Spirit. The Holy Spirit brings the theologian to a life of repentance (*metanoia*) and purification (*katharotēs*).[693] The gift of repentant sorrow (*penthos*), throughout much of the Byzantine tradition, but especially in the writings of Symeon, represents an integral stage in preparing the soul for the contemplation of beauty.[694] This spiritual cleansing marked by tearful repentance is the essential prerequisite, for both Symeon and Nicetas, preparing the theologian to engage in prayerful contemplation, and thereafter to obtain the (limited) ability to articulate the profundities of God.[695] The theologian, through the power of the Holy Spirit, possesses the temperance,

---

[691] *Contemplation of Paradise.* SC. 81.194.

[692] Nicetas describes the trinitarian life as a movement of dynamic interpenetration and participation, where the Son is in the Father and the Spirit, while the Spirit is in the Father and the Son, and the Father is in the Son and in the Spirit. Furthermore, the Father, Son and Holy Spirit interpenetrate one another without blending together or creating a confounding comingling or any other confusion. *Contemplation of Paradise.* SC. 81. 204.

[693] *Contemplation of Paradise.* SC. 81. 220. The Byzantine tradition has long valued the role of repentance and purification as a preparatory step leading to the contemplation of beauty. Spidlik explains that, 'With the Fathers, *katharsis* (purification) coincided with perfection as the restoration of our original, primitive condition...The first condition of contemplation is purification from sin, repentance, because 'the Bridegroom does not like to mingle with an alien soul'.' Spidlik. 2005. 176; also, see Gregory Nazianzen, *Carmina.* 2.45, v. 45; PG. 37.1356.

[694] In his profound appreciation for the gift of repentance, Symeon declares, 'Let us repent with our whole soul and repudiate not only our wicked deeds but even the twisted, defiled thoughts of our heart.' *Catecheses.* 5.49-52, cited in B. Krivocheine. *In the Light of Christ: St Symeon the New Theologian: Life, Spirituality, Doctrine.* SVS Press. Crestwood. 1986. 68.

[695] *Contemplation of Paradise.* SC. 81. 220. 56.3-6. For further discussion concerning the relationship between compunction and the spiritual life, see I. Hausherr. *Penthos: The Doctrine of Compunction in the Christian East.* Cistercian Publications. Kalamazoo. 1982.

which allows for the regulation of all the senses (*aisthēsis*).[696] As theologians fully participate in these divine gifts, they become full of mercy and replete with the good fruits of the Spirit.[697] This following passage from the *Paradise*, contains a concise synopsis of key elements recapitulated throughout Nicetas' mystical theology and sets out his schema for the soul's ascent towards beauty:

> As for the tree of the knowledge of good (*kallos*) and evil: it is the discernment of multiple branches, following the strong opinion expressed well by others having come before us in their philosophy. It is the discovery of our own structure and of our own nature; that which is good for us who have attained perfect (*teleios*) humanity and the measure of the stature of Christ, thanks to the absolute impassibility (*apatheia*) and the wisdom (*sophia*) of the Spirit; and by it we are turned back again toward the magnificence of the Creator in order to begin the contemplation (*theōria*) of the same beauty (*kallos*) of the creatures. For them, the cause of their progress is realized with time in the stable possession of virtue (*aretē*), and cannot succeed if it wanders from this property; because their work is firmly assured in the divine contemplation (*theōria*).[698]

Here Nicetas provides a precise summary of the archetypal eastern monastic sense of the ascetic movement (*kinesis*) of the soul; where one begins with considering the structures of the inner nature (*logoi*) of things and self; then in Christ through the Spirit, advances in stages of ascending contemplation. [699] The

---

[696] *Contemplation of Paradise*. SC. 81. 224.

[697] *Contemplation of Paradise*. SC. 81. 222.

[698] *Contemplation of Paradise*. SC. 81.170.

[699] Nicetas' structured analysis of the spiritual life reflects the wider Byzantine theological tradition. In his study on Maximus the Confessor, Lars Thunberg observes the progression of theoretical contemplation as follows: 'Contemplation, according to the early church, particularly in the East, starts in the ontological and ends in the mystical. Accordingly, contemplation is a threefold activity. It consists, according to Maximus the Confessor, in 'natural contemplation' (i.e., contemplation of natures), in spiritual contemplation of what is revealed through Scripture, and in mystical contemplation of the triune God himself.' L. Thunberg. *Microcosm and Mediator: The Theological Anthropology of Maximus the Confessor*. Open Court Press. Chicago. 1995. 363f.

golden chain of tradition, which is embodied in those who have 'come before us in their philosophy,' provides Nicetas and his fellow monks with a descriptive template for their own advanced contemplation (*theōria*) of beauty.

In another excerpt from the *Paradise*, the saints are described as responding to the Holy Spirit with an openness that facilitates an intimate connection with the divine life, thus allowing the disciple penetration into the sanctuary (*hagiasma*) through the royal door of contemplation (*theōria*).[700] In the sanctuary, that is the metaph-orical state of blessed contemplation, one advances in the knowledge of being and the recognition of both divine and human realities.[701] The Holy Spirit brings the faithful saints into perfect contemplation of the beautiful (*to kalon*),[702] where the efficacy of love and the quest for beauty (both being essential features derived from the Platonic notion of the soul's ascent) become heightened in Byzantine Christian theory as the faithful are seen as further empowered by the Holy Spirit with a perfect love (*agapē*) towards God.[703] In harmony with the older Byzantine mystical tradition, and his own spiritual father Symeon, Nicetas believed that the power and energy of divine love, measured in Christ and through the wisdom of the Holy Spirit, directs the faithful saints towards perfection.[704]

---

[700] *Contemplation of Paradise. Sources Chrétiennes*. 81. 218.

[701] *Contemplation of Paradise. Sources Chrétiennes*. 81. 218. The image is taken from St. Gregory the Theologian's image of the initiated (hieratic) soul penetr-ating behind the veil of divine unknowability in a priestly act of initiation. See: JA. McGuckin. 'The Vision of God in St. Gregory Nazianzen.' Studia Patristica. 32. (ed). E A Livingstone). Peeters. Leuven. 1996. 145-152.

[702] *Contemplation of Paradise. Sources Chrétiennes*. 81. 170.

[703] *Contemplation of Paradise. Sources Chrétiennes*. 81. 222.

[704] *Contemplation of Paradise. Sources Chrétiennes*. 81. 170. Regarding the centrality of charity or love (*agapē*) in Symeon's spiritual theology, Krivocheine concludes, 'Symeon's entire spirituality is characterized, permeated, even dominated by the spirit of charity (*agapē*), of which it is the cornerstone...Symeon describes charity as a divine quality, as Christ or God Himself. Charity is the greatest of the virtues, the first and the last.' Krivocheine. 1986. 371.

Conclusion

Symeon's teachings on the Holy Spirit were in agreement with the earlier eastern tradition, although his emphasis on the active role of the Holy Spirit is much stronger than many of his closer predecessors. For its part, Nicetas' *Paradise* is a tractate devoted to analyzing the quest for beauty using allegories and imagery associated with paradise (e.g. good and bad fruits), contoured by Hellenistic philosophy, the biblical story of creation, fall and redemption, the wider patristic tradition, and all steadily anchored in the doctrine of the Trinity. Perhaps, above all else, it is the Orthodox doctrine of the Trinity which indelibly shapes Nicetas' mystical theology. In his recent study on the history, doctrine and spiritual culture of the Orthodox Church, John McGuckin has offered this following cameo on the significance of the doctrine of the Trinity within Eastern Orthodoxy:

> As God the Father moves out to creation through the Son and in the Spirit, so it is meant and destined as the communion of our grace, that the highest levels of the creation (spiritual intelligences above all, though the pattern is noticed in other parts of the sensible creation) themselves move towards God the Father. The movement to the Father directly is impossible: such is his transcendence and glory that no creature can make that pathway without mediation. One moves to the Father through the promptings and guidance of the Spirit. The movement is perfected by the Spirit's incardination of each spiritual intelligence in the image of the Logos, whose pattern forms our substrate of being, and our perfection of enlightenment.[705]

On earlier occasions too, using patristic evidences, McGuckin has made similar observations regarding the central importance of this spiritual moving energy or *kinesis* that lies behind the eastern Orthodox understanding of the Trinity, as our progressive initi-

---

[705] JA.McGuckin. *The Orthodox Church: An Introduction to its History, Doctrine, and Spiritual Culture.* Blackwell-Wiley. Oxford. 2008. 125-26.

ation into the God who reaches out to us.[706] The point is an extremely important one for understanding the Orthodox doctrine of the Trinity; but it also has merit for rightly interpreting the trinitarian theology that is embedded throughout Symeon's *Ethical Discourses* and Nicetas' *Paradise* alike; and which is so often (mistakenly) dismissed as a mere trope by commentators. The Orthodox understanding of the Trinity is primarily about the mystery of salvation, which is grounded in the outreach of the Father, Son and the Holy Spirit, and realized within the liturgical, doxological, life of the Church. The doctrine of the Trinity is less a mathematical conundrum; much more an explication of the Christian experience of the communion of grace; not a philosophical obscurity as much as a shorthand for the divine movements of the Father, Son and Holy Spirit, which are bound up with energizing, for our sake, the economy of salvation.

The melody is a consistent one: we find it in the early fathers, in Symeon and Nicetas, as well as in later Orthodox reflection on the Trinity – that God is a restlessly creative energy and that the Holy Spirit ever prompts the faithful to move toward the Father, in Christ, ultimately leading disciples to the perfection of enlightenment; or, to refer back to the ancient term for sublime contemplation of the divine, the *theōria* of that which is truly beautiful.

---

[706] See, for example, JA. McGuckin. 'Perceiving Light from Light in Light: The Trinitarian Theology of St. Gregory the Theologian.' *Greek Orthodox Theological Review* 39. 1-2. 1994. 7-32.

Contributors

Dr. Stamenka Antonova holds a PhD in Early Christian History from Columbia University, where she has taught since receiving her doctorate in 2005. She has also taught Early Christian studies at Union Theological Seminary, New York University, and Seton Hall University in addition to actively contributing and publishing in Late Antique history.

Dr. Bruce Beck earned his doctorate in Early Christian thought at Harvard University, with a Dissertation on the use of the Book of Jonah in Christian and Jewish exegesis. He has since organized, as its Director, the Pappas Patristic Institute at Holy Cross, Brookline, and offers courses there in New Testament and Biblical hermeneutics.

V. Revd. Prof. Nicolae Dumitrascu is professor and Dean of the Faculty of Orthodox Theology *Episcop Dr. Vasile Coman*, in the University of Oradea, Romania. He has been a visiting professor in Croatia, Lebanon, Finland and Belgium and is involved in several international ecumenical partnerships. He is a priest of the Romanian Patriarchate and has written extensively in the field of Patristics, Missiology and Ecumenism. His Collected Essays: *Athanasius and Basil: Faith, Mission and Confession in Shaping Christian Doctrine* will appear in 2013.

Todd French is currently in the final stages of completing his doctoral researches in Columbia University's Religion Department, in the field of Early Christian thought and culture. He is a teaching fellow at Columbia, writing his Dissertation on the topic of Byzantine Hagiography.

Sergei Holodny is a free-lance student of history with close interests in the life and culture of Russia.

Lisa Radakovich Holsberg comes to theology from a professional life in the arts as a singer, composer, and music educator. She received her M.A. in theology from Union Theological Seminary and is now a Ph.D. student at Fordham. Her recent compositions around Byzantine texts: the *Akathist to Jesus Christ* for chorus, chanters, and congregation, and *Come, True Light: Prayer of St. Symeon the New Theologian* for voice, piano, cello, bells and cymbal, received their premières at the 2011 and 2009 annual conferences of The Sophia Institute. Her award-winning music peace project, responding to the tragic events of 9/11, may be found at: www.racetothesky.org.

Victoria K McCarty graduated from The General Theological Seminary where she now serves as Acquisitions Librarian for the Keller Library; she is an Associate of the Community of the Holy Spirit. She holds degrees from Michigan State University and the University of Louisville. Her article on the early Christian ascetics: 'Desert Wisdom for Spiritual Directors,' was recently published in *Presence*.

V. Revd. Prof. John A. McGuckin holds the Nielsen Chair of Church History at Union Theological Seminary, and is Professor of Byzantine Christian History at Columbia University, New York. He is a priest of the Romanian Orthodox Patriarchate serving in Manhattan. A Fellow of the British Royal Historical Society, he is an extensively published scholar whose latest works are: *The Orthodox Church* (Blackwell Wiley, 2008), *The Encyclopedia of Eastern Orthodoxy* (Blackwell Wiley, 2010), and *The Ascent of Christian Law: Patristic and Byzantine Reformulations of Antique Civilization.* (SVS Press. New York. 2012).

Maya Machacek, after many years as a professional educator, is currently completing her MA studies in Early Christian thought at Union Theological Seminary, New York, where she has made special researches into the writings of Origen of Alexandria.

Nicholas Marinides is a senior doctoral candidate in the Department of History at Princeton University, writing on lay piety in the early Byzantine Empire. He is currently a Bliss Prize Junior Fellow at Dumbarton Oaks Research Library for the academic year 2012-2013.

Matthew Pereira is in the final stages his doctoral level research into the writings of St. Cyril of Alexandria at Columbia University's Religion Department. He is a teaching Fellow at Columbia, and as well as currently writing up his Dissertation, he has published several articles on Patristic and Byzantine religious thought.

Rebecca Thekla Raney holds the Master of Divinity Degree from Holy Cross Greek Orthodox School of Theology where she integrated her background in social and cultural anthropology and her career experience in international humanitarian development with Patristic and Liturgical study, Social Ethics, and Scriptural Exegesis.

Kristen Leigh Southworth read Communication Studies at the University of North Carolina at Greensboro and holds the Master of Divinity Degree from Union Theological Seminary, with a concentration in theology and the arts. She has performed nationally as a professional

Indie-folk-rock singer-songwriter since 1998 and actively contributes to a number of projects that support the arts in both ecumenical and secular communities.

Sergey Trostyanskiy is in the final stages of his doctoral research at Union Theological Seminary, New York, focusing on the use of the Greek philosophers by the Church Fathers. His dissertation is concerned with the semantics of the Council of Chalcedon. He is the recipient of the Spears Scholarship for Early Christian Studies and is a Teaching Fellow in Church History at Union Seminary. He has authored several publications in the fields of ancient and modern philosophy, as well as the theology of Origen of Alexandria. His forthcoming book (2013) is entitled: *Seven Icons of Christ: The Theology of the Oecumenical Councils.*

Zachary Ugolnik is currently pursuing doctoral level researches in Columbia University's Religion Department, focusing on Early Christian and Byzantine theology and culture. He received his Master of Theological Studies from Harvard Divinity School in 2009 and worked afterwards with Harvard University's Pluralism Project in raising awareness for Eastern Christianity in America. His account of the project appeared in the 2011 Summer-Autumn issue of Harvard Divinity Bulletin.